Dry Place

Landscapes of Belonging and Exclusion

Patricia L. Price

D0099348

University of Minnesota Press
Minneapolis • London

"Unrefined," by Pat Mora, from *Chants* (Houston: Arte Público Press–University of Houston, 1985), is reprinted with permission from the publisher, Arte Público Press.

Portions of chapter 4 were originally published as "Inscribing the Border: Schizophrenia and the Aesthetics of Aztlán," *Journal of Social and Cultural Geography* 1, no. 1 (September 2000): 101–16. Reprinted by kind permission of Taylor and Francis Ltd., http://www.tandf.co.uk.

"Borderlining," "Angel," "Twin Cities," and "MV Coho," by Patricia L. Price, originally appeared in "Entre Amigos / Among Friends," *disClosure: A Journal of Social Theory* 13 (2003). Reprinted courtesy of *disClosure* and the Committee on Social Theory.

Photographs in this book were taken by the author, unless otherwise credited in the captions.

Published by the University of Minnesota Press
111 Third Avenue South, Suite 290
Minneapolis, MN 55401-2520
http://www.upress.umn.edu

Printed in the United States of America on acid-free paper

Library of Congress Cataloging-in-Publication Data

Price, Patricia L.
  Dry place : landscapes of belonging and exclusion / Patricia L. Price.
    p. cm.
  Includes bibliographical references and index.
  ISBN 0-8166-4305-9 (acid-free paper) — ISBN 0-8166-4306-7 (pbk. : acid-free paper)
    1. Mexican-American Border Region—Civilization. 2. Mexican-American Border Region—Intellectual life. 3. Narration (Rhetoric)—Social aspects—Mexican-American Border Region. 4. Mexican-American Border Region—Ethnic relations. 5. Group identity—Mexican-American Border Region. 6. Landscape—Social aspects—Mexican-American Border Region. 7. Mexican-American Border Region—Poetry. I. Title.
F787.P745 2004
972'.1—dc22
                                2003027594

The University of Minnesota is an equal-opportunity educator and employer.

12 11 10 09 08 07 06 05 04   10 9 8 7 6 5 4 3 2 1

Dry Place

This book is dedicated to my mentors
Joe Dennis (1911–2001)
and
Morgan D. Thomas (1925–2001)

Contents

Acknowledgments

The background for this book derives from my long interest and field experience in Mexico, and my familial roots in West Texas and a life-long connection to this dry place. Growing up in the dark, cold, and humid Pacific Northwest, yet visiting my grandparents often as a child, then living for six years in Mexico as a young adult, I often wondered about the relationship between place and identity. How is this relationship established? How is it maintained? How does it vary with the physical characteristics of the land, and with our journeys across its surface? How do we become *of*, not just *on*, the land, or do we ever really do so?

In crafting this book in response to those questions, I have benefited enormously from conversations with friends and colleagues in a variety of contexts. At Florida International University, John Clark, François Debrix, Damián Fernández, Paul Kowert, Rod Neumann, Lisa Prügl, Terry Rey, and Ted Young provided commentary on preliminary writings that eventually coalesced into an idea for this book. Gail Hollander and Nick Onuf read an early draft of this project, and their gentle yet incisive feedback came at a crucial time. Jennifer Gebelein spent precious time helping me with some of the photographs. Colloquia at Dartmouth College, the University of Washington, and the University of Kentucky offered arenas for presenting drafts of chapters and discussing them among a wide group of intelligent folks.

At the University of Minnesota Press, Carrie Mullen encouraged me to write a book and supported this particular attempt, even in its decidedly execrable early stages. Her vision, and that of the internal board at the Press, helped to guide the manuscript in its current direction. The detailed and thoughtful comments from two anonymous reviewers provided a sense of how to reposition this book for a broader audience. Melissa Wright, a third reviewer for the University of Minnesota Press, nudged me to make it speak more directly to the substantive concerns of geographers. As a copractitioner in a discipline that is not typically receptive to thinking outside the box, she was cognizant and supportive of the risk taking involved in this endeavor. I thank her for her ongoing encouragement and feedback.

The Latin American and Caribbean Center and the Department of International Relations, both at Florida International University, supported travel to Guadalajara and Los Angeles in 1999. A National Endowment for the Humanities Institute at Southwest Texas State University in June 2000, directed by Mark Busby of the Center for the Study of the Southwest, provided library resources and thoughtful colleagues. A Florida International University Foundation Award during the summer of 2001 funded field research in Ciudad Juárez, Culiacán, and Tijuana, Mexico, and El Paso, Texas. In Ciudad Juárez, colleagues at El Colegio de la Frontera Norte gave generously of their time and insights. César Fuentes, Alfredo Rodríguez, and Paty Mendoza at El Colegio, and Lety Castillo at Instituto Mexicano de Investigación y Planación (IMIP) were particularly helpful. In Tijuana, Manuel Valenzuela of El Colegio de la Frontera Norte probably spent more time than he should have visiting cemeteries, slums, and roadside shrines with me. He generously shared his work and thoughts on popular religion and popular culture in Mexico. Efraín González, acting caretaker of the Jesús Malverde chapel in Culiacán, spent several days with me recounting various versions of the life and times of Malverde. Bobby Cordero, Zeke Saldivar, and Doug Mosier at the border patrol offices in El Paso shared with me their visions of life and labor along the border, and in the process helped me to gain an appreciation for other perspectives. Finally, Sarah Hill was a friend and colleague in El Paso.

In Miami, the steadfast conviction of my department chair, Damián Fernández, that time off for research is a good thing for a junior scholar provided a semester's relief from teaching in the fall of 2001, which allowed me to begin this manuscript. A College of Arts and Sciences Research Award during the summer of 2002 supported the final stages of writing. My students in Miami are perennially interested about life along the "other" border, and their questions have kept me more honest than I otherwise might have been about the need to keep border theory and practice open to exploration in multiple sites.

Last but certainly not least, Ari, Nina, and Daniel were present throughout the research and writing of this book, and I owe them the biggest debt for simply keeping it all in perspective.

Introduction: The Ghosts of the Past and Claims to Place

This book is an exploration of how we relate (to) place. In general terms, I address place as a layered, shifting reality that is constituted, lived, and contested, in part, through narrative. More specifically, I examine some (though certainly not all) of the narrative threads that together weave the brilliant fabric of the area surrounding the boundary between the United States of Mexico and the United States of America. Though the lands in question are today deeply engraved by this powerful geopolitical legalism, they have long been divided as well as connected along social, political, cultural, and economic axes that predate this specific boundary. Thus, the geopolitical boundary constitutes a chapter, albeit a dramatic one, in the many-bordered story of this place.

To write of such a place, and of the identities, collective and individual, fashioned in narrative articulation with it, invokes a deeply problematic politics of speaking. Whose stories are told, from whose perspective, in whose voice? Whose stories, versions, and voices are left silent? Translated? Warped? Questions such as these have long and productively vexed anthropologists as well as scholars in other disciplines, particularly those who use ethnographic methods. They have also, at times, led to a scholarly aphasia of sorts, a reluctance to explore important avenues of inquiry for fear of the reprisal—real or imagined—that might follow. In my own work, for example, I have found the racialized and gendered guilt that often accompanies ethnographic exchanges and scholarly interrogations of these exchanges to be particularly limiting.[1]

Though this book is not a thoroughly ethnographic undertaking, my emphasis on narrative as well as the ethnographic basis of some of the research undertaken in the course of writing it has certainly brought issues of power and voice to the surface time and again. In weighing these questions, I have kept Nancy Scheper-Hughes's words at the forefront of my mind: "given the perilous times in which we and our subjects live, I am inclined toward a compromise that calls for the practice of a 'good enough' ethnography."[2] For Scheper-Hughes reminds me of what I already know, that power relations are very rarely straightforward or one-way. The recognition of this sometimes irreconcilable complexity should not lead one to abandon ethnographic inquiry altogether, to become so ridden with anxiety or guilt that one loses one's voice. These are indeed perilous times, and an imperfect politics of ethnography is decidedly preferable to no ethnography at all. What Scheper-Hughes (and others who have proceeded with ethnography despite the risks) does urge, however, is a careful exploration, to the extent possible, of one's own positioning within the intricately delicate and complex politics of knowledge construction. Here is what I can say about my own position in this project.

My parents married young and did their best to escape West Texas, which they did in short measure by moving as far away as they felt they possibly could to Washington State, south of Tacoma, on Puget Sound. My father still laughingly recalls my astonished mother stopping the car and taking pictures of the towering fir trees on their drive north. After several stops and many photos, he said, "Linda, I think they're everywhere up here."

My mother used her savings to purchase land perched on the edge of a precipitous drop to the Sound. My father, an architect, designed a low flat-roofed dwelling reminiscent of Frank Lloyd Wright's strategy of mimicking the contours of the surrounding landscape. The west wall juts to the cliff's edge and is transparent, glassed to echo the water and to bring it visually into the house. It must have been as lonely as it was lovely in those days. At that time, we had no neighbors save another couple; oddly, they were named Price as well. Nowadays the tall houses crowd one another, marching up the banks behind ours and straining to glimpse the water over the shoulders of their neighbors below. I vividly recall the wooded, cool expanses that surrounded the house in my childhood and offered a seemingly unlimited area to explore (now developed), pods of migrating orcas (now threatened) passing in front of the long windows, and the liquid calls of birds (now gone) on summer evenings.

One night, when I was still a baby and my mother was expecting my brother, my father awoke with a start. At the foot of the bed stood an old Indian woman. Her lined face was like a topographical map of the surrounding land. In her raised hand she held a meat thermometer with the sharp skewer end aimed at my mother. Terrified, my father lunged for her but his grasping arms clasped at nothing. My mother awoke to find him, his knees and feet scraped raw, sprawled on the sisal carpet. He told her of the vision he had had and how real it had seemed. Together they searched for the meat thermometer, which they had used that evening as they grilled a roast. Search as they might, they could not find the thermometer. When I asked him to tell this story to me again, my father wrote:

> Some time later I came across a book of nautical charts of Puget Sound, with references in the margins to events and historical happenings, including native legends and folklore. At about the spot where our house was built, overlooking the Tacoma Narrows, the reference said that the native people used to string nets from the edge of the cliff to tall trees below and trap birds in them as they flew by. Had our house construction disturbed a sacred place? Was the old Indian woman angry because we had ruined her bird-hunting spot? Or was it just a case of indigestion? You tell me. All I know is that to this day, 37 years later, we never have found that meat thermometer.

He ends his e-mail to me by saying, "I would be curious to see how you re-tell this tale." Indeed, there is no way that this retelling of his tale would be anything but curious. This particular story has likely grown more embellished with the passing years. In switching narrators from my father to myself, the story's focus and pace have doubtlessly shifted as well. And in my retelling here, I have a purpose different from any my father had ever imagined, and an audience he had never expected. Good stories have an opalescent quality; as they are polished and handled and turned they reveal vivid occlusions that flash forth unexpectedly. As with dreams, the lines between fiction and nonfiction, truth and fantasy, reality and illusion become blurred and one wonders what the difference really is.

Was the dream real? Did the woman really disappear into the night with the meat thermometer? Does she bear a grudge to this day? Though I won't pretend that I don't wonder about all of that when I visit my parents, who still live in the same house, I will suggest that the ontological status of the dream is not what makes it important. Rather, it is the way that this dream provides an entry point for thinking about place in general and claims to specific places—the epistemology of the dream, if you will—that makes it useful here. This is a ghost story. In it, an archetypical previous inhabitant—the old indigenous woman—appears in a dream to my father. She tries to kill my mother, whose purchase of this land has alienated it, and who will soon bring forth another white man, my brother, who like me was born on this land and is thus of it. My parents are ciphers themselves, stand-ins for wave after wave of white men and women who, for the past hundred years, have rolled into the far western United States in their wagons and trains and cars bringing their strange, devouring attitude toward the landscape with them. Not having much of a sense of the sacred, or a ready use for birds, the newcomers simply parceled out, sold, built up, and paved land such as these hunting grounds.

The plot structure of this ghost story holds that the land rightfully belongs to the aboriginal inhabitants, while my parents are usurpers with no true claim to belonging. But as Doreen Massey has so correctly pointed out, if one digs into the history of any place, one is bound to uncover layer upon sedimented layer of historic claims to places by people who had come from other places: "even the megalith builders had come to Corsica from somewhere else."[3] Chief Seattle himself had a similar, if ineffably sadder, view, observing that in the long reach of history

> Tribe follows tribe, and nation follows nation, like the waves of the sea. It is the order of nature, and regret is useless. Your time of decay may be distant, but it will surely come, for even the White man whose God walked and talked with him, as friend to friend, is not exempt from the common destiny. We may be brothers after all. We will see.[4]

More recently, Washington State has proved to be controversial ground yet again with the case of the so-called Kennewick Man. In July 1996, two college students stumbled across a skull while watching the hydroplane races from the banks of the Columbia River in the tri-cities area of Eastern Washington. Later investigation revealed a skeleton dating from 9,300 years ago. It is one of the oldest human remains found in North America, and one of the most complete. It also displayed unexpected physiognomic characteristics incommensurable with what scientists would expect from Native American remains of that period. Among them, Kennewick Man is taller and thinner than most ancient Indians, the skull is not flattened in the back, and his nose was high-bridged and large. Scientists variously hypothesize Kennewick Man's provenance to be as far-ranging as Southern Asia (as opposed to Northern Asia, the long-supposed origin of Native Americans), Iberia, Scandinavia, Japan, or Australia.

Citing NAGPRA (the Native American Graves Protection and Repatriation Act of 1990), Native Americans in the region want the remains to be handed over to them for reburial. It is a precedent in the United States that human remains dating from before the European conquest of the Americas are legally considered to be Native American, even if they cannot be definitively shown to possess a biological or cultural relation to modern people. For their part, scientists cite the Kennewick find as of singular importance given its completeness and age, and wish to study the remains further. As of this writing, four Northwest tribes, the Nez Percé, Umatilla, Yakama, and Colville, are appealing U.S. Magistrate Judge John Jelderks's ruling of 30 August 2002 in favor of a handful of scientists who wish to study the bones at the Burke Museum in Seattle, where the remains have been housed for several years.

So much more than the fate of a few old bones is at stake in this struggle. Did American Indians in fact displace other original residents? If so, their contemporary legal claims against whites who subsequently displaced them are diluted. Is this simply another manifestation of white men's imperial desires for native lands cloaked in the garb of science? Is there a related, but deeper, desire on the part of whites to claim a superior speaking position, not just legally but culturally as well? Jack D. Forbes, professor emeritus of American Indian studies and anthropology at the University of California, Davis, believes that "what it is is a wish on the part of some Europeans to be nativized, to have gotten here early, not late."[5] Or is this perhaps the expression of a long-lived fear of wildness, one that can only be assuaged (but of course can never really be exorcised) by grinding into the very bones of ancient Indians, much as the fat of dead Indians was used to dress the wounds of Spanish conquistadors?

Will history be rewritten? What structure will its plot assume? Whose tale will be told above and over all others as the official story? Whose voices will whisper around the edges of the canon, telling their heretical versions? Whose voices will be forcibly silenced, and whose will die out?

Who has valid claims to land and who does not? Who belongs and who is an outsider? What is the statute of limitations on all of this? Must one have been born of the land, or is it necessary too to have dead buried there? How many generations must one travel in order to be absolved of the sin of dispossession? Is it fair to take recourse to dead Indians, as I do here with the old woman's ghost, Chief Seattle, and Kennewick Man, to address such questions?[6]

What, pray tell, *is* race? How exactly is it linked to who may lay claim to what? And if it is as muddy a category as it appears to be, what does this mean for claims to place that are based in a purified notion of race? Indeed, isn't a more useful concept of race based on shared histories—in this case, a shared history of suppression, genocide, and dispossession—than the blood-based notions of racial purity rooted in the ugly slaving past of the United States?

Yet, here once again we are faced with difficult questions of boundaries, limitations, who's in and who's out. Even in my own history I have meandered far beyond blood-based definitions of race, beyond neat borders that could define what is just and what is a travesty. After I left the glass-fronted house overlooking the sea, I spent six years, off and on, living and working on Mexico's Gulf Coast, central Mexico, and most recently in the northern border region. Academically, I trained as a geographer specializing in Latin America. My dissertation research took a close, ethnographic focus on the daily lives of poor women trying to make ends meet, economically and psychologically, in slum areas of Mexican cities. As with many of us who spend large portions of our adult lives far from home, the far-away becomes progressively closer and the notion of home itself becomes problematic. My daughter was born in a hospital in Xalapa, Veracruz. She has both Mexican and U.S. citizenship and, thanks to recent legal changes, will not have to choose between her two citizenships when she turns eighteen. Her father, a Mexican national, has indigenous, European, and Arab ancestors. She is not fair-skinned but her hair and eyes are quite light. Her first years were hard for both of us, economically speaking. Graduate school is rarely a bounteous time, and, given her absent father, it was a lean time indeed. My dissertation was sped along by the twin devils of humiliation at receiving AFDC checks and food stamps and the well-founded fear that this support would be cut off before I could finish.

My own Anglo-Texan family, relieved at my daughter's fairness, was further relieved when I got a job in Miami, though they were not happy with the distance that now separates us. At least it wasn't Texas, where my father's mother had picked cotton as a girl, where my own parents had struggled so to escape from. In Miami, my daughter is an odd Mexican-gringa among Cubans. She refuses to speak Spanish.

Our accents are ridiculed. I do not wish to be buried here, mostly because the landscape is redolent with palm trees that sparkle like waxed houseplants in the sun, and I do not trust it. Ragged, wet, towering black firs still populate my dreams.

My own story hints, in however restricted a way, at how other variables—class, gender, ethnicity, and motherhood among them—intervene in the directness of claims to purity and place. In this book, I draw necessarily on my academic training, as well as on the experiences and proclivities that have been shaped over the course of my life, to explore the layered narratives that, together with the physical surroundings, constitute the storied landscape of the Southwestern United States and Northern Mexico. It is a place to which I am linked through collective familial ties of blood, history, longing, and revulsion. My family ties, academic training, and life experience do not provide my account with a privileged speaking position, but they have given me an appreciation for the importance, as well as the contested nature, of place and the tales that make it.

Chief Seattle was looking forward, while the Kennewick case takes us back in time, yet both directions reveal histories of ceaseless human displacement in the land, "like waves of the sea." The ghosts that wander these narratives—the old Indian woman, Kennewick Man— remind us of the layered quality of all places. No claims to land are straightforward. Rather, they are shrouded in categories that are themselves unclear, haunted by other voices, shadowed by guilt and grief and longing and regret. And there is some comfort in this. Perhaps we are brothers after all, if only in our propensity to employ mythic constructs to attempt to stop the waves through an appeal to timelessness. As Chief Seattle reportedly went on to remind the whites in his speech:

> And when the last Red Man shall have perished, and his memory among white men shall have become a myth, these shores shall swarm with the invisible dead of my tribe, and when your children's children shall think themselves alone in the field, the store, the shop, upon the highway, or in the silence of the woods, they will not be alone. . . . At night,

when the streets of your cities and villages shall be silent, and you think them deserted, they will throng with the returning hosts that once filled and still love this beautiful land. The White Man will never be alone. Let him be just and deal kindly with my people, for the dead are not powerless.[7]

All landscapes are haunted by ghosts. The stories told of those long displaced and dispossessed combine with the tales of those who claimed and possessed, and these tales shape, contest, and offer alternatives to the tales of those now living on the land. Some human geographers have spoken of landscapes as texts, but I wish to take this notion further in this book. Places, as well as the landscapes that allow us to grasp them, are thoroughly narrative constructs. They would not exist *as places* were it not for the stories told about and through them. Stories constitute performative, mimetic acts that conjure places into being and sustain them as the incredibly complex, fraught constructs that they are. Stories—particularly those tales we tell ourselves about ourselves—provide the weathered bedrock that binds human collectives to the lands we inhabit. Culture-stories form the very loam of the soil of identity from which human beings and the physical earth are inextricably intertwined. Blood and earth. Places without stories are unthinkable. Perhaps, as Brian Jarvis suggests, *geography* without stories is unthinkable: "Ultimately there can be no geographical knowledge without historical narrative. To know one's place and to change places it is necessary to listen to the meanings buried deep and wide across the storied earth."[8] Even more humbling, when we pause to consider the hubris behind the human propensity to view our role as that of shaper of places, is Paula Gunn Allen's provocative suggestion:

> One imagines that we impose our sense of place on the land, but given the oddly similar lines of these narrative strands as they work themselves out in the Southwest and elsewhere, one wonders: Is it we who invent the stories and thus inform the land, or does the land give us the stories, thus inventing us?[9]

In chapter 1, I develop this notion of place as narrative construct. I will suggest that places and the stories that compose them are deeply constitutive of our identities, both as individuals and as members of human collectives. More broadly, place emerges as a polyvocal concept, an unstable yet rich palimpsest where various visions of human identity through ties to land are negotiated, a concept at least as riddled with silences, dissenting voices, and differences as it is with unisonant consensus. The landscapes shaped by narratives are as real as those sculpted by the action of wind, waves, and glaciers. And it is precisely this coming together of the cultural and the material in a place that interests me in this book, and in broader debates under way in contemporary human geography. In chapter 1 I will suggest (and illustrate in the balance of the book) that the materiality of stories and the storied nature of materiality provides a productive way of thinking about, researching, and discussing place and identity. Stories matter.

Many—though certainly not all—of the modern narratives about this place have the nation-state as their principal plotline. In chapters 2 and 3, I discuss two of these modern narratives set in the U.S. Southwest. The westward expansion of Anglo-Americans in the nineteenth century, and the myth of the western landscape as empty as a central backdrop to this process, is examined in chapter 2. Chapter 3 undertakes an analysis of the counternarrative of Chicano nationalists in the 1960s and 1970s. Though this story was staged in the same physical location as that of Anglo[10] expansionists, details of the landscape imaginary of Chicano nationalists could not have been different from that of their Anglo-national counterparts of the previous century. While the landscape wishfully envisioned by Anglo expansionists was smoothed, a tabula rasa waiting to be inscribed with the narrative of a United States whose destiny it was to stretch from coast to coast, the landscape envisioned (also wishfully) by Chicano nationalists was saturated with mythic figures, events, and places that tied Chicanos to this land as rightful inhabitants. However, both the Anglo-American expansionists and Chicano nationalists shared a similar national plot structure, one where borders both geopolitical and more broadly conceived functioned to both exclude and include.

Focusing on certain stories necessarily excludes other stories. The role of this place in Mexico's own national myth of destiny, and of this place for the Native American peoples who also inhabited (and inhabit) it, could logically provide material for two additional chapters. I chose to focus on Anglo-national expansionism and Chicano counternationalism primarily because of my interests in Anglos and Latinos in the United States, itself likely born of my family history as Anglo-Texans living and working side-by-side with *mexicanos*, sometimes in tension, sometimes in solidarity. Six years of living in Miami have broadened my horizons regarding what counts and what is disallowed, racially speaking. I wonder how my daughter fits into or doesn't fit into this paradigm, how I fit, how my parents and grandparents and friends fit or not, and this doubtlessly fuels my research interests.

In chapter 4, I turn to contemporary place visions. The plotlines here are less clear. A common narrative involves the erasure of national borders, the decline of the nation-state, and the disappearance of distinctive places: a generalized condition of placelessness. This condition has been variously celebrated and feared. The celebrants range from the boosters of globalization who see the nation-state and its appurtenances as anachronistic inhibitors of free trade, to proponents of the so-called borderlands perspective who sense the liberating potential in the erosion of old structures of cultural and political power. Artists, performers, and poets have claimed the border not as a metaphor of separation but as an imperative for building bridges. In the fracturing of identity that the border has long occasioned, the scraps of a new, hybrid self can be assembled.

Among the fearful, a dominant response is to retrench, to inscribe old borders even more firmly on the landscape, and to erect new ones as well, in a desperate bid to stabilize the racialized Anglo-national self. The U.S.-Mexico border, and the area surrounding it, figures centrally in these various emplotments of the future. Legislation regulating the flows of goods, services, information, production, industrial contaminants, labor, and migrants has seized on this as the key geopolitical, institutional, and cultural barrier to be eradicated, fortified, and redefined. Nativist politicians and others in the United States have sought to strengthen the profile of the border between Mexico and the United

States, and since the mid-1990s the physical barrier between these countries has become ever-more impermeable: longer, stronger, higher, more omnipresent in the landscape.

In chapter 5, the space on and around the border between Mexico and the United States—the borderlands—is conceptualized as the stage, if you will, for the playing-out of the geopolitical Ur-plot of good versus evil. This is approached through a discussion of recent apparitions of the Virgin of Guadalupe, which are juxtaposed with the murders of more than 300 women in Ciudad Juárez since 1993. Good and evil struggle in the guise of the Virgin and the Devil, protagonist and antagonist in this uncertain tale, and they do so on the U.S.-Mexico border. Given the ambivalence about where we are headed and who "we" even are anymore in this postnational era, this storyline comes as no surprise.

Chapter 6 moves from the archetypes of the previous chapter—good and evil—to specific characters who inhabit the contemporary borderlands. These are Juan Soldado, patron saint of undocumented border crossers, Jesús Malverde, patron saint of narcotraffickers, and Elián González, a Cuban boy elevated to quasi-sainthood by Cuban exiles when he was rescued at sea and brought to Miami. These three figures are everyday fellows who have been elevated to unofficial sainthood because of contemporary needs. Their elevation and the needs that give rise to it bespeak a crisis of place, a claim to legitimacy, and a durable desire for stable spatial referents in times of uncertainty. Border crossing, drug trafficking, and rafters' desperate attempts to flee Cuba are contemporary realities that secular border institutions cannot or will not deal with. I will suggest that, among other things, Juan Soldado, Jesús Malverde, and Elián González function as trickster figures in contemporary narratives of place, nation, and identity. They work across borders in disruptive ways, circumventing legal structures, providing a measure of sanctity for clandestine activities, challenging us to think beyond the nation and, at least figuratively, see with the eyes of others. In doing so, they give us tools we need to survive in the world, tools that are desperately needed.

Chapter 7 concludes with poetry I have written. These are pieces I wrote during the year I drafted the manuscript for this book. At the time, they functioned as a creative outlet for issues that came up in the book but that I could not resolve directly through the prose itself. Thus, as strategies of resolution, they approach important themes obliquely, and by doing so are perhaps better equipped to grasp them than the expository tactics offered by traditional academic writing. It is this attempt to grasp and comprehend that is the essence of a conclusion and, I believe, what ultimately matters above and beyond the method one uses to do this.

Admittedly, by including my own creative writing I am focusing explicitly on my own voice and experiences. Does this mean that the book is more about me than the people and places that I write about? Is such a distinction between author and subject even a possibility? Should I be able to claim the right to tell my own stories alongside those of others? Am I merely making myself more transparent in this narrative about narrative, and is this a desirable thing? These are, again, political questions about authorship, voice, and the right to speak, and I won't attempt to resolve them here. However, I will concur with Roland Bleiker, who has noted how powerful poetry can be for addressing issues at the heart of change:

> Poetry is ideally suited for rethinking world politics because it revolves around a recognition that (aesthetic) form and political substance cannot be separated. . . . poetry lies at the heart of politics and social change, for it deals with the values that either enable or obstruct transformation.[11]

As with all challenges to established ways of doing things, to write differently one must take risks. And academia is a risk-averse profession. Taking risks is not encouraged among academics with our ceaseless, at times cruel, scrutiny of one another's work. For example, though "writing differently" and seeking "different voices" has been clamored for lately by many in academia, I have seen precious little published scholarship that actually attempts to do this. It seems to me that the time is ripe to push those boundaries. Perhaps then the voices of ghosts can be heard.

CHAPTER 1

Place Visions

Landscape is loud with dialogues, with story lines that connect a place
and its dwellers.

—Anne Whiston Spirn, *The Language of Landscape*

Seeing and Then Seeing Again

So where exactly *is* the place that is the focus of this book? Is this book
about the Southwestern United States? The West more generally?
Northern Mexico? The territory around the U.S.-Mexico border? Is it
useful or even fair to state that the book is both about all of these places
and about none of them?

These are important questions, to which the many and varied
forays into the nature of place, space, and landscape, by geographers as
well as nongeographers, attest.[1] Their explorations have proven anything but conclusive. For these are concepts whose boundaries overlap,
they are terms that are frequently used interchangeably: their meaning
is flexible, to say the least. I do not pretend, or even wish, to provide a
definitive theory of place, or clearly delimited distinctions between
space, place, and landscape, or an exhaustive account of all the ink that
has been spilt over such questions. Rather, in this chapter I will elaborate the notion that place—in general, as well as the specific place under
investigation in the balance of this book—is a processual, polyvocal,
always-becoming entity.[2] Apart from location as simply coordinates on
the globe, there are many possible negotiations of emplacement. The
same physical site may be dreamed, ignored, appropriated, or simply
lived differently by different individuals or groups simultaneously. It is
in this layered approach to place making, this simultaneity of stories,

and the politics of making one's voice heard, that place constantly, problematically materializes. Indeed, following the argument of the philosopher Edward Casey, I will suggest that there is no such thing as place qua place.[3]

This is a frustrating assertion. To say that there is no such thing as place echoes the contentions of many contemporary critical scholars: there is no such thing as "the body," there is no such thing as "culture," there is no such thing as "nature," there is no such thing as "race," and so on. As their critics have been quick to point out, at times such claims tend toward the banal. Writing of such criticisms of her work on the performance of gender, Judith Butler observes that "certain formulations of the radical constructivist position appear almost compulsively to produce a moment of recurrent exasperation, for it seems that when the constructivist is construed as a linguistic idealist, the constructivist refutes the reality of bodies, the relevance of science, the alleged facts of birth, aging, illness, and death."[4]

Yet perhaps the banality lies not in the claims themselves but in our deep reluctance to fully explore them, our susceptibility to "a devouring force [that] comes at us from another direction, seducing us by playing on our yearning for the true real."[5] For to truly accept that place, for example, is so thoroughly socially constructed that place qua place does not exist, we are faced with a necessary reinvention of what we do as scholars and how we do it. Analysis with the objective of getting to the bottom of things could not exist if there were no bottom to be got to. It's turtles all the way down.[6] No wonder we look for ways out:

> Would that it would, would that it could, come clean, this true real. I so badly want that wink of recognition, that complicity with the nature of nature. But the more I want it, the more I realize it's not for me. Nor for you either . . . which leaves us in this silly and often desperate place wanting the impossible so badly that while we believe it's our rightful destiny and so act as accomplices of the real, we also know in our heart of hearts that the way we picture and talk is bound to a dense set of

representational gimmicks which, to coin a phrase, have but an arbitrary relation to the slippery referent easing its way out of graspable sight.[7]

How then can we speak about something that isn't really real yet at the same time whose effects are really powerful and palpable, of something that we wish were really real yet that we quietly know cannot be, something that is not even a *thing* at all? What sort of language can we use that is not always already, as Michael Taussig asserts above, "bound to a dense set of representational gimmicks"?

Far from banal, Taussig's own oeuvre has kept a steady focus on just the sorts of questions that so concern the more pragmatic critical scholar: power, agency, materiality, resistance, and change. His long-standing strategy for dealing with these quandaries of representation has been to revel in this very taint itself as constitutive of political economic systems such as slavery, colonialism, and the state. Epistolary exchanges, official proclamations, popular lore, religion, myth, rumor, magical ceremonies: all of these coalesce into a tight bundle of texts, which, emplaced, constitute the fluid, contested, unstable, dynamic reality (but not *really* reality) under consideration. As Taussig remarks, this is a delicate and at times oblique undertaking. Invoking Conrad's narrative in *Heart of Darkness*, he likens the method to a glow that brings out a haze otherwise not visible, an exterior work of gentle, painstaking, ceaseless illumination rather than the neat distillation of meaning to fit inside the shell of a cracked nut:

> The formulation is sharp and important: *to penetrate the veil while retaining its hallucinatory quality*. It evokes and combines a twofold movement of interpretation in a combined action of reduction *and* revelation—the hermeneutics of suspicion and of revelation in an act of mythic subversion inspired by the mythology of imperialism itself. Naturalism and realism as in the aesthetic form of much political as well as social science writing cannot engage with the great mythologies of politics in this nonreductive way, and yet it is the great mythologies that count precisely because they work best when not dressed up as such but in their guise and in the interstices

of the real and the natural. To see the myth in the natural and the real in magic, to demythologize history and to reenchant its reified representation; that is a first step. To reproduce the natural and the real without this recognition may be to fasten ever more firmly the hold of the mythic.[8]

There are other answers to these questions and many more examples of scholarship that grapples with them. What is important is that work such as Taussig's has challenged critical scholars to explore new ways of thinking, seeing, writing, and doing research. He, and others, have pushed scholars who wish to assert that the something under scrutiny is in fact a social construction, to illustrate just how this is so and, most importantly, to convince us of the difference that understanding things this way makes.

In *Dry Place*, I do indeed assert that place is thoroughly socially constructed, that place qua place does not exist. Rather, narratives about people's places in places continuously materialize the entity we call place. In its materializations, however, there are conflicts, silences, exclusions. Tales are retold and their meanings wobble and shift over time. Multiple claims are made. Some stories are deemed heretical. The resulting dislocations, discontinuities, and disjunctures work to continually destabilize that which appears to be stable: a unitary, univocal place. Such an approach is very much consistent with Judith Butler's work on gender. If, for example, we were to substitute "place" for "sex" in the passage below, we approximate what I have in mind:

> As a sedimented effect of a reiterative or ritual practice, sex acquires its naturalized effect, and, yet, it is also by virtue of this reiteration that gaps and fissures are opened up as the constitutive instabilities in such constructions, as that which escapes or exceeds the norm, as that which cannot be wholly defined or fixed by the repetitive labor of that norm. This instability is the *de*constituting possibility in the very process of repetition, the power that undoes the very effects by which "sex" is stabilized, the possibility to put the consolidation of the norms of "sex" into a potentially productive crisis.[9]

As Paul Adams et al. have discussed at length, the reassertion of place in so much contemporary scholarship is both tied to the rethinking of place-related concepts such as "region" and "landscape" and is highly interdisciplinary.[10] In researching and writing *Dry Place*, I have deeply benefited from theoretical insights developed in a number of disciplines, particularly in the humanities: work on the social function of narrative in literary criticism, on sacred places in religious studies, and the "New West" studies emanating largely from history. From this last field in particular I have relied on the work of a growing number of scholars who are interested in the multiple ways that regions, regional identities, regional imaginaries, and the connections among regions are being recrafted in the contemporary world, with a particular emphasis on "the West."[11] As the best of this work so aptly illustrates, regions emerge through a sedimentary process. Depending on one's focus, the composition of the sediment in question varies. Layers of investment patterns, forms of labor, gender roles, migratory streams, and architectural styles: these among many other possibilities accumulate in sites over time. Often, they do so in constitution with one another, with other places, and across geographic scales. Each round of sedimentation cannot help but shape the subsequent round.[12] The place that materializes from this repetitive superimposition is never finished, never closed, never determined. Rather, places understood this way are processual, porous, and articulated.

It is the superimposition of common characteristics that overlap—but never exactly—at a site that lends places their apparent and thus meaningful (if temporary) coherence, both conceptually and experientially. Take, for example, Patricia Limerick's understanding of the West as a meaningful regional designation:

> This consensus—that the West exists, and exists as a real place—only works, some may think, if you are careful to avoid the question, "Where exactly is this region, and what are its boundaries?" The outward boundaries are, indeed, tough to draw, but, then again, drawing outward boundaries is probably the least useful way to define a region. What is

more useful is to keep in mind a set of common characteristics. These characteristics appear and overlap in many places between the Hundredth Meridian and the Pacific Ocean; they appear and overlap often enough to tie those places into a unit we can call the West.[13]

The West, for Limerick, emerges via the superimposition of multiple characteristics, ranging from aridity, the presence of Native and Mexican Americans, proximity to the Pacific Ocean and thus Asia, high levels of federal control over land, and so on. Rather than existing in a singular and static sense, the West is a layered collage that arises over time from interrelationships, from the coincidence of physical geography, ethnicity, and legal-institutional factors.

This approach, more than any other insight, is what lends a useful sort of newness to new regional geographies. It has led a number of contemporary scholars to utilize terms that indicate the complexity of place-based notions. Daniel Cooper Alarcón, in his scholarship on the mythic realm of Aztlán and its function in the Chicano imaginary, and Chris Park in his work on religion and geography, both write of landscape as a palimpsest, "a manuscript on which two or more successive texts have been written, each one being erased to make room for the next."[14] This inscription, erasure, and overwriting harken to the definition of place as textured:

> A place's "texture" thus calls direct attention to the paradoxical nature of place. Although we may think of texture as a superficial layer, only "skin deep," its distinctive qualities may be profound. . . . Etymologically, texture is associated with both "textile" and "context." It derives from the Latin *texere*, meaning "to weave," which came to mean the thing woven (textile) and the feel of the weave (texture). But it also refers to a "weave" of an organized arrangement of words or other intangible things (context).[15]

To take this a bit further, we might note the presence of the word "text" in "texture" and thus make the association between place as *textured* and *textual*. Place as palimpsest is inherently textual, written, erased, and overwritten, and it is in this process, which is akin to weaving, that the warp and woof of place is crafted and place granted its heft.

A related notion, pentimento, is also employed to evoke the multiple changes that characterize place. Lillian Hellman, in her book *Pentimento*, provides a picturesque definition:

> Old paint on canvas, as it ages, sometimes becomes transparent. When that happens it is possible, in some pictures, to see the original lines; a tree will show through a woman's dress, a child makes way for a dog, a large boat is no longer on an open sea. That is called pentimento because the painter "repented," changed his mind. Perhaps it would be as well to say that the old conception, replaced by a later choice, is a way of seeing and then seeing again.[16]

Belden Lane, in his exploration of the geography of American spirituality, writes of the deepened sense of place that a pentimento approach allows: "I see with greatest depth that which I observe from different perspectives at the same time."[17] Patricia Seed has utilized the notion of pentimento in her work on Native Americans and colonization, to indicate both the multivocal nature of place and the sense of repentance and loss embedded in the term. With pentimento as well as palimpsest, there is a ceaseless play of writing, erasure, and overwriting that occurs on and through physical sites. Place, in these approaches, materializes as a layered text of narratives of belonging and exclusion, always negotiated, always struggled over, never finished.[18]

To return to the original query about the place under scrutiny in this book, then, the boundaries and meaningful physical features of the land in question depend to a great extent on whose vision is prioritized. Rather than trying to evade the difficult task of defining for the reader the precise geographic boundaries of the place in question, then, I am instead suggesting that such boundaries do not exist *because a stable sort of place itself* does not exist. So the spatial focus of this book shifts as different stories are told, from the ever-advancing "border between savagery and civilization" of Frederick Jackson Turner's frontier thesis, the ever-receding West of the Anglo-American geoimaginary in the nineteenth century (and its recirculation in the cinematic national imaginary of the twentieth century), the central Mexico valley that is dreamed and smuggled to the U.S. Southwest in the counternational narrative of Chicano nationalists, the transborder region of Greater Mexico, and even South Florida, geographically discontinuous yet logically a part of the greater Southern borderlands of the United States. The focus of this book becomes, in the words of Akhil Gupta and James Ferguson, "place making,"[19] rather than a specified place.

This is not to say that boundaries do not play an important role in the various narrative iterations that together weave this place. As I have emphasized, the question of external regional boundaries is a slippery one. The role of boundaries more generally, however, is vital. For it is the differences *within* regions, the internal borders that unsettle what is already a loosely layered idea, that lend a dynamic quality to the contemporary study of places. And it is the multiple roles played by boundaries, borders, and borderlands in the negotiation of these dry lands that are central to this book. Much has been made lately of these concepts: both of the functions and renegotiations of geopolitical boundaries in late modernity, and the liminal spaces or "borderlands" that have emerged on and around the contestations of identity on and around geopolitical boundaries.[20] I do discuss both a specific geopolitical boundary—that long, powerful seam between Mexico and the United States—as being a central character in the tales of national identity, and the spatial performance of these tales, told by Anglo-Americans (chapter 2) and retold by Chicano nationalists (chapter 3). I also write of the borderlands, certainly a more fluid concept yet one that is also centered along the geopolitical boundary between Mexico and the United States, as constituting a particular set of approaches to understanding the role of difference in the negotiation of identities (chapter 4). Throughout this book, however, I centralize a far more encompassing approach to borders, understood as *"any place where differences come together,"*[21] because this definition allows the focus on collective human attachments to land to be broadened to include many constructions of difference: geopolitical, to be sure, but also cultural, racial, linguistic, gender, sexual, and so on.[22] It is in the confluence of these differences as they have been inscribed, negotiated, and resisted on and through place that has structured narratives of belonging and exclusion that, layer after superimposed layer, have sculpted this site as surely as the actions of wind and water.

The importance of geopolitical boundaries to the functioning and conceptualization of the nation-state provides an illustrative subset of the importance of borders to collective meaning making through the construction and management of difference. Geopolitical boundaries are central to the modern project of nation building precisely because they function to purify and stabilize a collective sense of self through both the erasure of internal difference and the demarcation of a constitutive outside through the expulsion of Other nations. We have only to witness the prevalence of modern conflict sparked by attempts to move or blur border lines to understand the importance of geopolitical boundaries in stabilizing a collective national self. In other words, geopolitical boundaries are so important for the modern nation-state because they are a peculiar, and particularly modern, subset of borders more broadly understood. As much recent scholarship across academic disciplines has noted, modern identities at all scales turn on starkly bordered dichotomies: inside/outside, us/them, civilized self/barbarian Other, here/there, and so on. Object-relations scholars, in particular, have underscored the centrality of borders of all sorts and across scales— from individual psyches to social collectives—to constructing identities.[23] Though I am not academically trained in psychology, and I make no claims to working within an object-relations tradition in a pure sense, I do agree that the maintenance of borders is not a particularly recent event in the ongoing negotiations between human collectives and the lands we inhabit.

Borders have an enabling function, both allowing the emergence of the modern nation-state and allowing the emergence of the identities that go along with this sociospatial formation. Borders have also enabled, and bedeviled, counter- and antinational narratives. As with place, it seems that borders are something that humans cannot get enough of, or at the very least cannot seem to get away from. Indeed, rather than signaling delimitation—for example, the end of the legal-institutional powers of the state—borders can also, perhaps more productively for our purposes, signal beginnings. As Heidegger noted, "A boundary is not that at which something stops but, as the Greeks recognized, the boundary is that from which something *begins its presencing*."[24] Textually speaking, we can attempt a broader understanding of borders as narrative elements, as tropes much like metaphors or similes, that turn the text-that-is-place in specific ways. In the narrative of the old global order, a moral text worked around a tightly jigsawed surface of national spaces arranged in continuous juxtaposition, national boundaries performed the clearly defined function of territorial demarcation.[25] Geopolitical boundaries also allowed a certain sort of nation—a modern nation—to be imagined, "because even the largest of them, encompassing perhaps a billion living human beings, has finite, if elastic, boundaries, beyond which lie other nations."[26] As I will explore in chapters 3 and 4, borders both literal and figurative are crucial to the counternational narratives of Chicano nationalists, as well as the antinational (or perhaps anational) narratives of globalizationists and denizens of "the borderlands" alike.

Thus, though particular borders may be far less permanent than we might like to believe, borders in general are here to stay. And it is their "staying" power—understood both as their durability as well as their ability to fix or stabilize—that makes borders so vital for establishing claims to place, place-based identities, and places themselves as articulated entities.

Place, Space, and Landscape

Reoccupying the Low Land: Edward Casey and Place

In his essay "How to Get from Space to Place in a Fairly Short Stretch of Time," Edward Casey queries the nature of the relationship between space and place:

Are we to believe that human experience starts from a mute and blank "space" to which placial modifiers such as "near," "over there," "along that way," and "just here" are added, sooner or later: presumably sooner in perception and later in culture? Or are we to believe that the world comes configured in odd protuberances, in runs, rills, and flats . . . all of which are traits of places?[27]

Casey employs a phenomenological approach to address this question, ultimately unsettling, indeed reversing, the common perception that space enjoys an a priori status vis-à-vis place, of place being merely a derivative apportioning of preexisting empty space. Rather, he argues, things are the other way around. Place is prior to space, and indeed space is derived from place. For space and time can only arise from the experience of place. Furthermore, there is no such thing as place knowledge, or having a sense of place, that can exist outside of *being* in a particular place: there is no such thing as a general experience of place. "The world comes bedecked in places; it is a place-world to begin with."[28] We are ineluctably, inescapably emplaced beings. Our grasp of place is thoroughly, specifically experiential, and this is mutual. As Robert Sack has reiterated, "Places cannot exist without us. But equally important, we cannot exist without places."[29]

Casey locates the impulse to conceive of space in terms of pure, formal essence as a habit particular to the modern Western mind. Foundational modern thinkers including Newton, Descartes, and Galileo saw space as an infinite, undifferentiated extension. Place itself was utterly discounted or, at best, seen as coterminous with space; space along with time assumed its monolithic status in modern thought, and secondary notions like place were all but abandoned. Thus getting back into place is, for Casey, of paramount importance, because it allows us to bypass some of the errors and omissions of modernism: "One way to avoid the high road of modernism as it stretches from the abstract physics of Newton to the critical philosophy of Kant and beyond is to reoccupy the low land of place. For place can be considered either premodern or postmodern; it serves to connect these two far sides of modernity."[30]

In particular, Casey finds troubling the modern penchant for divorcing embodied people from place through the privileging of an evacuated, unpopulated, purified notion of space. Thus he views the emplaced body as the vehicle by which to get back into place. Not only are the senses necessarily embodied and as such so is any experience of place; the lived body functions as a mediator between enculturation and emplacement, "their localizing agent, as it were. . . . As places gather bodies in their midst in deeply enculturated ways, so cultures conjoin bodies in concrete circumstances of emplacement."[31]

For Casey, gathering is not equivalent to simple accretion. Places hold things, even seemingly disparate things, in apparently orderly configurations. This is true for the human and nonhuman inhabitants of place, the physical features of the land itself, as well as such ephemera as memories. A place holds in and holds out, at once retaining its occupants and distributing them toward its horizons.

> Minimally, places gather things in their midst—where "things" connote various animate and inanimate entities. Places also gather experiences and histories, even languages and thoughts. Think only of what it means to go back to a place you know, finding it full of memories and expectations, old and new things, the familiar and the strange, and much more besides. What else is capable of this massively diversified holding action?[32]

Casey's elaboration of the gathering work done by place echoes previous work by geographers. In her essay "Home, Reach, and the Sense of Place," Anne Buttimer calls for more attention to insiders' ways of experiencing place, arguing that urban renewal programs had paid far too little attention to this in favor of detached descriptions of places by outsiders. Buttimer argues that *centering*, rather than *centralization*, holds the key not just for effective urban policy but for understanding the construction of place identity. It is a distinction that hinges on the difference between insiders and outsiders, one that has "more to do with everyday living and doing rather than thinking."[33] Centering invokes a to-and-fro motion, a tension between dwelling and reaching, between home and horizon, a tension that prefigures what Casey would explain in his notion of gathering as holding in and holding out. Buttimer writes of centering in organic terms, as akin to breathing: "centering suggests an ongoing life process—the breathing in and bringing home which is reciprocal of the breathing out and reaching toward horizon."[34]

The Dreamwork of Imperialism

Geographers who have pondered the term "landscape" tend to agree that it is as ambiguous as it is elusive. Yet most contend that a truth of landscape lies in its orderly visual patterning of the physical features of a portion of the earth's surface: a gathering, to use Casey's imagery. Long-standing definitions of landscape as a "portion of land which the eye can comprehend at a glance" or "a collection of lands"[35] allude to gatherings; in the first case, it is the sweep of the painterly gaze that gathers, in the second, it is a more administrative understanding of gathering together like objects. The earth's components are shaped, literally through physical transformations of them and figuratively through their cultural interpretations, in specifically intelligible ways. Landscape is a meaningful crystallization of place, the cultural framework with which human collectives may craft a specific understanding of place and their place in it. Yet landscape is processual, a verb rather than a noun,[36] never concluded or fixed but always becoming, materializing in tension and solidarity with the human collectives that shape it.

As with the argument above regarding place, there is no such thing as a land unfiltered by human agendas, land without landscape. Even the simple declaration of one's surroundings as pleasant or ugly or just plain is an assessment, albeit one that is subject to change over time, and to widely varying assessments by different cultures. There is no such thing as untouched land, either unshaped physically or in the human imaginary: "So comprehensive and powerful has been man's role in changing the face of the earth that the whole landscape has become an artifact."[37]

The modern usage of the term "landscape" has its roots in aesthetics, as a specific genre of painting that flourished in Western Europe from the fifteenth century to the late nineteenth century.[38] Its emergence coincides with the ascendance of the visual more generally in Western Europe. Tuan suggests that the rise of landscape signaled a broader axial shift in meaning, from the rigidly vertical cyclicality of "cosmos" to a horizontal, relational, linear worldview.[39] The particular form that this envisioning took hinged on the emptied, gridded space discussed above by Casey, an optic that allowed for the development of perspective. Here the issues become as much political as they are aesthetic. For perspective had the effect of shifting subjectivity to the viewer of the painting (his eye was the focus of the image)[40] and to the artist as creator, rather than to the images painted. The collectivity of the lives and the subjective experience of the individuals depicted were incidental; what was paramount was the ownership—literal or implied—of the land and its inhabitants by the viewer:[41]

> Perspective, then, was a device for controlling the world of things, of objects which could be possessed. It was related to a cosmology in the Renaissance which regarded creation as ordained by fixed geometric rules. The painter or architect could understand and apply these rules and thereby emulate the creative act.[42]

As Cosgrove elaborates in his important book *Social Formation and Symbolic Landscape*, landscape painting in Western Europe evolved hand-in-glove with capitalist relations of land ownership and specific forms of appropriation of labor. And this was intimately tied to imperialism, both overseas as well as internally (as with, for example, the enclosures in England). Landscapes were controlled representations of the nature and people dominated by Europe; they were visual narratives of conquest that not only depicted but also reinforced this domination. One of the purposes of landscape as a genre, and the way of seeing of which it is a part, is the effacement of the exploitative conditions that enable and sustain capitalism and imperialism, and the specific formations of racism, classism, and sexism that accompany them. Landscapes naturalize the particular patternings they depict; their intent is to make such depictions appear straightforward, orderly, unproblematic, and enduring. As Don Mitchell writes in his analysis of the making of the landscape of modern California: "Landscape is at once patently obvious and terrifically mystified. . . . The more the word landscape is used, the greater its ambiguity. And the greater its ambiguity, the better it functions to naturalize power."[43] It is this "darker, skeptical reading of landscape aesthetics"[44] that has given rise to the most illuminating critical landscape studies.

W. J. T. Mitchell broadens these ideas, contesting standard assumptions that landscape painting, as well as a landscape way of seeing, are specific to modern Western Europe. He notes that, for example, ancient Chinese landscape paintings far predate the landscape tradition of the European schools and belie the notion that the genre is peculiar to the West or particularly modern. Indeed, Mitchell observes, many imperial societies nurtured well-developed traditions of landscape painting: classical Greece and Rome, China, Japan, the seventeenth-century Dutch and French, and eighteenth- and nineteenth-century British. He goes on to suggest that the rise and flourishing of these traditions in each of these imperial societies coincides with the rise and flourishing of their imperial presence, while the specific decline of landscape painting in these societies tends to accompany the decline of their imperial profile more generally. Mitchell is at pains to note that both processes—the development and decline of landscape painting as well as imperialism—are in themselves highly complex and context dependent, and as such their interrelationship is far from straightforward or formulaic. In particular, Mitchell underscores the fact that neither dominant schools of painting nor modes of imperialism are seamless, uncontested monoliths. As with place, there are gaps and fissures that continuously undermine the illusion of stability, permanence, and naturalism:

> Landscape might be seen more profitably as something like the "dream-work" of imperialism, unfolding its own movement in time and space

from a central point of origin and folding back on itself to disclose both utopian fantasies of the perfected imperial prospect and fractured images of unresolved ambivalence and unsuppressed resistance.[45]

In sum, landscapes synthesize and make whole, they are collective and political products. They are attempts—always powerful, always partial—to freeze the blur of place, to gather together individual voices in a hegemonic vision, to tell a certain tale above all other existing narratives.

Landscape as Text

Some scholars have sought to explicitly conceptualize and analyze landscapes as texts. Early approaches to landscape as text were atheoretical or even antitheoretical: landscapes coded cultures in a relatively straightforward way, and all one really had to do was go into the field and decode what was already there:

> Our human landscape is our unwitting autobiography, reflecting our tastes, our values, our aspirations, and even our fears, in tangible, visible form. . . . All our cultural warts and blemishes are there, and our glories too; but above all, our ordinary day-to-day qualities are exhibited for anybody who wants to find them and knows how to look for them.[46]

In this view, the only real difficulty for the scholar (once she or he is trained to "see" landscapes as problematic in the first place) is that the pages of the text in question—the landscape—are often smudged, torn, or missing. Thus the only impediment to an exhaustive, complete, and accurate reading of the landscape is a reconstruction of a meaning that is already, albeit at times vexingly, hidden in the land.

More recent work on landscape as text shows a marked theoretical sophistication; in particular, questioning the scholar's ability to get below the surface of things and decode symbols to reveal a base stratum of underlying truth. This work draws on theoretical developments in literary criticism, in particular, that problematize the act of writing.

Since geography is, etymologically, "earth-writing," a problematization of writing is thus a problematization of what we do as scholars.[47] There is a productive slippage between signifier and signified, representation and the thing represented. There is, in other words, no way that what we write can provide a truthful mirror of what we are writing about. What's more, and as with the earlier discussion of place, there is no truly real *thing* that we may write about more or less accurately; there are merely different representations that in themselves and in tandem with other representations produce a gapped, fissured, powerful discourse. Writing itself is constitutive of reality; its process and products take center stage. Trevor Barnes and James Duncan assert that rhetorical devices or tropes such as metaphor, simile, and irony are powerful in themselves rather than as distractions to be gotten beyond; it is they, rather than an elusive bedrock reality, that should be attended to. Quoting Hayden White, Barnes and Duncan note that a trope "is the shadow from which all realistic discourse tries to free itself. This flight, however, is futile; for tropics is the process by which all discourse constitutes the object which it pretends only to describe realistically and to analyze objectively."[48]

This realization has profoundly shaped the work of some cultural geographers.[49] James S. Duncan's *The City as Text* provides an excellent example of this approach. Duncan explores the discursive construction of the early-nineteenth-century Sri Lankan landscape of Kandy. He approaches this landscape as a text, but not a text that can be read unproblematically. Rather, for Duncan, Kandy's landscape is composed of multiple texts that lend themselves to multiple readings. It is particularly in the contestation of the discursive field within which early-nineteenth-century Kandy materializes that Duncan finds his richest arena of inquiry. To explore these productive gaps, Duncan centralizes what he calls the rhetoric of landscape, "the mechanisms by which signification takes place within a landscape":[50]

> through the vocabulary of various conventional forms—signs, symbols, icons, and specialized tropes in the landscapes—people, particularly

powerful people, tell morally charged stories about themselves, the social relations within their community, and their relations to a divine order.[51]

The Kandyan landscape itself was constructed to reflect a divine order, a landscape of the gods, as set forth in the Sakran discourse. The cosmic Ocean of Milk, itself symbolic of the generative, cleansing powers of water, is echoed in the wavelike shape of the city's walls. The center of the palace symbolized the summit of Mount Meru, the *axis mundi* that joins heaven and earth. The city was partitioned to reflect heavenly divisions between sacred and profane spaces, and features of the landscape—the Temple of the Tooth Relic, the palace, the houses of commoners—were situated accordingly. Yet, as Duncan notes, the Kandyan landscape was not a static or closed entity; rather, it was built up, destroyed, and rebuilt many times, and in this process other, earlier cities both in Sri Lanka and in South Asia more broadly were referenced.

Duncan contends that landscapes are powerful constructs, illustrating empirically how a landscape has the ability to "act back" and shape the very politics of place from which it arises. In the Kandyan case, the urban landscape "was consciously designed to foster a certain hegemonic reading that spoke of the power, benevolence and legitimacy of the kings in their capital."[52] Yet the Kandyan landscape that was constructed in the early nineteenth century was read by some as providing visual evidence of the king's neglect of his duties, which enabled his opponents to rally the peasantry against him. The landscape and the story it told were interpreted differently than intended, and challenged, with profound material consequences for the king himself and the institution of kingship more broadly in Kandyan society:

> The changes that the king made to the landscape of Kandy lay at the heart of this controversy and revealed the contradictions within the larger discursive field of kingship. They prompted the nobles and the peasants to reconsider and shift their thinking about abstract conceptions of kingship. . . . The irony of this is that the king had hoped that his

city-building project would solidify his power by reinforcing both his charisma and magical power.[53]

In Duncan's book, it is the representation, construction, and play of interpretations of landscape that is geographically and politically powerful, not some static reality of the site itself, a deep cultural or placial bedrock that he succeeds in uncovering. Duncan's approach is a deeply textual one, very much informed by theories and methods of textual analysis found more readily in the humanities. One can imagine, however, a landscape approach that retains Duncan's appreciation of the polyvocality of landscape and his reluctance to seek the really real, yet that shares more theoretically and methodologically with a materialist perspective.[54] However, in some of the most recent and otherwise well-crafted critical cultural geography, there remains the nagging sense that the landscape as cultural and material construction merely obfuscates something deeper, something more solid, something worthy of uncovering. For example, Don Mitchell asserts that "landscapes transform the facts of place into a controlled representation, an imposition of order in which one (or perhaps a few) dominant ways of seeing are substituted for all ways of seeing and experiencing."[55] Mitchell's *The Lie of the Land* is a brilliantly detailed historical tracing of this imposition and its implications for California and, more importantly, Californians. That there is a powerful, hegemonic force at work in imposing one (or a few) dominant ways of seeing and experiencing is without question. But what are these facts of place that he refers to? Again, it seems, we are asked to believe in an enduring substrate, a straightforward power of place that undergirds, drives, and is effaced by its representations.

Such questions are at the heart of a debate within cultural geography. In contemporary critical approaches to landscape, a hardening schism is unfortunately developing among cultural geographers, between those whose focus is on the material construction of specific landscapes, and those whose approach emphasizes landscape's representational aspects.[56] On the one hand we have those who have apparently grown unmoored from the vital concerns of peoples and places, seduced instead by the siren call of poststructural theories that do away altogether with reality and, it is implied, the social scientist's duty to attend to the ethical and material underpinnings at the place under study. On the other hand are the excessively deterministic scholars, those whose writing suggests that there is a matereality of place as evidenced by a univocal, unifocal landscape that holds forth scant potential for alternative readings, even less so for agentic ones. For example, Don Mitchell categorizes Duncan, Cosgrove, and Barnes as "new cultural geographers," "the most extreme forms of [whom] have abandoned all interest in the world outside language and symbolic structure, outside representation."[57] Such geographers, in their stubborn insistence on the thoroughly constructed nature of place, have headed in the wrong direction: "More than from labor, much cultural geography is disconnecting itself from a concern with material spaces, sometimes arguing that since 'brute reality' is unknowable, cultural geographers should concern themselves with how landscapes are *only* representations, *only* ideology."[58] Their work, it is implied, is empirically, theoretically, and ethically wrongheaded—even pointless—and their energies would be far better spent developing a landscape praxis that emphasizes the political, material aspects of landscape and how these shape the real lives of real people in real places. Geographer Dick Walker reiterates Mitchell's concerns, admitting to feeling "a bit uneasy" and "concerned" about what he perceives as a turning away from "the old cultural geography [which] had a healthy respect for the evidence of material culture, which is in danger of slipping away in the reinvention of the field."[59]

For both of these geographers, a symbolic or representational approach to landscape is seen as decidedly secondary, even dangerously distractive. At the root of both Mitchell's and Walker's criticisms is the fear that a focus on representation will divert our collective critical attentions away from "material reality." There is here the implication that materiality—most often viewed in work by human geographers through the lens of labor—is somehow more singular, real, and hence more immediately important for a critical understanding of landscape than are representation and ideology. By contrast, there is something lacking in the softer representational approach, as if it just weren't quite legitimate. As Walker puts it, "Decoding the ideology of landscape and stripping away the cultural veil over the hard machinery of political economics is not easy."[60] There is here a separation of the "hard machinery of political economics" from culture, which is simply a veil to be "stripped away." There is also a gendered hierarchy of science at work, wherein stories and other figurative or poetic approaches are a flimsy feminine veneer—or worse, fail to show their "healthy respect"—while the hard language of fact and logic is coded as masculine, rational, and more valid for the serious tasks at hand.

Being myself one of those cultural geographers whose approach to landscape is through representation, I find the dismissiveness—not to mention the gendered coding—of this criticism unhelpful. I can nevertheless appreciate the frustration with scholarship that never seems to root its analysis in the lives, concerns, triumphs, and hardships of real people in real places. And in all fairness, Mitchell, too, recognizes that one "cannot understand a landscape . . . independent of how it has been represented."[61] Yet I fail to see, for example, how Duncan's work in *The City as Text* can be dismissed as lacking in significant political content: the book is centrally about the relationship between landscape iconography and political change. Indeed, I feel that the debate itself is sketched in far starker terms than are necessary. Both Mitchell and Duncan have more in common that it might seem. Reading both of their books, I am struck by the wealth of sound empirical research, their constant attention to issues of importance to the everyday lives of people in places, and the foregrounding of the political dimensions, both broad and narrow, of the powerful interrelationship between land and life. In other words, there seems to be a middle ground between a deterministic, univocal read of reality hidden in the landscape, and an infinite multiplicity of possible readings with each as valid as the next.

I do, however, take issue with the suggestion that there is an unproblematic, factual substrate of place that may be uncovered by carefully stripping away the veil of representation. For to attempt to prise apart fact from fiction not only constructs a hierarchy whereby "fact" is prioritized above "fiction," it also assumes that such a separation is possible. Yet as I will suggest here, the narrative construction of landscape is so tightly bound to material processes that to separate the two, let alone relegate stories to a secondary role, would be to profoundly miss the point. To assert that place is a narrative construction is not to deny that it is a materially powerful sort of construction, one rife with (perhaps predicated upon) conflict, and that this narrative tension results in tangible changes wrought upon both the human beings and the physical spaces with which we share the planet. To deny the materiality of place would be not only difficult, it would be politically irresponsible. To assert that places are narratively constructed is in fact to assert that they are power constructs, always processual, usually contested, and deeply performative. Stories can be powerfully real and really powerful.

Might we understand, for example, the geological explanation of landscape morphology as a story of sorts? The division of long time into periods (chapters), the recounting of teleological events such as the hydrological cycle, plate tectonics, the rise and subsidence of seas, the layering of rock upon rock, the action of wave and wind and river, and so on, all toward a known end-point "now" (plot), the rise and fall of successive empires of bacteria, lizards, mammals, and man (protagonists) and their grand tussles with meteors, glaciers, and viruses (the epic struggle between good and evil): all these events no less real or true, simply seen differently.

Or consider the weight of stories told about human claims to particular pieces of land. Charlotte Black Elk, for example, believes that the bones of her Lakota ancestors make up the Black Hills in present-day South Dakota. According to Lakota creation legends, place is centrally important in distilling the meaning of life: "When the universe was created, all of the universe was given a song. Each piece of the universe holds a piece of that song, but the entire song is located only in the Black Hills."[62] The massacre at Wounded Knee was the direct result of the strength of these claims to place. Paula Gunn Allen recalls a story that her Laguna Pueblo great-grandmother, Meta Atseye Gunn, told her about how "a couple of very large sandstone rocks—one roughly round, and the other rectangular, almost cylindrical" were in fact the head and the body of a wicked giantess, flung there by two young men with special powers after a mortal battle to vanquish the giantess.[63] Allen notes, ironically, how identity shifts and becomes, for her, unsettled as the same landform, "Tse'pina, or Veiled-in-Clouds, the old woman mountain" is written on Anglo maps as Mount Taylor, "named after the old Indian fighter and president of the United States, Zachary Taylor, changing the meaning, gender, and our relationship to that mysterious, beautiful place."[64] Robert Layton's scholarship focuses on the landscape construction of Aboriginal peoples of the Uluru region of Australia's Western Desert, where rocks and waterholes are spoken of as relatives or as embodying ancestral beings, and the undulating lines along the flank of Uluru (Ayers Rock) mark the passage of the Kuniya pythons and their very bodies are long, tubular boulders.[65] As with the Lakota and Laguna Pueblo place stories in the emerging United States, these Australian place stories have precipitated deadly struggles over meaning and legitimacy in the landscape. Stories matter. They can move mountains. They can inspire the ultimate sacrifice.

The Narrative Construction of Landscape
Emplotting Place
Landscapes are scripts that discursively construct particular understandings of place. As with stories, landscapes render a series of things, be they events or physical features, meaningful. They synthesize and connect, lending a holism to what would otherwise be a disparate collection of objects or events. As Roland Barthes points out, narratives are ubiquitous features of human societies; it is thus unsurprising that narrativity shapes human understandings of their places in the world: "Narrative is present in every age, in every place, in every society; it begins with the very history of mankind and there nowhere is nor has been a people without narrative."[66]

By thinking of landscape and narrative as working in tandem, we understand that when culture-stories are physically inscribed in the land, they are accorded a fixity. Landscapes not only allow us to tell stories about ourselves to ourselves and thereby construct collective identities, they also allow us to write them down. In telling tales through landscape, speech becomes writing. This is a powerful act. Drawing on the work of Paul Ricoeur, Clifford Geertz notes the importance of the act of inscription and the fixation of meaning this achieves: "When we speak, our utterances fly by as events like any other behavior; unless what we say is inscribed in writing (or some other established recording process), it is as evanescent as what we do."[67] Here, I will suggest that landscape provides just that sort of alternative recording process. This claim is reiterated by Kenneth Foote, when he asserts:

> This concept of memory provides an important bond between culture and landscape, because human modifications of the environment are often related to the way societies wish to sustain and efface memories. More to the point, the very durability of the landscape and of the memorials placed in the landscape makes these modifications effective for symbolizing and sustaining collective values over long periods of time. . . . In effect the physical durability of landscape permits it to carry meaning into the future so as to help sustain memory and cultural traditions. Societies and cultures have many other ways to sustain collective values and beliefs, including ritual and oral tradition, but landscape stands apart from these—like writing—as a durable, visual representation.[68]

Take, for example, Keith Basso's fascinating book *Wisdom Sits in Places*. In it, he discusses the durable nature of stories written on and through the landscape as he came to understand this through his field research with a group of Western Apache in Cibecue, New Mexico. There are two major categories of place names for the Western Apache: those that refer to physical features, such as Juniper Tree Stands Alone, or Line Of Blue Below Rocks, and those that refer to sad or tragic events that serve to remind people of proper behavior. A place named Shades Of Shit, for example, acquired its name from a group of ancestors that would not share their corn with a less-fortunate group and was eventually forced by the second group to remain inside their shades (or shelters), forced even to defecate inside them until the stench made eating terribly unpleasant. When the first group finally agreed to share their food, they were allowed out and immediately moved to a new place, never to return to the site that figuratively, if not literally anymore, reeked. To this day, the name Shades Of Shit reminds their descendants of the social consequences of stinginess.[69]

Basso notes that the land has a deep moral purpose for these people, because stories of correct behavior told through place names act as a corrective to those who would drink, philander, or try to imitate the ways of whites. Place names inscribe and enforce a social order, one that some Western Apache feel is fundamental to their collective survival. Basso recounts speaking to a young Apache woman whose grandmother had "shot an arrow" at her two years previously. Of course, the grandmother did not literally shoot an arrow at her granddaughter; she had merely told a story intended to remind the girl of proper ways of behaving. In this case, the girl had attended a puberty ceremony with pink plastic curlers in her hair, a practice she picked up at school in Utah. This went against the custom of wearing one's hair free-flowing as a sign of respect, respect that was essential to the ceremony's power to provide girls with the qualities they would need as adults. The grandmother waited quietly for two weeks, then, in the presence of a large group, casually told the tale of an Apache cattle rustler who had tried to act like a white man. In the story, he was released by the police at a place called Men Stand Above Here And There. The grandmother did not explicitly direct the story at her granddaughter, but she and the rest of those present knew whom the arrow was aimed at. The story had a powerful and lasting effect on the girl's sense and practice of herself. She threw away the curlers, which she now understood to be an attempt on her part to act white. More importantly, as she drove with Basso past Men Stand Above Here And There two years later, he asked her if she recalled the incident of the story. She replied, "I know that place. It stalks me every day." In the words of Nick Thompson, one of Basso's key informants, it is the lasting nature of stories thus written that makes the land so important:

It's hard to keep on living right. Many things jump up at you and block your way. But you won't forget that story. You're going to see the place where it happened, maybe every day if it's nearby and close to Cibecue. If you don't see it, you're going to hear its name and see it in your mind. It doesn't matter if you get old—that place will keep on stalking you like the one who shot you with the story. Maybe that person will die. Even so, that place will keep on stalking you. It's like that person is still alive. Even if we go far away from here to some big city, places around here keep stalking us. If you live wrong, you will hear the names and see the places in your mind. They keep on stalking you, even if you go across the oceans. The names of all these places are good. They make you remember how to live right, so you want to replace yourself again.[70]

Landscapes are an ordered form of writing. They have the basic elements of stories: plot, sequenced events, and characters. To return to my father's story, for example, in his fraught understanding of the place where he was building our house, the prominent plotline is constituted by white guilt, though it was so far sublimated it had to be dreamed. Yet, as I suggested, the understanding of the place changes depending on who is doing the telling. When I tell this story, I cast it in terms—white guilt, for example—that my father does not agree with. For his part, he sees clear protagonists—my mother and himself—and an antagonist, the angry old woman. In his telling, the storyline is one of vengeance. I, on the other hand, and perhaps some of my readers, am more inclined to see the principal action as one of dispossession on my parents' part (though that plot twist puts me in a rather uncomfortable position). Antagonist and protagonist change places in my version. My parents are thieves, while the Indian woman is rightfully indignant. Chief Seattle had still another emplotment in mind when he took the long historical view of what had happened to lands that used to be his, their dispossession merely constituting one among many in the ceaseless rise and fall of civilizations. In Chief Seattle's telling of this place—in his landscape, that is—there is no clear antagonist or protagonist, only people at the mercy of larger forces they cannot control. He speculated that we might be brothers after all in our shared powerlessness in the face of the course of history.

Conjuring Place, Claiming Identity

There is a master narrative at work in all place stories, one that constructs identity at individual as well as collective levels by laying claim to land through stories. We are, in a profoundly important sense, who we are because of where we are, and vice versa. Indeed, culture itself, the very essence of humanness, is rooted in the land. As Casey notes, "To be cultural, to have a culture, is to inhabit a place sufficiently intensely to cultivate it—to be responsible for it, to respond to it, to attend to it caringly."[71] Behind such an assertion lies Heidegger's idea of dwelling as a process that is necessarily of the land, a process upon which Being itself is predicated.[72] Some, including Simone Weil, have gone so far as to suggest that the need for place is among those basic to human existence, on a par with food: "To be rooted is perhaps the most important and least recognized need of the human soul."[73] Phenomenologists in general assert the connections between dwelling in a place, caring for it, and constructing an identity that is deeply place-based. As Barbara Bender notes, "By moving along familiar paths, winding memories and stories around places, people create a sense of self and belonging."[74]

Little wonder so much of contemporary social theory centralizes anxiety over displacement, the human consequences of dispossession of land, diaspora, being lost, and attempts to construct individual and collective identities in what is seen to be a generalized context of placelessness. Much emotive energy is bound up in these ties to place, in forging them, keeping them, reclaiming them. Land, both in the possession of it and possession by it, evokes an affective response, one that can turn bitterly angry if one's claim is challenged. Yi-Fu Tuan termed this propensity for developing deep attachments to land "topophilia." Broadly defined, topophilia encompasses "all of the human being's affective ties with the material environment," ranging from aesthetic enjoyment to a "more permanent and less easy to express" experience, manifest in "feelings that one has toward a place because it is home, the locus of memories, and the means of gaining a livelihood."[75] Topophilia is a distilled term, appropriate for my suggestion that landscape, narrative, and identity are bound together in place. It is these claims legitimated through stories, and the passionate senses of self that are forged, recreated, and contested therein, that are at the heart of *Dry Place*.

Collective memory is the process that shapes these stories and keeps them alive. As Joseph Davis reminds us in his analysis of narrative in social movements, the telling and retelling of tales is a social exchange whereby "my" story eventually becomes "our" story. In other words, stories are a method by which community can be constructed through remembering together.[76] In this remembering through landscape and landscape shaped through narrative, there is a mutual sustenance. Christopher Tilley notes: "If stories are linked to regularly repeated spatial practices they become mutually supportive, and when a story becomes sedimented into the landscape, the story and the place dialectically help to construct and reproduce each other."[77] Or, as Matthew Potteiger and Jamie Purinton have asserted,

> The term landscape narrative designates the interplay and mutual relationship that develops between landscape and narrative. To begin with, places configure narratives. Landscape not only locates or serves as background setting for stories, but is itself a changing, eventful figure and process that engenders stories. A road establishes a sequence while opening the possibilities of chance encounters. The scale of space becomes the scope of an epic or the confines of a personal drama. Traces in the landscape hold secrets and invite interpretation. Trees, rocks, ground, weather, or any elements can serve as emblems in a narrative. In this manner people map landscapes into the very texture and structure of stories. In turn, every narrative, even the most abstract, allegorical, or personal, plays a critical role in making places. It is through narrative that we interpret the processes and events of place. We come to know a place because we know its stories.[78]

To return to Basso's example, the very history of the Western Apache is written not in books but in litanies of place names that recount what happened where and why it is important. Together, place names and the narratives they hold act to gather and reproduce the community; they give it a sense of we-ness, of a shared past and a common destiny. Another example of this emergence of collective belonging through the narration of collective memory through the landscape is provided by Simon Schama, as he recounts his visit to the Polish wilderness, the *puszcza*, a landscape that appears repeatedly in Polish literature. In his explorations, Schama came upon a mass gravesite enclosing the bodies of Poles executed by Stalin's security police in 1945:

> What filled my own field of vision formed the shape of a window or a painting, a rectangular space, composed of horizontally layered scenery. Here was the homeland for which the people of Giby had died and to which, in the shape of their memorial hummock, they had now been added. Their memory had now assumed the form of the landscape itself. A metaphor had become a reality; an absence had become a presence.[79]

The importance of memory for constructing spatialized collective identities has not escaped the notice of geographers, despite the fact that narrative per se is paid scant attention in the discipline.[80] Much of this work focuses on the construction of national identity through collective memory. In this, these cultural geographers acknowledge a deep debt to the foundational work of Benedict Anderson, whose analysis of the emergence of modern nationalisms through print journalism insisted that modern nations were in fact "imagined communities," where "imagined" is not equivalent to "imaginary." Anderson is at pains to underscore the deadly sway of modern nationalism. In the same fashion, geographers who have examined the discursive construction of nation on and through the landscape have noted that for all its constructedness, the landscape is anything but passive, inconsequential, or subordinate. Rather, the landscape and the identities contested therein are at the center of some of the bitterest human conflict.

The act of naming the land is a critical gesture in the formation of national identity and of ongoing struggles over national identity. Because the question of "who are we?" is always vexed, the landscape is not solely the locus of these negotiations, but more often than not it is the very means of such contentions over identity. Catherine Nash, for example, has illustrated the difficult contest between Gaelic and Anglicized place names in Ireland to underscore the complexity of the politics of place and national identity. [81] The designation of symbolic sites on the landscape, in the form of monuments, battlegrounds, plaques, and so forth, can also be understood as a form of naming, or designating that which is significant by speaking it through the landscape. Tim Edensor investigates the contentious performance of Scottish national identity through the constant reworking of the myth of medieval heroes Robert the Bruce and William Wallace, and the spatial negotiation of this narrative revision through heritage tourism, monuments, and museums.[82] Kenneth Foote examines the designation of places of diverse valence on the landscape of the United States, noting that a politics of remembering and of forgetting is at work when some sites are set apart from others, or alternatively, when they are consciously effaced in an attempt to erase what happened there from national consciousness. [83]

The repetitive performance of nation on and through the landscape can lend a measure of sanctity to the events, people, and places in question and thus to the nation they stand for. Thus the nation as sacred space is constructed in no small measure via the construction and emplacement of historical memory, itself an act of narration and counternarration. Likewise, to contest the emplacement of historical memory is often understood as an act of desecration. Thus, though it may be enacted symbolically, the negotiation of national identity is a contention frequently waged on terms no less portentous than the struggle between the sacred and the profane. As David Chidester and Edward Linenthal note, "a space or place is perhaps revealed at its most sacred when people are willing to fight, kill, or die over its ownership and control."[84] Their contention echoes Anderson's discussion of the power of the nation as imagined community, wherein the fact that the nation is imagined in no way diminishes its ability to recruit sentiments of place loyalty so strong that one is willing to sacrifice one's life based on them.

The naming, memorializing, and ritualization of place in turn constitutes a sort of *conjuring*, a bringing into being of place and with it, a specific and scripted understanding of collective identity tied to that place. If place is conjured—in other words, if there is no such thing as place qua place—place can be understood as an empty signifier, a signifier that lacks a signified and thus can be invested with potentially infinite meanings.

> When space or place becomes sacred, spatially scarce resources are transformed into a surplus of signification. As an arena of signs and symbols, a sacred place is not a fixed point in space, but a point of departure for an endless multiplication of meaning. Since a sacred place could signify almost anything, its meaningful contours can become almost infinitely extended through the work of interpretation. . . . Due to the inherent surplus of signification in "the sacred," no appropriation can ever be final, no exclusion can be total, and, therefore, conflict over ownership and control of the symbolic surplus remains endemic in sacred space.[85]

To say that place is conjured is not to say that place, landscape, and identity are somehow powerless or immaterial. It is, rather, to note that the power of place lies in the politics of its production, and that such politics is suffused with, not apart from, narrative, myth, and ritual. Claiming space, the ownership of sacred symbols, and the right to name the land constitute powerful authorial gestures in the scripting of collective identity. Contesting such claims, often through the same narrative, symbolic, and ritual modes that are employed to make them initially, is at the heart of a politics of the relationship between identity and place.

CHAPTER 2

A Blank White Page

Americans in some manner will cling to the traditional idea that
they suddenly came upon a vacant land on which they created the
world's most affluent society. Not only is such an idea false, it is absurd.
Yet without it both Western man and his religion stand naked before
the world.

—Vine Deloria, *God Is Red*

Nation-State and Narratives of Belonging and Exclusion

One of the central plotlines that has shaped modern landscapes is
the nation-state.[1] The emergence of the familiar modern (Eurocentric)
world order in which the earth's surface is thought of and practiced as
a tightly jigsawed surface of nation-states has involved at its very core
the weaving of an elaborate tapestry of tales, myths, and dreams. The
nation-state has provided a durable narrative framework for claims to
place and identity, one perhaps rooted in ethnic and religious solidarities that predate (and will surely outlast) modernity, one so ubiquitous
and ritualized that some scholars have perceived the nation-state as
a sacred, even magical, sort of landscape.[2] To approach the modern
landscape of nation-states through stories is to attempt to denaturalize
one of modernity's key sociospatial institutions, to attempt to plumb
the vastly complex web of difference upon which the mythic unity of
the nation-state is constructed. "From the margins of modernity, at the
insurmountable extremes of storytelling, we encounter the question of
cultural difference as the perplexity of living, and writing, the nation."[3]

To centralize the role of narrative in understanding the crafting
of national (and postnational) landscapes is never to imply that there
is only a flimsy form of fiction at work that has somehow duped us all,
for as Anne McClintock has so correctly observed, "nations are not simply phantasmagoria of the mind; as systems of cultural representation

whereby people come to imagine a shared experience of identification with an extended community, they are historical practices through which social difference is both invented and performed."[4] One has only to witness the contemporary liberation struggles of Palestinians, Quebequois, Irish, Aborigines, First Peoples, and Native Americans, among others, to appreciate the grim reality of the blood shed and the hearts broken over such stories. These struggles are undeniably material events. Yet they are driven, ultimately, by stories, tales that root the claims of peoples to particular pieces of land, often in direct conflict with the equally mythic, divine, or timeless claims of other groups.

The organizing motif of the nation-state, with its borders, capital cities, and vivid patchwork of contrasting colors in elementary school textbooks, has been the most important sculptor of the geopolitical landscape of the modern world. Given our durable propensity to develop deep attachments to land, however, it is wholly legitimate to expect politicized claims to place to outlast modernity; and furthermore, that the ways we construct and contest difference will be reworked outside the framework of the nation-state. Perhaps the nation-state is always already in crisis, excessive, endlessly contested and in flux. In the modern West, nation (understood as a supralocal collectivity often rooted in ethnic and religious solidarities) and state (the legal-institutional appurtenances that allow the spatial expression of the nation) are expected to seamlessly coincide territorially, culturally, ethnically. A great deal of official and extraofficial work goes into assuring that they appear to do so.[5] Yet often nation and state do not overlap; indeed they frequently work at cross-purposes. As Sarah Radcliffe and Sallie Westwood explore in their fascinating study of the production of contemporary national identities in Ecuador, a constant tension exists between the desire for a centered nation (where nation and state coincide) and the reality of "the fragility of these attempts at centering and the strength of the fractures."[6] Perhaps it is only through these ongoing performances of sameness and difference that the nation itself can be imagined. It is in the play between the narrative agenda of imposing national borders as enclosures of homogeneous national spaces, and the tensions that inevitably arise because difference cannot be fully suppressed—those ghostly voices—that the nation-state can be appreciated as an inherently, immanently unstable entity.[7] As Homi Bhabha has noted, this interplay of stabilization and destabilization is profoundly narrative in nature:

> Counter-narratives of the nation that continually evoke and erase its totalizing boundaries—both actual and conceptual—disturb those ideological maneuvers through which "imagined communities" are given essentialist identities. For the political unity of the nation consists in a continual displacement of its irredeemably plural modern space, bounded by different, even hostile nations, into a signifying space that is archaic and mythical, paradoxically representing the nation's modern territoriality, in the patriotic, atavistic temporality of Traditionalism.[8]

The modern nation-state, and, before it, other spatial expressions of nation rooted in ethnic or religious solidarities, have long engaged dual gestures of internal smoothing and external striation. This ceaseless, productive oscillation between smoothness and striation is centralized in the work of Gilles Deleuze and Félix Guattari. Utilizing the Lacanian understanding of how the smooth body of the infant becomes striated, or progressively marked with sensual and social meaning and thus differentiated, forming the development of one's sense of separateness in the world, Deleuze and Guattari extend the idea spatially. *Spaces* also move from smooth to striated, but they can move back to again to smoothness. Spaces can be both smooth and striated at once. Smoothness and striation invoke one another; indeed, they allow each other to exist: "we must remind ourselves that the two spaces in fact exist only in mixture: smooth space is constantly being translated, transversed into striated space; striated space is constantly being reversed, returned to a smooth space."[9] Tellingly, Deleuze and Guattari utilize the example of textiles—felt, quilting, knitting, embroidery, and crochet, as well as woven fabrics—to illustrate this interplay, an analogy that harkens back to the previous chapter's discussion of place as textured.

Constructing and maintaining (at least the semblance of) internal homogeneity was for modern nation-states, as Víctor Zúñiga has noted, "a precondition for constituting themselves as liberal, representative democracies."[10] Yet the internal smoothness could only function as such by contrast, by juxtaposition with an outside, kept comfortably at bay by a geopolitical border, "a spatial wrapper surrounding the nation-state":

> The eradication of internal frontiers implies the homogenization of space in social, political, and cultural terms. The imposition of external borders, however, implies quite the opposite, that is, the promotion and maintenance of spaces that are socially, politically, and culturally distinct. . . . The creation of modern states included a dual geographic exercise: level and divide. It is for this reason that the promises of modernity suppose, on the one hand, secure external frontiers that are unmovable, functional, and linear. On the other hand, they suppose that the spaces within national frontiers will be homogeneous, ordered, level, contiguous, and isolated from other national spaces, just as they appear on grade school maps.[11]

For the nation-state, smoothness, ease, and internal homogeneity are but a recurring wish for intact fullness. The geopolitical border may be firmly in place, but real differences are always there, sometimes internal, sometimes external, perhaps driven underground, silenced, cloaked or stifled, absented but never finally absent. They create a constant din of dissent from the literal and figurative margins.

In the words of Anthony Burke, writing of geopolitical borders and security, the modern nation-state is distinguished by a sharp, necessary contrast between what he terms "the jagged and the smooth," the recursive tension between ideal and harsh reality, "the smooth experience of life—consensual, pleasurable, and safe—that security has historically promised and enacted, with the jagged history that has enabled and underpinned its dreams of prosperity, order, and realization."[12] Burke's analysis brings to the fore the repressive element involved in enacting the state's desire for intact fullness, and this is an important consideration when speaking of the ways that the United States of America has constructed, solidified, and maintained its smooth-surfaced vision of sameness-in-difference, of a leveled social, economic, and political playing field adorned (but never marred) by cultural difference.

Burke's analysis also, unwittingly, dances around the possibility of internal differences that arise *within* the nation-state to disrupt its smooth surface, a point that harkens back to Bhabha's, above. Burke's description of smoothness turns on what can be read as an androcentric description of a desirable sexual experience, in his words, "consensual, pleasurable, and safe." He describes smoothness as "emotional, tactile."[13] Constructing internal smoothness in these terms signals the very important possibility that not all will experience the nation-state with the same degree of smoothness, or that what is smooth for some may well be jagged for others, or even that smoothness *turns on* jaggedness in (what Burke terms, though again with no eye to the gender dynamics implied) "a profound, functional embrace."[14] Internal borders—borders that at once reflect and structure gendered, sexualized, racialized, ethnicized, religious, class, and other differences—inevitably ruffle the surface of smoothness, regardless of how seamless the external, geopolitical boundaries may be.

A foundational myth in the evolving geoimaginary of the young, expanding United States of America in the nineteenth century turned on constructions of the Western landscape as empty. The histories of both this landscape and the nation-state of which it is a part tell of the ceaseless, productive oscillation between smoothness and striation, bordering and debordering, deterritorializing and reterritorializing. Such a rhetoric of emptiness has allowed an array of stark, transformational, and sometimes violent acts—bombing, nuclear testing, damming, mining, polluting, dispossession, fencing, and the construction of Indian reservations and military bases among them—to be committed upon the land and its inhabitants. For example, the coding of Nevada's arid lands as "vacant" and "worthless" was reflected in a 1989 U.S. Navy publication that quipped, "If you find the surface of the moon congenial,

[Nevada] ain't bad."[15] The statement was used to legitimate the appropriation of these lands by the U.S. Navy as a bombing range, a gesture that has too-close parallels to the earlier coding of Native American land as "surplus" and its subsequent appropriation by the U.S. government for military establishments and white settlement a century previous. In both cases, a space is deemed blank with the intent to permit its striation in particularly violent fashions. This irony has been much examined by scholars, particularly New Western historians. As Patricia Limerick has noted, "The legacy of the overland trail was a judgment of arid vacancy. That legacy lasted into the twentieth century and up to the present. . . . defense projects made it clear that an 'endless sea of nothingness' had its uses."[16]

The rhetoric of emptiness could not have operated without particular sorts of striations: borders. Borders provide an essential trope that structures this particular narrative. Though the tale is one of smooth passage westward, of borderlessness, it could only be enacted with the aid of borders both external and internal. So though, for example, the raconteur par excellence of expansionism, Frederick Jackson Turner, could argue that it was the very smoothness of Western spaces, the *limitless* supply of *free* land, that was translated into the limitless inventiveness and unbounded energy of the (Anglo) American character, he fails completely to mention that the establishment of a geopolitical boundary with Mexico in 1848 had enabled this expansion in a legal-institutional sense in the first place.[17] Turner's account is, however, rife with references to internal borders, specifically, the endless conflict between Native and Anglo Americans. Indeed, his very conceptualization of the frontier as, ultimately, the border between savagery and civilization invokes a border in the larger sense that I wish to use it throughout this book. However, Turner continues to write of the West in terms that emphasize its borderlessness. In particular, he utilizes metaphoric references to water: American social development is characterized by its "fluidity" (2) the advancing frontier is "the outer edge of the wave" (3), miners trekking to California are a "tide" (8), westward migration "flowed" over already taken eastern lands (18), and so on. Turner also describes the frontier as "elastic"; "it does not need sharp definition" (3): in other words, it is soft, a term that evokes Burke's implicitly gendered description of smoothness.

Thus the Ur-tale for understanding nothing less than the American spirit—a story that captures considerable attention to this day—itself turns on the oscillation between smoothness and striation.[18] Tellingly, some of the most incisive critique of Turner's frontier thesis points to how his analysis glossed the centrality of Western cities (striations) in favor of presenting a view of the West as wholly rural (smooth). For example, though he does not use the terms "smoothness" and "striation" in his analysis, William Cronon emphasizes how the striations of urban development necessarily constitute what Turner chose to emphasize, the smooth rurality of the Western landscape: "Frontier and metropolis turn out to be the same sides of the coin."[19]

This chapter explores the rhetoric of emptiness, understood here as a particularly important mode of landscape construction vis-à-vis the spatial and ideological enactment of the expansionist (Anglo) nation-state. As explored in the previous chapter, borders are approached broadly as the expression, sometimes formally spatial but often neither formal nor spatial, of the coming together of difference as an integral process in the construction of identity at all scales. In the specific case of the westward expansion of the United States of America in the nineteenth century, borders both internal and external, formally spatial and not, were vital to the spatial enactment of a nation that, at least narratively, was predicated on a form of smoothness understood as emptiness, as a lack of borders. Thus the history of the United States is one of tension between borders and borderlessness: a long tale of border conflict.

Smooth Space in the Colonial Geoimaginary

Though it is not commonplace to set the history of white Americans and their nationalism in the context of fables, it is apparent that promised lands, mythic odysseys, and the fulfillment of divinely ordained destinies are woven into the earliest threads of the nation that would become the United States of America. From its formal founding as a colony of religious refugees, the emergent nation of the United States of America considered itself exceptional. The Puritans who initially colonized New England in the early seventeenth century were part of a tradition of English Protestantism that saw England as apart from, and morally superior to, the rest of the European continent, "a place divinely singled out for higher missions."[20] The Separatists who voyaged across the Atlantic saw themselves as still purer sorts who needed to break away from an England that had not fully parted with its popish ways. The New World had been provided by God that the Puritans might forge a utopian future in a pure place, physically and spiritually far from England. Nearly a century later, Thomas Jefferson sustained a biblically rooted notion of American exceptionalism, likening the exodus of the Puritans from England to the chosen of Israel and their deliverance from Egypt to Canaan.[21]

Manifest Destiny—the idea that there existed a preordained, God-given mandate for white, English-speaking Europeans to expand and fill the North American continent—constituted a decisive era in this assertion of American exceptionalism. Though the phrase "manifest destiny" was first penned by John L. O'Sullivan in 1840, the *idea* that America's bright future was continental in extension dates from the Revolutionary period, itself thought to be a clear sign from God that the new nation was marked for greatness.[22] The United States of America would not only capture a finer, higher destiny than that of decadent Europe, it would do so in a way that would appear inevitable, and thus innocent, because of its divine ordination.

Manifest Destiny was predicated upon the territorial expansion of civilized, English-speaking white men, not just pell-mell across the face of the continent, but *westward*. This westward movement would complete a long historical cycle that had seen human civilization move inexorably toward the setting sun. The movement west was understood as a sort of natural law that applied as equally to human beings as to inanimate earthly phenomena. Thomas Hart Benton, who served as a senator and Democratic party leader, declared in 1818–19,

All obey the same impulse—*that of going to the West*; which, from the beginning of time has been the course of heavenly bodies, of the human race, and of science, civilization, and national power following their train. . . . In a few years the Rocky Mountains will be passed, and "the children of Adam" will have completed the circumambulation of the globe, by marching to the west until they arrive at the Pacific ocean, in sight of the eastern shore of that Asia in which their parents were originally planted.[23]

The tale of nation was an epic saga of desti-nation, one which turned on a particular landscape construction that turned on the interplay of smoothness and striation. This smoothing of spaces constructed a blankness that was at the heart of dominant landscape attitudes in colonizing societies more generally. Understanding polar, jungle, ocean, and desert spaces as smooth was a gesture of colonization, a crucial aspect of empire building, one that sought to erase prior claims to places and allowed a direct, unmediated inscription of the colonial worldview.

The blankness was consciously, narratively constructed. It shaped a landscape that could be more easily (dis)possessed. The polar, jungle, desert, and ocean regions were erased in the collective imperial geoimaginary, so that they could be overwritten with a narrative of expansion, civilization, and extraction. Rather than writing of these landscapes as smooth spaces, then, it is more appropriate to use instead the modifier "smoothed," for this invokes the active processes at work in rendering a landscape featureless. If the landscape is understood as that place produced in-between the human and nonhuman worlds as they work at trying to make sense of one another, there can be no such thing as a landscape that is truly and utterly devoid. The rich diversity of the world is, for the most part, in the eye of the beholder. To *not* see this involves a choice, perhaps not a wholly conscious choice given that dominant landscape attitudes train vision and craft language that can help, or hinder, our perception. Yet it is a choice nonetheless.

Joseph Conrad's literary treatment of West-Central Africa as "the heart of darkness" illustrates this gesture. Marlow, the shipboard raconteur, describes the lure of this blankness for him as a small boy:

> Now, when I was a little chap I had a passion for maps. . . . At that time there were many blank spaces on the earth, and when I saw one that looked particularly inviting on a map (but they all look that) I would put my finger on it and say, When I grow up I will go there. . . . But there was one yet—the biggest, the most blank, so to speak—that I had a hankering for.[24]

In the same passage, Marlow describes a crucial turn, that moment in his youth when the blank spaces on the map begin to fill with names and symbols and topographical features. In the case of West-Central Africa, the focus of his tale as related in *Heart of Darkness*, this filling-in lent the place a terrifying aspect. For, though more was known about the physical geography of the place once Marlow had grown to manhood, what was known of the human geography was sufficient to render the place unintelligible to the European mind. In the black-and-white, darkness-and-light leitmotif of Conrad's novel, "It had ceased to be a blank space of delightful mystery—a white patch for a boy to dream gloriously over. It had become a place of darkness."[25]

It was for Belgium to bring light to this dark place (and for Conrad to poetically shed light on the darkness of the colonizing heart). The colonizer, that Prince Valiant of smooth spaces, would illuminate this space by marking it, striating it with the laser-sharp beams of abstract partitioning. With his phallic sword of empire, he would draft national borders, categorize the local flora and fauna, hack of meaning out of the relentless smooth ebony forest. He brought structure and rationality to the formless jungle, imposed meaning on chaos.[26]

Polar explorations, as well, provide ample illustration of the colonizing imaginary that willed the human and animal life of these lands nonexistent, seeing only the blankness of snow and sea and ice unfolding miserably in all directions. And terrifying these spaces seemed for explorers from Russia, England, and the United States in search of the Northwest Passage, for further details of lands claimed, and, at times, for any trace of previous expeditions. Lieutenant Maxwell, a member of Vitus Bering's second polar expedition, is quoted as saying, "You never feel safe when you have to navigate in waters which are completely blank."[27] The blankness of the northern waters emerged as particularly frightening, with entire expeditions and hundreds of men swallowed into the pack ice and dragged into the endless night beyond the horizon of Europe. At times only their skeletons were found, while grim reports of mutiny and madness and cannibalization slowly surfaced from journals and ship's records later recovered. Other times, no word at all ever emerged.

Writing of polar expeditions, Annie Dillard links the perceived austerity of the landscape directly to the task at hand: "Polar explorers— one gathers from their accounts—sought at the Poles something of the sublime. Simplicity and purity attracted them; *they set out to perform clear tasks in uncontaminated lands.*"[28] As with the heart of darkness described by Conrad, these frightening tales were accompanied by the irresistible allure of the poles. Some, like the naturalist John Muir, were pulled to the poles by the magnetic taxonomizing force of being the first to scientifically catalogue and classify these lands.[29] Others, like the officers and men aboard the lost whaler *Jeanette*, which the *Thomas Corwin* sailed in search of in 1881 with Muir aboard, found the attraction of the poles to be in the lucrative hunting of whales, seals, sea otters, and walrus, and soon in the glitter of the Yukon gold fields. Still others saw their duty in terms of knowing and mapping these blank spaces in order to claim them for their country, planting flags and building stark cairns on lonely islands in an emphatic striating gesture of national expansion. The poles were harsh tokens to be possessed for the ultimate enrichment of the nation diligent enough to grasp them, holding forth a "vision of a vast northern empire, rigorous and stern to its children but kindly in its very rigour, rich in resources, not such as to fall into the idle hand and nourish the languor of inertia but such as come as the reward of effort and courage."[30]

Along with the ocean, outer space in the postwar expansionist geoimaginary of the United States, and perhaps cyberspace in today's emerging informatics empire, the desert provides a final example of a smooth landscape par excellence. In the early decades of the nineteenth century, the North American desert and semidesert lands (indeed, much of the Western United States) was in Spanish, then briefly in newly independent Mexican, hands. Few Anglo-Americans had reason or desire to traverse it. By the conclusion of the U.S.-Mexican War in 1848, the United States had exchanged a mere $15 million dollars for roughly half of Mexico's national territory at the time.[31] In the bargain, the United States acquired a significant amount of truly arid land.[32]

As with polar regions, the desert was initially approached as lack: devoid of water, of life, of variation let alone beauty, of economic potential, of any goodness whatsoever.[33] Yet, California beckoned on the other side of the continent, that lush coastal strip of balmy climate, fertile land, abundant space, rich gold fields. Thus the great American desert region in-between "had the primary function of connective tissue; something, after all, had to connect Texas to California."[34] In the mid-nineteenth century, the desert was a landscape to be passed through and at best merely survived. It was not a place to settle, and certainly not a space of aesthetic contemplation. The ordeals endured by some overland travelers were so trying as to be understandable to them only in biblical terms. The term "desert" harkens to the Judeo-Christian understanding of deserts as wildernesses, comprising any uninhabited (deserted) places, regardless of relative humidity.[35] Biblical wildernesses serve metaphorically as crucibles of excess (lust, temptation) and thus tested the mettle of the faithful in ways that were viewed as analogous to the trials of early Euro-American desert crossers.

An initial perception of vacancy was in part understandable on the part of the newcomers, who were accustomed to midlatitude landscapes long shaped by sedentary agricultural practices and relatively overt topographical and vegetative contrasts. European and Anglo-American explorers, scientists, prospectors, soldiers, religious separatists, and colonists had to learn to see and speak desert landscapes: they were not natives. As Barry Lopez notes, "a local language discriminates among the local phenomena, and it serves to pry the landscape loose from its anonymity."[36] And by the end of the nineteenth century, as David Teague has explored at length, there arose a "desert aesthetic" in the United

States that enabled just this sort of discrimination of the difference in American arid environments, and an appreciation of their particular, sublime beauty.[37] Yet, despite the development of a desert aesthetic, deserts have endured in the American geoimaginary as devoid of any obvious benefits, aesthetic or otherwise. "Deserts, for many people, remain simply blank areas on the map—wasted paper, wasted land."[38]

It was no accident that the acquisition of significant territory through the Treaty of Guadalupe Hidalgo in 1848, and the surveying and delimitation of an international boundary between the modern nation-states of Mexico and the United States of America that closely followed, occurred at the beginning of the second half of the nineteenth century. Though westward Anglo-American expansion has, as we saw with Turner's frontier hypothesis, typically been conceived, practiced, and even critically analyzed as an unbounded process, it was the southern geopolitical boundary with Mexico that in the end made this expansion possible, both legal-institutionally and in the larger geoimaginary of the second half of the nineteenth century. The border proper has since its inception been a source of conflict and uncertainty. Even more conflictual, however, are the internal borders that have riven the smooth space so diligently, and violently, forged westward across the national territory of the United States of America. Here, "race" and sexuality provide for two brief meditations on internal border conflicts that have long interrupted the hegemonic plot of Anglo-American expansionism.

Inside and Out: Race and Smooth Space

In the history of Anglo-American expansionism in North America, *smoothing* space has involved violence. This violence was discursive in terms of ignoring, forgetting, and silencing nonwhite peoples and unfamiliar components of the nonhuman world.[39] It was also quite literal—though it is a bit disingenuous to attempt to separate the discursive from the literal—involving quick deaths of human populations by European and African diseases and incursions by the U.S. cavalry, or slower obliterations through encampment on reservations, forced assimilation, and displacement by successive waves of newcomers. Overhunting, overgrazing, fencing, and the introduction of railroads and nonnative species worked their destructive magic on the desert's nonhuman populations. The West was, literally and figuratively, wiped clean to make way for the forcible, uncompromising, direct style of narrative inscription typical of Anglo-American nationalism.

It was the perceived *blankness* of the Western landscape in the national geoimaginary—a form of borderlessness—upon which white expansionism was predicated. Indeed, as I noted earlier, modern empire building in general turned on the a priori rendering of non-European landscapes as empty. A liberal, Lockean outlook held that lands that were not being used for cultivation by sedentary peoples were in fact wilderness, and as such open for appropriation by civilized peoples (that is, those who would engage in sedentary cultivation).[40] In addition, the lands in question were seen to be devoid of Christians and were, for all intents and purposes, understood as empty and free for the taking.[41] Indigenous human beings were classed with the other wild beasts in a howling wilderness, and as part of this incomprehensible and hostile nature, they could simply be felled along with the trees. Indians became part and parcel of the *void* that characterized the landscape constructed from the rhetoric of emptiness.[42] Anglo-Americans, argues Richard Drinnon, brought a European-derived asceticism west with them, characterized by what he terms, drawing on Herman Melville, "the metaphysics of Indian-hating, those deadly subtleties of white hostility that reduced native peoples to the level of the rest of the fauna and flora to be 'rooted out.'"[43] Only in wiping the landscape clean of all traces of fallen nature—including indigenous human beings, "bodies *in* that wildness"[44]—could the epic mastery of Anglo-Americans over fallen nature, good over evil, civilization over chaos be assured in their new surroundings.

One of the key gestures in taming the desert's emptiness, and the burgeoning nation of which it was quickly becoming symbolic, was through the drafting of a geopolitical border with Mexico to the south. Establishing geopolitical borders involves a particular form of marking, one predicated on *naming*. The power to name is the power to possess; thus we see the array of blank landscapes—deserts, ocean floors, polar

regions, the moon—depicted on maps as surfaces that are tightly partitioned by networks of straight lines and punctuated by place names in
an effort to wrest a particular sort of meaning from nothingness. Narratively speaking, "naming both situates things within narratives and
marks the beginnings of narratives."[45] The (re)naming of the arid lands
wrested from Mexico in the mid-nineteenth century constituted their
(re)situation in a different narrative, one of desti-nation emplotted by
Manifest Destiny and enabled by the rhetoric of emptiness.

At the conclusion of the U.S-Mexican War, on 2 February 1848,
the Treaty of Peace, Friendship, Limits, and Settlement was signed
between the United States of America and Los Estados Unidos Mexicanos at Guadalupe Hidalgo.[46] The settlement apparently had less to
do with friendship and more to do with limits, for it brought nearly half
of Mexico's territory—the formerly Mexican states of Alta California,
Nuevo México, and northern portions of Sonora, Coahuila, and Sonora—
into the legal-institutional orbit of the United States of America. The
newly added territory was now formally opened to Anglo-American
advancement and settlement. Overnight, *mexicanos* became second-class
citizens in a foreign land, subject to discrimination, harassment, brutality,
and land theft.[47] The line legitimated the marginalization of *mexicanos*,
who since 1848 (north of the Rio Grande) were in theory American
citizens with legal rights to their lands as well as to citizenship more
generally. But they were Catholics, and descendents of that intermixed,
debased crossing of indigenous American and European. At the very
least, the intermixing had weakened the already hopelessly papist Spaniards to the extent that the *mexicanos* were simply incapable of managing
these lands to their fullest advantage. Thus O'Sullivan could comfortably remark that "[Texas] was disintegrated from Mexico in the natural
course of events, by a process perfectly legitimate on its own part,
blameless on ours; and in which all the censures due to wrong, perfidy
and folly, rest on Mexico alone."[48]

The geopolitical boundary between the United States of America
and the United States of Mexico rendered stark the separation between
Anglo-America and a discrete space of otherness, Mexico. Since the

mid-nineteenth century, the hegemonic rhetoric regarding Mexican-descended people north of the line has been, assimilate quietly or leave. This is partly why the counternational discourse of Chicanos in the 1960s and 1970s—which turned on a refusal to do either, as I will explore in the following chapter—was so apparently radical. The border made possible the construction of Mexico as a constitutive outside, a bounded Other whose presence facilitated a purified ideal of smoothed national space in Anglo-America.

As Pablo Vila has illustrated, such a construction of Mexico-as-Other operates to this day to facilitate sharp spatial differentiations of Mexico and Mexicans as intruders in the U.S. Southwest, as the source of all poverty and social problems enumerated by Vila's interviewees on the U.S. side of the border. This sentiment was at times so extreme that Vila writes:

> [In this interview] we encounter what was prominent in most of our interviews with Anglos: the idea of "otherness" they feel in relation to Mexicans is so profound that it is not enough to talk about El Paso and Juárez as belonging to two different *countries*. They have to remark that both cities belong to two different *worlds*.[49]

The establishment of a geopolitical border constructed a dichotomous understanding of political space, one that had no room—literally or figuratively—for Native Americans. Subsumed and spatially confined within the national space of the United States of America, Indians were relegated to the official status of outsiders within. Both the Mexican and United States governments considered Native Americans dangerous pests to be exterminated. Yet many were clearly not content with being rendered invisible, and Indian raiding constituted a principal source of border friction between the United States of America and Mexico throughout the second half of the nineteenth century.[50] Reports on the actual process of surveying the geopolitical boundary between the two countries, for example, repeatedly express concerns over Indian defacement or removal of the boundary markers as acts of protest.[51]

By the end of the nineteenth century, modernity and all of its challenges, anxieties, and discontents was in full swing on both sides of the Atlantic. In the United States, the literal frontier of settlement had been declared closed and many feared that this would have wider cultural implications, that the American empire would soon pass its peak and slip into decline, both morally and physically. As Mary Douglas has reminded us, societies often sharpen their borders at precisely the times when they feel most under siege.[52] Douglas, and other object-relations scholars, works with a broad understanding of borders as involving distinctions between self and Other. Racialized and ethnic understandings of inside and outside are a common way that societies draw boundaries. Border conflict in nineteenth-century Anglo-America was thus both inside and out. It was external, as the fraught undertaking of claiming, marking, and maintaining a line between the United States of America and Mexico attests.[53] Border tensions were also internal, in the sense of racialized conflict resulting in part from the silencing of Native Americans in the hegemonic narrative of belonging and exclusion told from the mid-nineteenth century onward. As Thom Kuehls has pointed out, the very legal status of Native Americans as nations within a nation disrupted the smoothed national surface: "The presence of an 'Indian Nation' within the sovereign borders of the United States ought to explode the assumption of the unambiguous sovereign inside. It should raise questions concerning the nature of sovereign territory and the concept of space that accompanies it."[54]

Additionally, border conflicts arose along the contested lines of gender and sexuality. Both the geopolitical boundary between the United States and Mexico, and the particular geoimaginary that shaped the arid Southwestern landscape, turned on often violent constructions and suppressions of gendered and sexual difference.

Outside In: Gender and Smoothness

Unrefined

The desert is no lady.

She screams at the spring sky,

dances with her skirts high,

kicks sand, flings tumbleweeds,

digs her nails into all flesh.

Her unveiled lust fascinates the sun.

In this poem, Pat Mora offers powerful insight into the systematic coding of the desert as female, and the ways in which writers and artists have attempted to rethink such codings. Chapter 4 will explore aspects of contemporary borderlands rewritings of the Southwestern landscape, of which Mora's work is a fine example. In this section, it is the initial coding of the desert as female, and what this says for the larger argument developed here regarding the smoothness of the space of the Southwest, that are of interest.

The landscape has been conceptualized in the modern, Western geoimaginary along dichotomous lines that hold that the physical earth is part of nature.[55] In this schema—an oppositional practice of making meaning that is inherent to a colonizing worldview—nature is a subordinate term to culture and is elided with other subordinate terms such as the body (opposed to the mind), wildness and disorder (opposed to civilization and order), irrationality (opposed to rationality), and, importantly, female (opposed to male). The association of women with nature implies passivity, stasis, and an absence of directionality and change; while the masculine principle represents a striating force: active, forward-moving, linear, progressive. The landscape is thus smoothed in gender terms: it is lack, void, inert. Nature, the landscape, and the feminine principles they embody are both literally and figuratively smooth spaces.

By coding the Western landscape as female, the masculine Anglo-American subject was able to emplot himself as the protagonist in the national mythology. There was no place, literally or figuratively speaking, for women in the geoimaginary of the West and of the national mythology for which the West stood. It is no accident that the prototypes for the iconic national figures in the narrative of the West—the cowboy, the miner, the hunter, the pioneer, the prospector, the cavalryman—were male. To be sure, they had their female variants, but they were just that, odd variants on the (male) prototype. The Western landscape was feminized in order to render it open to the advances of male protagonists. These advances could be chivalric, as in "saving the honor" or the "purity" of the land (a discourse that is still quite prevalent today in some conservationist circles). Frequently, too, the rhetoric was overtly or subtly (hetero)sexual in nature. The term "virgin land," the likening of the contours of landscape to those of the female body, and the often uneasy eroticism that abounds in Western landscape depiction invokes what Krista Comer has termed a romance narrative with respect to the gendering of the Western landscape:

> this romance narrative and sexual fantasy genders the explorer/citizen male, the land (and object of the citizen/subject) female, and the sexual attraction heterosexual. Man is the sexual actor, woman is passive recipient, the national sex act is intercourse. It all adds up to "possession."[56]

Patricia Seed expands this idea, sugging that the term "virgin land" allowed the relationship between white men and the land they cultivated to be understood in racialized as well as sexualized terms, exclusive terms that served to further dispossess Native Americans of their land. In Seed's view, for white males who tilled the land, the act of cultivation stood in for the act of sexual possession:

> Calling uncultivated land "virgin" land frequently encouraged a masculine fantasy of the initial plowing as a carnal act. Descriptions of tilling the ground regularly appeared as a male erotic role—plowing the field or furrowing. And imagining sexual intimacy between male colonists and the land effectively excluded others from the relationship, including the natives.[57]

Comer has noted that "the most often celebrated feature of western space is its spatial *non*containment, its expansiveness, its vastness, its sheer, weighty limitlessness."[58] The vastness of the desert could appear— as women often are seen to—mystical, sensuous, and healing. This is a long-standing theme in Anglo-American, as well as Native American and *mexicano*, perception of this landscape.[59] In the Anglo-American geoimaginary at the turn of the last century, the desert held forth the potential to cure the national fear writ (male) individual. The desert could provide the sort of "strenuous life" seen, at least by Teddy Roosevelt, to be sorely needed by those in dire danger of going "soft":

> The old iron days have gone, the days when the weakling died as the penalty of inability to hold his own in the rough warfare against his surroundings. We live in softer times. . . . if either man or nation wishes to play a great part in the world there must be no dallying with the life of lazy ease.[60]

The vastness could also be perceived as fearsome, much as a woman who is not bounded or constrained by male authority. And it is particularly in the uneasy eroticism of landscape construction that the instability of the coding "female" emerges. To be constructed as void is to be constructed as potentially terrifying. Smooth spaces are not neuter; at best they are castrated, at worst (from the viewpoint of the masculine subject) they are *castrating*. Western landscapes functioned as Other through constructing them as at once desirable and fearsome, much as spaces have always been constructed in eras of expansion and conquest. The empty spaces ever-west of (white) civilization provided an explicitly spatial challenge to be met by expansionist Anglo-America. These spaces beckoned, lured, dared, intimidated, and invited, the blankness functioning much as the sea monster–infested map margins had centuries before. Such limitlessness could potentially lead to a loss of the (male) self through being swallowed by the all-consuming *Deserta dentada*, succumbing to death or madness. Desert adventurer John Annerino writes, "There is nothing but silence and a luminescent white light that enshrouds a vast desert which patiently awaits to swallow me alive if I stray beyond the point of no return."[61]

The desert, in particular among other blank landscapes, has been harshly judged as a sterile, punishing sort of woman (a phallic mother); or, alternatively, a particularly magical, alluring, and beautiful woman (a lover). The desert can arouse and fulfill, emasculate or cure, cycling between love and hate, pleasure and peril. The oscillation of the landscape between the roles of lover and mother is an Oedipal emplotment of an uncertain masculine relationship to this landscape, inviting "erotic mastery or infantile regression" in what Annette Kolodny has described as the "psychosexual drama" of the Western landscape.[62]

Perhaps in part because of the mysterious, dangerous forces perceived to be at work on individual men in the desert, men seemed to prefer to stick together in the extreme homosociality that is typical of Western myth. Roosevelt had sought refuge in the West upon the sudden loss, at twenty-six years of age, of the two most important women in his life: his mother and his wife, who both died unexpectedly within a day of one another. His health always fragile, Roosevelt felt himself restored by the tonic climate of the West. He developed an enduring appreciation and respect for the "manliness" of the men he met there, particularly the cowboy, who, he felt, would make a fine cavalryman (his subsequent assemblage of the Rough Riders grew directly out of this sentiment). Roosevelt's accounts of the West describe his delight in the closeness to other men and abound with rich descriptions of generic profiles of individuals who embodied those "manly virtues" that Roosevelt deemed so vital to the ongoing health of the nation, as well as characteristics of individual men of whom he was particularly fond.[63]

In a contemporary illustration of the durability of the fear/desire motif of the feminized desert and the protective male bonding that can occur therein, Charles Bowden, a journalist and self-proclaimed "desert rat," expresses his last wish to be buried in the desert.[64] Writing of his ostensibly chivalric desire to create a nature preserve of untouched desert straddling the U.S.-Mexico border, Bowden describes the desert as a place of retreat alone or with other men, an endangered environment to be saved from the press of other human beings attempting to locate the sharp pieces of themselves that have been rent asunder by the industrialized, urban world, and in the long run of things, as a site of rebirth and reconnection with history and the men who made it. He describes his first experience of the desert as the place where "Julian and I became friends. The desert and I became lovers."[65] He curls up in sleeping circles thousands of years old, "to feel the bodies of the ancient ones."[66] A particular walk through the Sonoran desert with his friend Bill Broyles was so important for him, as a combined personal endurance challenge in the summer heat and as a retreat into the "blue desert" of his fantasies, that he required his estranged wife to schedule her radical mastectomy so that it wouldn't interfere with his trek with his buddy.[67] Yet, it becomes apparent that Bowden's surface association of the desert and male bonding has an undercurrent: the association of the desert with woman; more specifically, with his fears and desires regarding women. Well into the desert and delirious, Bowden attempts to come to grips with his fear of his ex-wife's cancerous breasts and their surgical removal, and his grief at the loss of his wife though their estrangement and her possible death. He undergoes this process by shutting his flesh-and-blood ex-wife out of the space he traverses. Not surprisingly, he never tells us what happened to his ex-wife, preferring instead to contemplate the hypothetical circumstances of his own death at length.

In his burial wish, Bowden is echoing Edward Abbey, who was laid to rest in an unmarked, uncovered desert grave, in order that he might be consumed by vultures and become one with them, soaring freely above the earth.[68] Bowden hopes to be united forever with his fellow (male) desert rats, in perpetual homosociality, "out there with Ed Abbey and Julian Hayden and Ronald Ives and Malcolm Rogers and early Americans."[69] His desert death wish invokes a type of return to the womb, though the mother/lover in question is an eternally punishing one: "[The desert] scowls, washes my face with its furnace breath, and at night pounds my head with a billion stars hanging down like ornaments. It doesn't give a damn about me."[70]

This uneasy erotic is also symptomatic of a larger unease at expansionism, dispossession, and exploitation of the land as the basis for

Anglo-American nationalism. If the West is constructed as an irrational Other, wherein the (white masculine) self had to be inserted in order to make sense of it, and if the objective was, more often than not, opening up the earth to dispossess it of inner treasures, then these powerful striating gestures of surveying and marking a geopolitical border, of plowing and sowing and reaping, and of mining, might be conceived along the lines of rape. Thus, concealed in Comer's "romance narrative" is a darker script, a rape script.[71] Indeed, Kolodny remarks that the "uncomfortable sense of bearing witness to a vanishing Eden runs like a leitmotif through nineteenth-century writing" and notes that much of the discomfort expressed was in terms of a particularly "male anguish at lost Edens and male guilt in the face of the raping of the continent."[72]

It is little wonder that the border between the United States and Mexico is frequently referred to in somatic language that invokes female genitalia: the border is a wound, a gash, it bleeds. The Chicana writer and scholar Gloria Anzaldúa likens the border to "*una herida abierta*" (an open wound),[73] performance artist Guillermo Gómez-Peña has termed it "the fissure between two worlds, an infected wound,"[74] while Mexican author Carlos Fuentes asserts, "The U.S.-Mexico border, some of those who cross it say, is not really a border but a scar. Will it heal? Will it bleed once more?"[75] The border is a sexualized striation, a gesture of splitting, marking, naming, and penetrating: rape. To return to Burke's inadvertent references to smoothing as (hetero)sexualized pleasure, the jaggedness that follows is the violence necessary to possess and maintain the smooth inside intact. It bespeaks the deepest fears of the (masculinist) state.

The Slippery, Slippery West

In 1890, the Superintendent of the Census declared the American frontier so interrupted by settlement that it was, for all intents and purposes, closed. With the closing of the literal frontier, the fantasy of the frontier took root and flourished in the geopolitical imaginary of the United States, becoming a cornerstone of American identity and a rich source of national symbol and myth.[76] Iconic features of the arid Southwestern landscape—saguaro cactus standing in their mute, anthropomorphic inscrutability, blowing tumbleweed, burning sands, ghost towns, and crimson sunsets—became displaced onto "the West" more broadly understood.[77] The arid Southwest as a place began to expand and become progressively unhinged from the literal landscape, eventually circulating in the collective imaginary as synechdochal for "the West," the 'American spirit,' and progress itself. As Leonard Engel and John Gourlie write, "Landscapes tell stories. Those of the American West relate narratives that have become part of our individual and national identity, often producing stories so powerful they have seeped into our mythic consciousness. . . . Symbolically, this landscape has always transcended region and spoken to the nation as a whole."[78] Though David Teague has argued that the desert Southwestern backdrop in the writing and imagery of such diverse nineteenth-century artists and writers as Mark Twain, Frederic Remington, and Frederick Jackson Turner was "incidental," that "the actual land, the desert itself, was little more than a stage upon which people moved," he is wrong.[79] The desert is anything but incidental. Its perceived, yet forced, smoothness functions to obfuscate the crucial role of the landscape in the exercise of power, while at the same time saturating the landscape with meaning.

In the West, myth and history became refracted through the prism of place and emerged as a potent combination in the American geo-imaginary. Myth and history often work together to the point that there exists little productive distinction between them. Indeed, the idea that there is ever a clear separation between event and the representation of that event ("history" and "myth") is debatable. Myth and reality, as these coalesce around the slippery entity of the West, bear such a close relationship to one another that trying to separate the two would prove infinitely frustrating. And it is precisely in this spatial and temporal indeterminacy that the power of the West lies. Where, exactly, does the West begin, and end, in both time and space? Though the term utilizes a specific geographic referent, it is an incredibly difficult place to pin down: the West is an immanently *dis*placed region. "The West was quite literally nowhere—or everywhere, which was to say the same thing."[80] It is precisely the smoothed nature of the West, as we have explored it here, that makes it so defiant of bounding, yet at the same time allows it to exert such power, on both the collective national imaginary of the United States, and on the reality of the actions of the United States in the contemporary world.

Around the time the Western frontier was officially declared closed, the West began to take on the symbolic, larger-than-life connotations it still retains. The paintings of Frederic Remington,[81] the dime novels of "Ned Buntline,"[82] railroad advertisements for scenic desert destinations,[83] and theatrical (re)enactments (and later, film and television)[84] of the "Wild West"—all displayed, with varying degrees of inventiveness that shaded into utter fabrication, a West infinitely more glossy, entertaining, and fabulous than it could have ever truly been.

One of the most popular attractions at the World's Columbian Exposition in Chicago was Buffalo Bill's Wild West.[85] It netted over a million dollars in profit in 1893 alone, traveled throughout the United States and Europe, and became one of the largest and most popular endeavors in commercial entertainment for more than thirty years, from 1883 to 1916.[86] It was also one of the first contexts in which the mythic figure of the cowboy was presented as such.[87] In a series of skits, a parade of iconic figures—wild beasts, Indians, colonists, pioneers, soldiers, cowboys, and later, Teddy Roosevelt and his Rough Riders—enacted the definitive epochs of American history, according to Cody. At times, the historic figures played themselves, as Cody managed to hire, at various points in the show's trajectory, Geronimo and Sitting Bull, Indians and regular members of the U.S. Cavalry fresh from battling one another in Indian Territory, and thirteen members of Roosevelt's Rough Riders.[88]

The perpetual displacement of the place Cody touted as the West is at the heart of its power. Indeed, Cody himself insisted that his performance not be called "Buffalo Bill's Wild West *Show*," because it was not a "display" or mere "entertainment," but a *place*.[89] By definition, the show was a traveling attraction, and was meant in no small measure to advertise the West as an attractive place of settlement to prospective immigrants, both within the United States and from abroad. Cody's

Wild West as a place was immanently *displaced*, and at the heart of this was a marketing campaign.

The exchange of real-life and mythic figures in the casting of the Wild West productions also represented a perpetual displacement, a cycling between myth and fantasy that underscored the growing inseparability of the two. Cody himself, discovered and fictionalized by Ned Buntline in a series of dime novels and execrable theatrical productions from 1869 to 1871, became "Buffalo Bill, the King of the Border Men" in the endless performance of himself. Buntline, later jettisoned by Cody, was nevertheless "the father of the frontier romance story who convinced others that the American West was a wild place populated by savages and beasts locked in mortal combat with noble white knights dressed in buckskin."[90]

In 1899, Roosevelt's Rough Riders' charge up San Juan Hill displaced Custer's Last Stand as the final definitive epoch in American history in Buffalo Bill's Wild West. In so doing, it inducted this act of imperial aggression into the pantheon of the Wild West, illustrating how the violent smoothing and possession of territory had been transported, in the collective American geoimaginary *and* in American military and political practice, to the international arena. As Richard Slotkin has quite correctly noted:

> This exchange of names between the agents of real-world imperialism and the mythmakers of the Wild West defines a significant cultural and political relationship. . . . By the terms of this exchange, the categories of myth shape the terms in which the imperial project will be conceived, justified, and executed; and the imperial achievement is then reabsorbed into the mythological system, which is itself modified by the incorporation of the new material.[91]

The West and its narrative characters continue to inhabit contemporary discourses that, in reality, have precious little—if anything at all—to do with the Western, let alone the arid Southwestern, United States of the nineteenth century. Metaphoric references to "the West" became common in framing a diverse array of conflicts. Note, for example, the persistent, explicit cowboy-and-Indian dialogue woven into Roosevelt's charge up San Juan Hill, the Cold War, the "space race," the Vietnam War, the Gulf War, the development of the Internet as an entrepreneurial horizon, and our current national obsession with "smoking out" savage, Middle Eastern terrorists. Despite, or perhaps because of, the impossible displacement of the West in these discourses, the durability of the national mythos is revealed. Richard Drinnon, for example, painstakingly exposes the narrative parallels between the official rhetoric of the U.S. government regarding Vietnam and that employed by the same government in campaigns waged against Native Americans in the previous century. Vietnam, according to Drinnon, constituted but an extension of a long Anglo-American tradition of Indian hating. Air and ground operations bore names such as "Daniel Boone," "Rolling Thunder," and "Sam Houston." Quang Ngai was referred to as "Indian Country."

> Elsewhere a My Lai veteran equated "wiping the whole place out" with what he called "the Indian idea . . . the only good gook is a dead gook." The Indian idea was in the air of Vietnam. Specialist 4 James Farmer, a soldier from a different battalion, put it this way: "the only good dink is a dead dink." And from within the Marine Corps came this echo: "the troops think that they're all fucking savages."[92]

Here is the same narrative of epic struggle between civilization and savagery, darkness and light, good and evil, cast in the mythic terms of the Wild West and transported wherever there is space to be had, literally and figuratively. Here too is the attempt, once again, to smooth space through wiping it clean of difference, in order to striate it with an imperialist, expansionist narrative. The West is transported through time and space, in word and deed, to enable a contemporary enactment of imperialist nationalism. The West continues to exert a powerful influence over the collective geographic imaginary of the United States, one that, in its hegemonic form, is profoundly racialized, gendered, and deeply imperialist.

The space of the West and, particularly, the desert Southwest, became at one important level perpetually displaced.[93] In its ability to telescope space and time, it acquired a strange, powerful dimensionality that verges on science fiction:

> Never forget that it was in the Mojave that the first claimed UFO sightings took place, and the pioneer conversations with little green men from Venus. In a landscape where nothing officially exists (otherwise it would not be "desert"), absolutely anything becomes thinkable, and may consequently happen.[94]

High tech security think tanks and alien encounters alike spring as contemporary twin tales from these dry lands, providing new layers of oscillation between smoothness and striation. The hegemonic Anglo-American exercise of power in the name of the nation-state has constructed a baleful landscape wherein smoothness is tantamount to wiping out any traces of difference, regardless of the human or ecological costs involved. Others, however, have seen in this arid landscape more progressive, even liberatory, possibilities.

CHAPTER 3

Debordering and Rebordering in Aztlán

Everywhere the wind moaned with the name of their homeland. They sat with old caciques who told the stories of the past, and always the four directions were pointed out, and in the center stood Aztlán. They moved north, and there Aztlán was a woman fringed with snow and ice; they moved west, and there she was a mermaid singing by the sea; and always, beneath the form in the vision they heard the soft throbbing of her heart. They walked to the land where the sun rises, and there by the side of the sea where the morning star and the sun played upon the waves before day entered, they found new signs, and the signs pointed them back to the center, back to Aztlán.

—Rudolfo Anaya, *Heart of Aztlán*

Searching for Other Stories

As I drove my tiny rental car through the desert Southwest during the hottest and driest part of the summer, I received many odd looks when, asked where I was headed, I replied, "I'm searching for Aztlán." For everyone who knows of Aztlán knows that it is a bit like the Land of Oz: a magical place that does not necessarily appear on maps. Rather, to seek Aztlán is to seek a spiritual reality, where ultimately one does not find a geographic destination but instead circles back to a rooted and renewed sense of self, community, and nation. Writes Luis Leal: "whosoever wants to find Aztlán, let him look for it, not on the maps, but in the most intimate part of his being."[1]

Aztlán is both old and new. In classic Mexican mythology, it is a region of whiteness, of herons, the mythic place of seven caves from which the ancient Aztec peoples of Mexico emerged and moved southward to the central highland valleys of Mexico to conquer established indigenous populations and to found the grand city of Tenochtitlán (now

Mexico City) in 1325. Though the geographic location of ancient Aztlán is the subject of much debate, it is generally thought to have been located somewhere to the north of Tenochtitlán, but has been variously placed in the modern-day Mexican state of Nayarit (on the Pacific coast about 400 miles northwest of Mexico City), in the contemporary U.S. states of Wisconsin, Florida, New Mexico, or California, and as far away as China.[2]

In the more recent Chicano nationalist discourse of the 1960s and 1970s in the United States, the idea of Aztlán was proposed as the contemporary homeland of the Chicano people.[3] Its geographic location was firmly conceptualized as that territory ceded to the United States by Mexico via the Treaty of Guadalupe Hidalgo in 1848—nearly half of Mexico's national territory at the time—now located in the Southwestern United States. The mythic tale of Aztlán was utilized as a contemporary political strategy, to geographically ground a homeland for Chicanos that was rightfully located within the United States. Without Aztlán, note Rudolfo Anaya and Francisco Lomelí, "we would be contemporary displaced nomads, suffering the diaspora in our own land, and at the mercy of other social forces. Aztlán allows us to come full circle with our communal background as well as to maintain ourselves as fully integrated individuals."[4]

Aztlán is a story. It illustrates the mythopoetic invention of nation whose spirit, and methods, variously contested the Anglo-American version of the national story. Chicano nationalists consciously sought to rewrite the tale of belonging and exclusion as it was written in the nineteenth century. As I have argued earlier in this book, and as Paul Routledge reminds us in his analysis of song as contestatory strategy in India's Baliapal movement, it is important to keep in mind that dissent is frequently conceptualized and enacted culturally.[5] As with Chicano nationalists, the Baliapal residents' geopoetics of resistance to the proposed construction of a test base for missiles in their rich farmlands used song, theater, and stories as narrative tactics to establish and legitimate their a priori claims to the land. To discount the mythopoetic dimensions of resistance would be, in both the Chicano and Baliapal examples, to present an anemic and distorted picture.

"The West" of the Anglo-American account and Aztlán of the Chicano nationalists both constituted attempts to root collective belonging to the land, and thus to the nation, through symbol and myth. Though its intent was to contest the hegemonic, Anglo-American narrative, Aztlán also shared important axes with it. In particular, both are border(ed) stories. Chapter 2 explored the importance of literal and figurative borders to the Anglo-American tale of the West. In this chapter, I will suggest that although Chicana/o scholars have explored the exclusions of Aztlán, their analysis has yet to be situated within a larger context of the long-standing narratives of border conflict that have so profoundly shaped the landscape of the Southwest. In addition, both the Anglo-American and the Chicano nationalist narratives turn on the oscillation between debordering and rebordering. In the Anglo-American account, told so well by Turner, the empty landscape allowed Anglo Americans to flow over the land, possessing it and marking it with their violently bordered nationalism. In the Chicano nationalist counternarrative, it is the geopolitical boundary between Mexico and the United States that is challenged, as well as the internal, racialized borders erected in the supposedly smooth space of Anglo-nation. Yet both were narratives of belonging and of exclusion; they erected new barriers— rebordering—within their smoothed spaces.

Furthermore, the significance of Aztlán as an explicitly *spatialized* tool of resistance has not yet been adequately explored. With the geo-imaginary concept of Aztlán, Chicano nationalists set their sights on the same arid expanse of the Southwestern United States as Anglo-Americans had claimed for their version of desti-nation in the previous century. Chicano nationalists envisioned an entirely different landscape, albeit still a nationalist landscape, from that of the Anglo-Americans whose vision, and reality, they were challenging. The freshly extended storyline of contemporary Aztlán legitimated the presence of Chicanos in what was now an alien Anglo-nation as part of a long-standing entitlement to the land through historic origins. Rather than constituting an invasion, the growing Chicano presence in the U.S. Southwest, understood in this way, constituted instead a reverse diaspora of sorts, a rightful return to a historic homeland that completed a necessary step in the destiny of the Chicano nation. Aztlán, because of (not despite) being a story, was deployed in a carefully, powerfully strategic fashion to contest the dominant Anglo-American narration of the United States of America. Aztlán as a mythic idea was consciously projected onto the desert terrain of the U.S. Southwest as a way to legitimate, root, and define the presence of Mexican-descended peoples residing in that region. The Chicano nationalist recovery of Aztlán as a precisely located geographic entity telescoped and focused the fuzzy geography of ancient homelands to serve a concrete political agenda. Aztlán illustrates well my claim that place stories can be powerfully real and really powerful.

Yet despite its apparently radical stance, Chicano nationalism shared the same exclusions that modern nationalisms everywhere contain. Aztlán's romantic national poesis silenced at the same time it spoke up.

> A geopoetics of resistance discerns that articulations of collective identity can themselves be abstractions that efface differences and inequalities within particular places and within the movements themselves. Place is a heterogeneous social construct, a dynamic locus of community, which frequently involves a variety of exclusions . . . as well as inclusions. . . . While celebrating the poetic imaginaries of resistance, it thus behooves academics and activists to remain grounded in the material spaces and spatial practices of those who resist.[6]

Many contemporary Chicana/o scholars and writers have become disenchanted because of what, and whom, Aztlán left out. Unresolved tensions of race, gender, and sexuality have undermined the strategic usefulness of Aztlán, much in the way that Chicanos of the 1960s and 1970s had hoped to implode the hegemonic Anglo myths and practices that had historically oppressed Chicanos. Ultimately, Aztlán was a utopian idea that rested on an uncritically romantic gesture of reversal, rather than a reinvention, of oppressive power structures. Aztlán erased Anglo-American claims to the region and overwrote the newly smoothed space with a backward-looking mythology of belonging. Yet border conflicts, both internal and external to the counternational space envisioned by Chicano nationalists, plagued Chicano nationalism. Aztlán provides a wonderfully rich example of how myth can be deployed to stake material claims to a place, to contest hegemonic borders both external (the geopolitical boundary between Mexico and the United States) and internal (the racialized exclusions of Anglo-nation). Yet, like nationalisms everywhere, Aztlán was riven by sexual and racial difference and by border conflicts of its own making, and ultimately imploded as a useful political concept. Aztlán illustrates that no story is wholly inclusive, even those stories that arise in direct contest to other tales in an attempt to overcome repressions, exclusions, and silences. Place visions are always partial.

A Space of Magic: Aztlán as Place of Origin

The Aztec people migrated from the north around the ninth or tenth century C.E. They arrived when Mexico's Central Valley was already densely populated, and no one wished to take them in. Relegated to a bit of rocky, marginal land known as Tizaapan, they were understood to be lowly *Chichimecas* (sons of dogs),[7] called the people without a face,[8] and often recruited to work as mercenaries because of their reputation for fierceness. Yet they flourished and assimilated the dominant Toltec culture of the valley. By the mid-fifteenth century, they had largely conquered and controlled the densely settled lake region of Central Mexico.

The ancestors of these pessimistic warriors had been compelled to leave their homeland. Michael Pina speculates that this migration may have arisen from a conflict in leadership between two male heirs upon the death of their father.[9] Doris Heyden's notes to Spanish Friar Diego Durán's account from the late sixteenth century suggest that the group left because they were subjugated to other Aztecs. Rather than accepting the ongoing humiliation of subjugation, they decided to emigrate.[10] Most accounts of the pilgrimage also hold that the warrior sun god Huitzilpochtli had promised the Aztec people a triumphant destiny in the south as rulers of a new empire, conquering and receiving tribute. To move southward was thus a chapter in their destiny as chosen people. "He wishes to extol his own name and raise the Aztec nation to the heavens. He will make us lords of gold and silver and of all metals, of splendid feathers of many colors, and of precious stones of great value."[11] Along their trek south, the Aztecs, under the guidance of Huitzilpochtli, received technology and knowledge (bows and arrows, spear-throwers, and nets for hunting and fishing) and were imbued with a sacred authority to rule over others.[12] As Pina notes, "Within this context the Aztec journey from Aztlán does not correspond to an escape from disgrace, nor a nomadic wandering, but rather assumes the sacred aura of a pilgrimage directed by a supernatural being."[13]

The northern region from which they originated was the subject of much curiosity for Moctezuma Ilhuicamina (Moctezuma the First), ruler of the Aztec empire from 1440 to 1469. According to Durán's account, Moctezuma Ilhuicamina sent sixty of his most powerful sorcerers northward in search of this homeland, Aztlán, desiring to know the place that their ancestors had left behind, and to greet Coatlicue, the mother of Huitzilpochtli, if she still lived. According to their accounts, the sorcerers used magic to turn themselves into animals and quickly cover the vast distance to Aztlán. Upon the wizards' return, Moctezuma Ilhuicamina listened to wondrous tales of a mountain rising up from surrounding waters, with caves or grottos in its side. Aztlán was described as a paradisiacal pre-Columbian Garden of Eden with abundant food crops, birds, enormous and beautiful fish, and the refreshing shade of many trees. In Aztlán, there was no sickness, strife, suffering, poverty, old age, or death. Encountering Coatlicue, the sorcerers were given a demonstration of how this magical place worked. Coatlicue's servant, an old man, began to descend the hill. Before the astonished eyes of Moctezuma Ilhuicamina's priests, he grew younger and younger as he descended. "When he reached the Aztecs, he appeared to be about twenty years old. Said he. . . . 'Behold, my sons, the virtue of this hill: the old person who seeks youth can climb to the point on the hill that he wishes and there he will acquire the age that he seeks.'"[14]

Importantly, the myth of Aztlán is inextricably entwined with the mythic enterprise of historical recovery. Upon conquest in the early sixteenth century, the vast majority of indigenous peoples and their constructions were destroyed in a sweeping attempt to stamp out the pagan profile of the Indians of the New World. Spaniards slaughtered Indians by the hundreds of thousands, tore down their temples, and burned pictorial records of indigenous history. Only a precious few preconquest codices (accounts painted on deerskin or bark) survived the Spanish immolations. Other versions were written shortly after conquest, often by Spanish clergy in tandem with indigenous peoples.[15] Furthermore, the Aztecs themselves may have earlier burned their own historical records in 1433, shortly after their decisive conquest of the Tepanecas of Azcapotzalco (part of the lake system in Mexico's Central Valley). This would have allowed them to rewrite history and put forth a new version, one more favorable to the imperial power that the Aztecs were swiftly becoming.[16] Finally, tales of a glorious land "to the north" could well have been embellished, even wholly invented, by indigenous peoples anxious to rid themselves of meddlesome sixteenth-century Spanish explorers. The legends of Cíbola and the Seven Cities of Silver, of an island of gold called California and ruled by an Amazon queen, and of a golden land called Quivira beckoned in the minds of Spaniards as a receding horizon of fantasy, drawing them ever northward in search of riches. As John Chávez explains:

> A fabulously rich Quivira had probably never been part of the local Indian conception of the plains area, but had been invented purely for the imaginations of the Spaniards. Since the Spanish had conquered and brutally occupied the Pueblo villages, the Indians most likely fabricated the urban wealth of Quivira in order to lure Coronado into a wilderness from which they hoped he would never return.[17]

Thus, the "true story" of Aztlán has been subject to recovery, partiality, and political strategization since preconquest times. The

Chicano utilization of Aztlán, then, can be seen as part of an ongoing reinvention of this mythic place for diverse political ends.

A Landscape of Struggle: Aztlán and the Chicano Movement

The Chicano Movement, or *El Movimiento*, arose in the United States in the mid-1960s, inspired in great part by the African American civil rights struggles occurring at that time.[18] The Chicano Movement was focused in those states bordering Mexico—California, Arizona, New Mexico, and Texas—though there were also active Chicano communities in Colorado and in Chicago. *El Movimiento* was broad based, encompassing rural farm workers and Chicano youth in urban barrios and universities. Chicanos fought for political, educational, linguistic, labor, and cultural reforms that would elevate and dignify the status of people of Mexican descent dwelling in the United States.[19]

To call oneself a Chicano was (and is still) not simply to underscore one's Mexican heritage; many people of Mexican descent in the United States chose to call themselves "Mexican Americans" rather than Chicanos. To be a Chicano also entailed a profound political statement. Chicanos agitated for radical social and political change, based in an ethos of self-help and solidarity understood in racialized terms. Chicanos argued that decades of pressure to assimilate into the Anglo mainstream of the United States had wrongly devalued the long, proud history, culture, and values of Mexican Americans. This had in turn impeded economic progress for Mexican Americans and resulted in a sort of cultural self-destruction.[20] To call oneself a Chicano thus indicated a rejection of earlier liberal, assimilationist, or accommodationist agendas vis-à-vis the Anglo-dominated social, economic, political, and cultural milieu.[21] Finally, the term "Chicano" was also closely associated with the working class and identification with one's indigenous heritage.[22]

Some leaders, particularly during the early years of *El Movimiento*, were political nationalists who advocated the secession of the Southwest from the Anglo republic of the United States of America, if not fully, at least locally with regard to Chicano self-determination in local governance, education, and means of production.[23] Inspired by Cuban and Vietnamese nationalist struggles at the time, many Chicano nationalists used a model of internal colonialism to understand the situation of an indigenous population (as they saw themselves) annexed by the expansionist U.S. hegemon and dispossessed of their land and capacity for self-determination. For example, Rodolfo Acuña, author of the canonical Chicano studies text *Occupied America*, drew on the core-periphery models of Andre Gunder Frank, Samir Amin, and Immanuel Wallerstein to argue that the annexation and exploitation of the indigenous land and labor of the Southwest had provided the wealth necessary for the economic expansion of Anglo-dominated United States.[24]

Most Chicano nationalists, however, did not express the extreme desire for secession from the United States, and the nationalism they expressed weighed more heavily toward the broadly cultural than the explicitly political:

> Chicanos interpreted their nationalist cause as more than a political movement; they were involved in the regeneration of sacred time and space, as the ultimate concern of Chicano nationalism sought to transcend the existent temporal and spatial barriers and establish a homeland patterned after the primordial homeland from which the Aztecs originated. This would be a spiritual nation rooted in a sacred landscape charged with the power of an indigenous spirituality and justified by the validity of their national liberation struggle.[25]

Yet for some Chicano nationalists, like the leader of *Alianza Federal de Mercedes* (Federal Land Grant Alliance), Reies López Tijerina, the only viable solution was to fully repossess the Southwest: culturally, economically, and politically. During the *Alianza*'s occupation of New Mexico's Echo Amphitheater in 1966, López Tijerina stated, "Fidel Castro has what he has because of his guts. . . . Castro put the gringos off his island and we can do the same."[26]

Aztlán surfaced in the Chicano Movement in the *Plan Espiritual de Aztlán* (Spiritual Plan of Aztlán), a document written in Denver at the

First Chicano National Youth Conference in 1969.[27] The *Plan Espiritual* constituted the ideological framework of the Chicano Movement, emphasizing nationalism and self-determination. The first sentence of this key document states the fundamental Chicano nationalist goal of reclaiming Aztlán as the land of the Chicano ancestors and as such the rightful homeland of the Chicanos, land that was brutally and wrongfully invaded by the *gringos*. Rudolfo Anaya views the claiming of Aztlán as a naming ceremony, and as such it constituted "one of the most important acts a community performs."[28] Aztlán might be seen as a parallel, powerful gesture. Indeed, Aztlán became a key organizing concept for *El Movimiento*:

> The appropriation from the elite lore of ancient Mexico of such a seminal emblematic device as Aztlán was the most brilliant political maneuver of the Chicano cultural nationalists. Nothing their critics have done has managed to surpass or equal this feat of organizational strategy. Under no other sign or concept, derived from the left, center, or right, were as many Chicanos mobilized and as much enthusiasm galvanized into political action—except for the concept of Chicanismo itself. For a movement hungry for symbols that could both distinguish it from other movements and unite it under one banner, Aztlán was perfect. So perfect, in fact, that almost two decades after it was unfurled it is still the single most distinguishing metaphor for Chicano activism.[29]

The spiritual and political homeland of Chicano nationalists was clearly designated as those lands annexed by Texas in 1845 and ceded by Mexico in 1848 in the Treaty of Guadalupe Hidalgo (including the contemporary U.S. states of Texas, New Mexico, Arizona, California, Nevada, Utah, and parts of Colorado, Wyoming, Kansas, and Oklahoma). According to Chicano nationalists, this "lost land" had been colonized time and again: by Spain, France, the Lone Star Republic of Texas, the California Republic, the Confederacy, and the United States of America. Yet, by virtue of an understood blood relationship to the indigenous inhabitants of this region, Chicanos claimed that these lands were in fact their historical birthright. By identifying a fixed geographic homeland, Chicanos were making a powerful claim to space, to legitimacy, and to an identity culturally and politically independent of Anglo-America. The power exercised by Anglo-Americans was thus illegitimate, "because in reality, if you were born in Texas, California, New Mexico, Arizona, or Colorado, you were not born in the United States of America, but in occupied Mexico."[30] Chicano nationalists had made an important reversal: the invaders were in fact the invaded; Anglo-Americans, who have no blood ties to the land or its indigenous inhabitants, were both alien and illegitimate. In taking back the Southwest, Chicanos sought restitution of their land and the identity that they perceived to be fundamentally tied to this place.

The mythic dimensions of Aztlán were not stripped away by contemporary Chicanos, particularly those who considered themselves cultural nationalists. They were instead utilized as unifying factors, in an attempt to create a smooth space (albeit a far different sort of smooth space than that envisioned by Anglo-Americans in the nineteenth century). The Aztec narrative of a paradisiacal place was deployed by Chicano nationalists to provide a narrative framework for their political and cultural vision. Aztlán was proposed as the site for building a bright future, built on "brown power" and newly revitalized pride in the indigenous culture, values, and social structure understood by Chicanos to be at the root of their identity. Though the more materialist Chicanos found the paradisiacal hopes for Aztlán too fanciful,[31] many envisioned Aztlán as "a social, political, economic, and cultural utopia, free of liberal politicians, welfare programs, police brutality, discrimination, poverty, and identity crises."[32]

Chicano nationalists in the United States saw Aztlán as a common ground for Chicanos who, geographically, politically, and spiritually, existed in diaspora. One of the crucial gestures of claiming Aztlán involved the perceived need to overlook differences among Chicanos in favor of the greater good arising from unity. Concepts of unity were central to understanding the Chicano movement and notions of the Chicano Movement as one large family ("*La Familia Cósmica*" or "*La*

Familia de La Raza"), *carnalismo* (brotherhood), and *La Raza* ("the race," "the people," or "The Bronze Race" in the *Plan Espiritual*). Ralph "El Duke" Peterson understood the Chicano Movement to be like a stone, in that it was formed of diverse particles that were "welded together by years of outside pressure and tempered in the fires of slavery and oppression."[33] Utopias are by their very nature smooth spaces. Indeed, their impossibility derives from the inadmissibility of striation. And it is precisely this inadmissibility of internal borders that would lead to the eventual implosion of Aztlán:

> Aztlán has been used to obscure and elide important issues surrounding Chicano identity, in particular the significance of intracultural differences, despite the admitted failure of social scientists and historians who have attempted to create models of Chicano ethnicity based on ethnic commonalities.[34]

A Home(land) Divided

In geographically affixing the floating homeland of Aztlán for a concrete political purpose, Chicano nationalists attempted to reverse what they understood to be a fundamentally race-based apartheid lived by Chicanos in the Anglo-dominated Southwest. Yet the views of Chicano nationalists from the mid-1960s to the mid-1970s reflected the largely male, working-class, and mestizo background of the majority of Chicano nationalist activists and scholars.[35] This particular positionality led to exclusions that would eventually undermine the integrity seen as necessary and desirable to maintain a unified Chicano vision of home. Race, gender, and sexuality constituted cracks in the (counter-) hegemonic discourse of unified Chicano struggle. Native Americans in the Southwest had also long claimed the desert Southwest as their homeland, yet they were included only rhetorically by Chicanos anxious to invoke a genealogy that tied them to this land. Chicana feminists and queer Chicanas/os, who did not fit comfortably (or at all) into the patriarchal family tale proposed as the template for Aztlán, were in a sense left homeless. These pressures led, ultimately, to an implosion of Aztlán.

AlterNative

In contrast to Anglo-American nationalism, which forever sought to purify itself of the Indians, indigenism has been at the rhetorical heart of the Chicano Movement from the beginning. *El Movimiento*'s narrative valorized a glorious indigenous past as constituting a purity of historical origin understood to have subsequently become corrupted though European colonization. This plotline is drawn directly from the post-revolutionary Mexican indigenist movement. In the 1920s, as Mexico began to reconstruct its economic, political, and social structures after the devastation of the Mexican Revolution (1910–1917), a form of cultural nationalism known as *indigenismo* arose whereby "Mexico's revolutionary elites asserted their commitment to the moral and economic elevation of the Indian, who they claimed was central to the national experience."[36] Yet in both the Mexican national reconstruction and the U.S. Chicano Movement of a half-century later, "the Indian" operated in a highly problematic fashion, one which reworked, but did not eliminate, the deep anti-indigenous racism of the dominant mestizo groups in question.[37]

For Chicano nationalists of the 1960s and 1970s, a central political gesture involved explicit territorial claims to the U.S. Southwest as their lost homeland. Yet these claims squarely overlapped the claims of Native American nations to the same lands. Furthermore, the "real" Aztlán of Aztec myth probably, unromantically, lay far to the south of the contemporary U.S. Southwest, somewhere in the Mexican state of Nayarit. In order to skirt these thorny issues, Chicano historians such as John Chávez constructed what Daniel Cooper Alarcón has termed an "odd" argument, one that "tries to shore up the Chicano claim to that region by rewriting Chicano genealogy and linking it to the ancient Cochise civilization" in the U.S. Southwest.[38] Similarly, the Native American scholar Jack Forbes, who considers Chicanos to be "our lost brothers," argued that Chicanos, or *Aztecas del norte* (Northern Aztecs), constituted "the largest single tribe or nation of Anishinabeg (Indians) found in the United States today."[39] Chávez went so far as to make the dubious claim that "since Chicanos are racially 70 to 80 percent Indian, they do indeed have much in common with Native

Americans."[40] Modern-day Aztecs (Chicanos) were, according to those Chicano scholars anxious to emphasize their ties to Native Americans, undeniably linked to Southwest Native Americans through language and shared cultures of food, folklore, and values.[41] Long before the arrival of Europeans, American Indians in the present-day United States Southwest were influenced by Central Mexican ceramics making, maize cultivation, language, and blood exchange, spread by extensive trading networks. These cultural, historical, and blood alliances, it was argued, naturally united the Native American and Chicano in their claims to the Anglo-dominated Southwestern United States. Yet Native Americans made solely cameo appearances in Chicano nationalist discourse. Critiquing John Chávez's *Lost Land* specifically, Alarcón notes how "Native Americans are not included in his discussion about the region, except when he requires their presence in order to legitimate Chicano claims to the Southwest."[42] Native Americans cast only blurry shadow-figures, functioning as a "dehistoricized fetish" that gave "a veneer of 'origin' and 'authenticity'" to Chicano nationalist discourse.[43]

Chicano nationalist discourse suffered from a related lack of specificity regarding the hugely varied Native American populations of the Southwest, as well the historical, geographic, racial, and class diversity among Chicanos themselves. In this lack of specificity, real claims to space, and identity, were erased on all sides. Some who were rhetorically included in the Chicano tale didn't consider themselves to be Chicanos, or to have Mexican ancestry, or to be indigenous in the slightest. New Mexican *hispanos*, for example, viewed their heritage as predating Mexican immigration to the Southwest and harkening directly back to a centuries-old lineage of Spanish conquistadors. Sizable groups of Chicanos living outside the Southwest borderlands proper (for example, in Chicago) saw their potential claims to space silenced through the insistence on the Southwest as homeland. Most Native Americans in the Southwest did not consider themselves to be modern-day Aztecs, Chicanos, or Mexican Americans. Discussion did not even begin to mention Asian Americans and African Americans, who could also potentially assert historical claims to the region.

The simultaneous invocation of a glorious indigenous past and the erasure of specific Native American, as well as other, claims to the Southwest points to the incredibly fraught relationship to the Indian in the American imaginary more generally. "Going to the Indians for their healing power and killing them for their wildness are not so far apart."[44] The reinscription of the Indian-as-Other into the very heart of Chicano nationalist narrative was ironic, since the "nation within a nation" internal colonial model was the framework through which some Chicanos understood their own subordination in Anglo society. Yet Chicano mestizos by definition were themselves also colonizers, if history were allowed to reel backward prior to 1848 (and it wasn't, in foundational Chicano nationalist texts), to speak of *mestizaje* as involving both Spaniard and Native American. The *Plan Espiritual de Aztlán* does not deal with this discomfiting role-reversal in which colonized becomes colonizer in the historical long view. Nor does the *Plan* explore the realities of Aztec expansionism and their own brutally colonial presence in Mexico's Central Valley prior to Cortez's arrival:

> The prospect of thinking about Spanish-speaking men dominating Native Americans simply muddies the picture of Anglo-Mexicano relations too much for the internal colonial model to embrace. Internal colonialism, in fact, has never been able to satisfactorily explain how to deal with the complex problem of mestizaje between Spaniards and Native Mexicanos. By picking up the story in 1848, internal colonialism avoids the problem and can simply label all the inhabitants of the recently conquered territory as Mexicans.[45]

The Chicano nationalist tale was thus deeply racialized in ways that were not made explicit. For truly considering Native Americans and their claims to land as viable and different from those of Chicanos, themselves diversely located socially and spatially, would have threatened to destabilize what was, ironically, a deeply bordered narrative of belonging and exclusion. Thus the racialized debordering that was attempted through the Chicano nationalist narrative was haunted by a racialized rebordering.

Women and Queers: The Others Within

Another sort of rebordering was enacted in the Chicano nationalist narrative, one that involved the minds, bodies, and labor of Chicana women and queer Chicanas/os. Aztlán was understood by Chicano nationalists to be modeled on the ideal(ized) Chicano family structure, with male leadership, *carnalismo* (a fictive kinship likened to brotherhood, "nationalist yet blatantly patriarchal in practice"),[46] and the respect of elders both providing a hierarchical, patriarchal leadership structure as the basic organizing principle of the Chicano political collective. The Chicano utopia would be a decidedly male utopia, with the Chicano male's privilege and power over Chicana women intact, even strengthened. For example, Armando Rendón, the author of *The Chicano Manifesto*, clearly connected his personal sense of honor and masculinity with a nationalist discourse: "The essence of machismo, of being macho, is as much a symbolic principle for the Chicano revolt as it is a guideline for family life. . . . Macho, in other words, can no longer relate merely to manhood but must relate to nationhood as well."[47] The Chicano nationalist vision was, in addition, deeply *hetero*patriarchal, with the family-based father-mother reproductive dyad providing the fundamental moral foundation of the Chicano community and political movement. To question the patriarchal family or heterosexuality as an organizing principle of the Chicano Movement constituted a betrayal, not only of the Chicano nation (*La Raza*) as conceived by its founding fathers, but also of the Chicano family, traditional gender roles, and heterosexuality themselves as the understood moral backbone of the larger political movement.[48]

As feminist scholars have recently argued, nationalism tends to draw upon stereotyped and limiting views of women and men, often rooted (and legitimated) in heterosexual, patriarchal family structures.[49] Patriarchal families are rarely comfortable or even safe sites for women, children, or nonheterosexuals. In this, Chicano nationalism of the 1960s and 1970s was no exception. For Cherríe Moraga, the heterosexuality enforced in Chicano families and the control of Chicana women are tightly bound together, and this is what has made the critique of power relationships nurtured within Chicano families such an untouchable topic:

We believe the more severely we protect the sex roles within the family, the stronger we will be as a unit in opposition to the anglo threat. . . . [Yet the Chicano] too, like any other man, wants to be able to determine how, when, and with whom his women—mother, wife, and daughter— are sexual. For without male imposed social and legal control of our reproductive function, reinforced by the Catholic Church, and the social institutionalization of our roles as sexual and domestic servants to men, Chicanas might very freely "choose" to do otherwise, including being sexually independent *from* and/or *with* men. In fact, the forced "choice" of the gender of our sexual/love partner seems to precede the forced "choice" of the form (marriage and family) that partnership might take. The control of women begins through the institution of heterosexuality.[50]

Elizabeth Martínez states that "Aztlán has always been set forth in ferociously macho imagery,"[51] an imagery that buttresses the material practices of patriarchy and homophobia in Chicano nationalism. Alluding to the huge paste-on wall murals that decorate Mexican restaurants in the United States, Martínez describes the kitsch scene of the Aztec warrior holding the swooning Azteca princess in his arms as he gazes off into the horizon as a landscape of sexualized possession that holds an enduring appeal to the secret fantasies of "the average Chicano."[52] The idolization of male iconic figures of resistance—Che Guevara, Fidel Castro, Pancho Villa, and Emiliano Zapata—has likewise legitimated the masculine heroism of *El Movimiento*'s political agents.[53] These strengthened the already deeply rooted suspicion that Chicana women were fundamentally apolitical and should be concerned foremost with the private (feminine) space of the home and not the public (masculine) space of politics. Within *El Movimiento*, a women's place was understood to be parallel to her place within the patriarchal Chicano family: to selflessly serve men. "Mujeres [women] in the Movimiento were indeed sin nombre [nameless], anonymous workers and theorists pushed to the background, kept in their places."[54]

As with leftist political movements more generally, issues of gender subordination within the Chicano movement were seen by the

Movement's leaders to be nonexistent at best, divisive at worst. Gender concerns constituted a sort of false consciousness, one that could be reduced to the class (and for Chicano nationalists, race as well) oppression that drove the oppression of all Chicanos, male and female. Once class and race divisions were overcome, gender inequalities would naturally melt away because they were secondary oppressions, derived from the fundamental inequalities of race and class.[55] Insisting on gender as intrinsically important was seen by the leaders of *El Movimiento* as unnecessarily divisive, sapping the strength-in-unity represented by Aztlán.[56] Indeed, to question the masculinism of the Chicano Movement was to question one's loyalty to Chicano men, and to risk being seen as a betrayer of *El Movimiento*. "You are a traitor to your race if you do not put the man first."[57]

However, the infinite delay of coming to terms with what many Chicanas saw as illegitimate gender-based inequalities in the workplace, home, and *El Movimiento* became a source of intense border conflict.[58] "The predominantly male-centered authoritative discourses . . . promised to include Chicanas in the cultural record of the practices of ethnic resistance if they accepted their exclusion as female subjects and dwelled only on their ethnic similarities with Chicano males. . . . these promises rarely materialized."[59] For many Chicanas who grew weary of seeing their intellectual and physical labor on behalf of *El Movimiento* remain un(der)valued, and their concerns silenced, the notion of Aztlán-as-home was soured. For the home was lived as a source of profound ambivalence: as both "a genuine bastion of Raza self-defense against a hostile society,"[60] and, at the same time, as a persistent locus of female subservience to the political concerns and careers of Chicano men.[61]

For lesbian and gay Chicanas/os, the idealized notion of home held dear by Chicano nationalists was arguably even more profoundly alienating than it was for straight Chicana feminists. For in the hetero-patriarchal home, there was no place at all for the queer Chicana/o. In her hugely important *Borderlands/La Frontera*, Gloria Anzaldúa centers her discussion on the evolution of her identity as a Chicana lesbian feminist, the physical and spiritual exile that this evolution required, and her longing to return home. She writes of homecoming in terms of *homophobia*: "Fear of going home. And of not being taken in. We're afraid of being abandoned by the mother, the culture, *La Raza*, for being unacceptable, faulty, damaged."[62] As Sonia Saldívar-Hull has commented in her review of Anzaldúa's work, choosing to be queer in the borderlands constitutes "the ultimate exile,"[63] while Anzaldúa herself refers to the repercussions of her choices as an "intimate terrorism."[64]

Lesbianism, in particular, was perceived to deeply threaten *La Familia*. Refusing to go along with traditional gender roles was seen to strike at the root of the male privilege sown and nurtured within the heteropatriarchal Chicano family, to potentially contribute to the genocide of *La Raza* through a perceived refusal of heterosexual reproduction (regardless of whether Chicana lesbians chose to have children or not), and to blaspheme against the teachings of the Catholic Church.[65] Queerness had the potential to rip open the foundation of Chicano nationalism—the individual Chicano family, as well as *La Familia de La Raza*—from the inside. Woman-identification and queerness were viewed not just as betrayals but also as a sabotage of Chicano identity, culture, and politics.

Some Chicano nationalists viewed homosexuality as white society's most formidable tool of deception, as "*his* [the white man's] disease with which he sinisterly infects Third World people, men and women alike."[66] Yet many feminist and queer Chicanas/os were acutely conscious of their transgressions and viewed these as a deliberate critical strategy for opening the movement up from the inside. Writes Rafael Pérez-Torres: "One cannot assert the wholeness of a Chicano subject when the very discourses that go into its identity formation—be they discourses surrounding the mutability of gender identity, sexuality, class and cultural identification, linguistic and ethnic association—are incommensurably contradictory."[67] The difficult reconciliation of *El Movimiento* with its own homophobia thus becomes imperative for the reassertion of politics and identities based in Chicanismo. As Cherríe Moraga elaborates:

> I guarantee you, there will be no change among heterosexual men, there will be no change in heterosexual relations, as long as the Chicano community keeps us lesbians and gay men political prisoners among our own

people. Any movement build on the fear and loathing of anyone is a failed movement. The Chicano movement is no different.[68]

A Second Departure?

Aztlán illustrates the power of narrative to contest political processes and the material construction of meaning and belonging that surround the ongoing negotiation of collective claims to place. The Aztlán of Chicano nationalists staked an explicit claim to place, and via this claim, to an identity, presence, and legitimacy that was not derivative of or subordinate to the Anglo-American majority. To claim the Southwest as the rightful homeland of Chicanos was a key gesture, one seen by many as providing the necessary grounding, understood both literally and figuratively, for *El Movimiento* to unite Chicanos under the banner of a common cause.

Yet by bounding and fixing Aztlán geographically, and emphasizing the color line dividing Chicanos and Anglos, *El Movimiento* constructed identity, and solidarity, in profoundly bordered terms. Other differences, both exogenous and endogenous to the Movement, were exiled from Aztlán lest they disrupt the painstakingly leveled terrain of *Chicanos unidos* against the uniform Anglo oppressor. But erasures of class, race, gender, and sexuality were never truly buried; they were instead merely *dis*placed. In fact, the suppression of internal difference by Chicano nationalists brought to the forefront the fractures among Chicanas/os along lines of gender and sexuality. The pressures that these suppressions gave rise to ultimately led to an implosion of Aztlán as a generally useful political, spiritual, and geopolitical construct. By the late 1980s and early 1990s, many Chicanas/os felt that Aztlán had become "very much an empty symbol," and there was talk of a "second departure" from Aztlán.[69] "There is no turning back to racial utopias which polarize the forces of oppression along ethnic lines and create fictitious narratives of domestic bliss with the concept of a male-centered familialism."[70]

Aztlán as the geoimaginary cornerstone in a counternational narrative sought to erase and overwrite Anglo-American claims to the same lands, while it intersected in problematic ways with historic and contemporary Native American narratives centering on this region, excluded claims of Chicanos located elsewhere, and silenced the voices of queers and women. In overwriting prior narratives and silencing others, a flattening of historical texture and a suppression of difference is inevitable. Perhaps counterhegemonic nationalist claims to space, claims that must of necessity flatten the layers of historical narration in order to present a unified voice vis-à-vis the dominant nationality, are inherently risky:

> Nationalisms work through such *differentiae* because they have to, caught as they are in the conflicts of *modernity* and *modernisation*, in conditions of uneven development that, within the spaces of colonialist domination, may yield no resources but the geographical, ethnological and cultural peculiarities of a region which, in the rhetorics of nationalism, become the indices of origins, roots, hidden histories and shared heritages. . . . Whatever momentum of reidentification and reterritorialisation nationalisms make possible, they always turn on their own strategy of terror: their own interiorisation of a centre, their own essentialising of a dominant frame of differentiation, their own pogroms and expulsions.[71]

In this, the Aztlán of Chicano nationalists is in keeping with many other minority and Third World national projects that draw on tradition and folklore, involving "a process of selecting one of many possible sets of experiences from their history, in order to narrativize it linearly and frame it as the 'authentic representation.'"[72] As I have suggested earlier in this book, perhaps the modern nation-state itself is immanently unstable. If the modern nation-state is predicated on bordered difference, then exclusion is always present. It cannot be otherwise. Aztlán represented an attempt to heal the wounds left by exclusion from the Anglo-American national discourse. Yet, because Aztlán was forged on the same template as all modern nationalisms, it too was born of difference and exclusion. Aztlán was profoundly, fatally, bordered.

The Chicano movement of the 1960s and 1970s was, at the end of the day, a nationalist movement and suffered from the same flaws as other nationalisms. The failure of Chicano nationalism is not due to external factors but to a crisis or paradox that is internal to modern nationalisms everywhere. Despite a good-faith effort at contesting, and eventually displacing, the hegemonic Anglo-American nation, Aztlán did not constitute moving beyond the nation. Rather, it was a tale that was haunted, in important ways, by its own ghostly voices from the margins.

Yet Rafael Pérez-Torres has suggested that Aztlán has become not just an empty symbol (as Alarcón suggests) but an empty *signifier*, and as such, is paradoxically saturated with meaning:

> Aztlán as borderlands marks a site that both belongs to and has never belonged to either the United States or Mexico. . . . As an empty signifier, Aztlán names not that which is or has been, but that which is ever absent: nation, unity, liberation. . . . the term Aztlán consistently has named that which refers to an absence, and unfulfilled reality in response to various forms of oppression."[73]

In Pérez-Torres's vision, Aztlán has come to provide a sort of ever-receding north, a contemporary Quivira that by its very slipperiness compels constant movement. In its transversality, the paradoxical space of a potentially refigured Aztlán very much echoes, and is spatially superimposed upon, the slippery West of Anglo-American nationalism. Thus, as with the West, Aztlán's potential for reinterpretation, reinvention, and recirculation remains strong.

By the mid-1980s, a shift in master symbol was underway, one involving the inevitable movement suggested by Pérez-Torres, away from the Aztlán of Chicano nationalists to "the borderlands" of many Chicana/o writers, scholars, and artists (as well as non-Chicana/o scholars). This exchange of master symbol is indicative of a larger shift in mainstream Chicana/o praxis, away from a decidedly modern, national project to a postnationalist, perhaps even postmodern sort of project. The borderlands hold forth a promising vision of a newly smoothed space. Itself contested, again from within, the borderlands perspective is accompanied by other contending scripts for the future, parallel place visions that are themselves also vexed by the difficult interplay of smoothness and striation.

CHAPTER 4

Alternative Narratives and the Uncertain Cartography of the Present

> . . . it may be best to conceive of places and place-based consciousness
> not as a legacy of history or geography, the givens of time and space
> that provide the context for intellectual and political activity, but as a
> project that is devoted to the creation and construction of new contexts
> for thinking about politics and the production of knowledge.
>
> —Arif Dirlik, "Place-Based Imagination: Globalism and
> the Politics of Place"

Narrative Exhaustion and the Loss of Place

A fair number of scholars have suggested that contemporary human societies are experiencing an identity crisis that is based in a deeper crisis: a crisis of place. These contentions are diversely articulated, and their proponents differ politically as well as theoretically. At their core, however, these contentions share the notion that collective attachments to place have eroded, thanks to rising levels of human mobility, the prevalence of electronic media, the radical decentralization of production, heightened levels of transnational cultural and economic exchange—all broad forces that are often gathered together under the umbrella term "globalization"—and what many perceive to be the concomitant demise of the nation-state's traditional role as the principal mediator between people and larger cultural, social, economic, and political forces. As modernity has progressed we have become uprooted, and the nation-state to which we might cling as a sheltering claim to place (or, alternatively, from which we have always been alienated; or, alternatively, which is now sorely outmoded) is no longer (or never was) able to provide a stable moorage in the midst of such a sea change.[1]

Marc Augé, for example, is critical of the effect on subjectivity wrought by what he terms "supermodernity." Specifically, he finds the superficial, impersonal, and shallow character of human connections to each other and to place in today's world troubling. Augé begins his discussion using the example of a frequent flier, the bulk of whose life is situated in transitory, nondescript nodes: airport lounges, airplanes, hotels, and so on. Augé terms such sites "non-places": "If a place can be defined as relational, historical and concerned with identity, then a space which cannot be defined as relational, or historical, or concerned with identity will be a non-place."[2] Importantly, Augé suggests that this condition of placelessness is not exclusive to the wealthy or the Western, noting that temporary abodes typify the supermodern landscape, spanning the socioeconomic gamut from impoverished slums to five-star hotels, providing at all levels a dense network of transitoriness and solitude that is conducive to the substitution of signs for real communication, emptiness for human connections to places, and thus to each other. The supermodern subject, wealthy and poor alike, inhabits a liminal zone, where s/he is continuously, uneasily "at home" while never really having a home, in the meaningful sense of the word, at all.

Belden Lane echoes Augé's concern with loss of meaning and identity in modern society. Additionally, Lane underscores the disembodied aspects of deterritorialization, emphasizing a theme broached also by Edward Casey in his concern for the disembodied quality of space that so fascinates the modern mind. Lane writes:

> Personal identity is fixed for us by the feel of our own bodies, the naming of the places we occupy, and the environmental objects that beset our landscape. But the effects of modernity, the impact of the technological society, and the various sea changes in our manner of travel and communication have all tended to separate us in the last century from the three-dimensional realities of our world. We feel out of touch, without a place.[3]

For Lane, placelessness involves a loss of physical and emotional contact with the day-to-day activities of one site, with the practice of *dwelling* as conceptualized by Heidegger. Yet because place-based belonging is, according to Lane (and others), a deep human necessity, an impulse characteristic of postmodern societies is the search for roots. Lane's contention is buttressed by Philip Sheldrake:

> People in the West are increasingly an exiled and uprooted people, living "out of place." Social geographers suggest that while it is essential to have "place identity," we have since the Second World War de-emphasized place for the sake of values such as mobility, centralization or economic rationalization. The global relativity of space dissolves a human sense of place. . . . It is this sense of placelessness that makes the contemporary Western quest for meaning so concerned with roots.[4]

Arjun Appadurai's analysis of groundedness and displacement in modern societies is specifically focused on the demise of the nation-state; as such his contentions are of particular interest here given the previous two chapters' focus on national narratives, and through them important modern claims to place and identity. According to Appadurai, it is mass migration and mass media in particular that have of late led to deterritorialized, unstable subjectivities that "confound theories that depend on the continued salience of the nation-state as the key arbiter of important social changes."[5] These forces have provoked a rupture with the nation-state as "electronic mass mediation and transnational mobilization have broken the monopoly of autonomous nation-states over the project of modernization" (10). Indeed, Appadurai feels that the demise of nation-state as a cultural and political form is imminent: "I have come to be convinced that the nation-state, as a complex modern political form, is on its last legs" (19). Appadurai sees in this rupture with the nation-state, and its eventual demise, the potential for agentic cultural and political repositioning of the subaltern (those individuals and groups excluded, or inserted in subordinate positions, in the narrative of the nation-state) enacted transnationally, or even postnationally, through collective spatial imaginaries:

> Fantasy can dissipate . . . but the imagination, especially when collective, can become the fuel for action. It is the imagination, in its collective forms,

that creates ideas of neighborhood and nationhood, of moral economies and unjust rule, of higher wages and foreign labor prospects. The imagination is today a staging ground for action, and not only for escape.

In Appadurai's view, film, television shows, and music have long provided subversive micronarratives that can be—and have been—expressed in a range of oppositional movements. He gives as examples the Shining Path in Peru, Habitat for Humanity in the United States, various green movements in Europe, Tamil nationalism in Sri Lanka, and Chechen separatism in the Balkans. Thus the idea of narrative is central to Appadurai's thinking about how best to address this "need to think ourselves beyond the nation" (158) through tapping the power of collective imagination.

As Appadurai's examples illustrate, concerns with crisis (of identity, of place, of the nation-state) and its resolution frequently invoke the importance of place, locality, or the scale of the local in envisioning attempts to mediate—and for some reshape—the global. Arturo Escobar suggests that globalization can be equated with precisely the sort of evacuated spatiality that typifies modernity. Though usually ignored in the discourse of globalization, local economies and cultures in fact offer sites of reworking and resisting the environmental, economic, and cultural damage wrought through globalization. According to Escobar, "place specificity . . . enables a different reading of culture and economy, capitalism and modernity."[6] It is this different reading that affords us a critical distance on the global and offers the chance to resist its excesses. Utilizing the example of Afro-Colombian rainforest social movements, Escobar makes a strong argument for an intellectual and political commitment to place as a potentially progressive counter to globalization and its effects.

However, and along with others, Escobar notes the tendency to uncritically romanticize the local, cautioning against the dangers that lurk therein: "Local knowledge is not pure or free of domination; places might have their own forms of oppression and even terror."[7] In a related caveat, Escobar also finds himself in good critical company when he underscores the need to differentiate between *place-based* and *place-bound* when conceptualizing locally based strategies of resistance.[8] Through what many have termed "glocality," *place-based* politics works across geographic scales, from local to global and back again, and thus can (potentially, at least) avoid the parochialism, spatially limited results, and possible oppressions of a *place-bound* strategy.[9] Conceptually, the dichotomization between global and local is seen by many scholars as obfuscatory, in that it hides the profoundly articulated nature of the co-construction of global and local in ways that are detrimental to both the construction of theory and political practice necessary to understand, and reshape, the cultural, political, and economic contours of the contemporary world. Instead, what is key are the processes by which certain scales (global, regional, national, local, or other) become important and shift over time, and the repercussions this has for people and processes acting at other scales. This has led Erik Swyngedouw to state, "I would, in sum, advocate the abolition of the 'global' and the 'local' as conceptual tools and suggest a concentration on the politics of scale and their metaphorical and material production and transformation."[10]

Reclaiming places and meaningful human ties to them involves reconstructing identities, both individual and collective. Because of my emphasis on narrative, I will suggest here that the labor of reconstruction in this time of crisis is narrative at its heart. Indeed, if—as I have argued throughout this book—place is narratively constituted, then the crisis of place is itself a crisis of narrative. We live in interesting times, when the tale of the nation-state and its variants (for example, the counternarrative of Chicano nationalists discussed in the previous chapter) no longer seem as useful as they once were. To paraphrase Gramsci, crisis is that liminal period when the old is dead and the new cannot yet be born, a period characterized by the morbid symptoms of death and at the same time the promising glimmers of new opportunities. Thus the present crisis can be viewed as productive as well as destructive, as offering an opportunity for moving beyond as well as leaving behind. Yet crisis is still always an uncertain time, and this uncertainty is clearly reflected in the ambivalence of the accounts surrounding the changing relationship between people and places. Is globalization ultimately harmful, an extension on an unprecedented scale of the destructive tendencies of capitalism and imperialism? Or are these changes potentially progressive, even liberating, of the strictures of modernity? Is the nation-state truly withering away, or is it coming back with a quiet vengeance? Is deterritorialization erosive or constitutive of meaningful subjectivities?

This chapter examines three narratives that have been offered up as solutions to the current crisis: globalization, the borderlands, and a nativist reprise on the nation-state. All three of these narratives are set in what has come to be, for academic theorists and policymakers alike, the Ur-stage on which the drama of the future, at least for the United States, is set to unfold: the southern boundary with Mexico. This long divide between the two countries today looms so large in the geoimaginaries of so many in part because it challenges us so, it dares us to rethink its usefulness in light of unprecedented levels of migration, trade, cultural exchange, and the political maneuvering that takes these forces into account. As Kathleen Staudt and David Spener have suggested, "If formerly the perspective we gained from the border was that of looking from the margins of history back toward the center, now the border stands at the center and offers us a front-row view of history's drama unfolding."[11]

The globalization narrative, and the neoliberal economic fable that nurtures it, provides a newly smoothed vision of the future. Proponents of globalization have a hopeful attitude, seeing on the horizon increasing prosperity, a lessening of economic inequality, and a causal linking of economic abundance to a flourishing democratic political culture. Though the economistic taproot of the globalization perspective, its inherent social, political, and economic conservatism, and mainstream (rather than oppositional) history clearly diverge from the critical foundations of the borderlands perspective and its practitioners, advocates of the globalization approach also hold dear the idea of a borderless world. Geopolitical boundaries between countries, and the state apparatus of which they are a part, are crumbling as the inevitable, and desirable, outcome of a new world order that no longer needs such anachronisms. The space of North America—and eventually the Americas from pole to pole—is smoothed of the rusty machinery of the old world order and overwritten with an economically driven narrative that sees us as progressing together beyond the nation-state. Smoothed of literal and figurative barriers, advocates of globalization see the logical emergence of supra-, trans-, or subnational regional blocs, a rhizomic space of logical nodes and decentralized networks, where people work together and follow the directives of that figurative smooth space par excellence, the global marketplace, in a new world order that is inherently competitive, fair, and frictionless.

Likewise, but in a very different and more nuanced genre, what Pablo Vila has called the mainstream borderlands perspective also centralizes a narrative of border erasure through the emergence of hybrid spaces-in-between Mexico and the United States literally, and figuratively, as signaling a pathway beyond the dichotomous construction of identities as either/or choices.[12] Such borderlands proponents take as axiomatic that Mexico proper has, for decades, steadily driven a cultural, demographic, linguistic, political, economic, and social wedge into the territory of the United States. Américo Paredes, the great border musicologist, called this region "Greater Mexico" to refer to "all the areas inhabited by people of a Mexican culture—not only within the present limits of the Republic of Mexico but in the United States as well—in a cultural rather than a political sense."[13] Greater Mexico is seen to present profound challenges to the legitimacy of dominant Anglo-narratives of the United States of America, challenges that are, in some important ways, different and more complex than those posed by Chicano nationalists. Greater Mexico constitutes a new sort of region, one that both draws upon and defies geopolitical boundaries. It also constitutes a new geoimaginary that holds forth the potential for new identities associated with it. Greater Mexico picks at the wound that is the nation-state in late modernity, it disrupts rather than mirrors the modern landscape, and it is actively rewriting human relationships to the land in this place.

Proponents of this approach note that it is in the borderlands that raced, classed, and sexed differences are being profoundly contested, as evidenced by contemporary aesthetic production in song, performance, and the plastic arts. In much of this work, the contemporary contestations of belonging and exclusion on and around the geopolitical boundary between Mexico and the United States construct a productively liminal space that allows for new identities to emerge, identities that forge wholly new subjectivities that are not bound by outdated notions of "here" and "there." The borderlands represent a move away from dichotomous constructions of collective identity rooted in difference, and toward a multiple and contingent subject positioning. They provide spaces-in-between, spanning both the literal border between the United States and Mexico and metaphorical borders of difference that have also divided and excluded for so long. In the borderlands, the social relations of power are conceptualized as reaching laterally across difference rather than hierarchically, reifying difference, and are thus seen as less oppressive. The borderlands provide a smooth space that turns on a deliberate erasure of borders both literal and figurative. Erasure is a transgressive, contestatory, liberatory gesture in the borderlands. The borderlands, like globalization, invoke a newly smoothed space where dichotomous constructions of belonging and exclusion are no longer viable. As with globalization, but in a very different way, proponents of the borderlands narrate a progressive vision of the future.

However, in the discourses of both the boosters of globalization and the proponents of a borderlands perspective, vestiges of old narratives of belonging and exclusion remain. Anglo-American expansionism and the contemporary globalization narrative share an uncannily imperialist, expansionist script. For their part, scholars and artists taking a mainstream borderlands approach in fact share much with their Chicano nationalist precursors, particularly the cultural nationalists, in their combination of aesthetics and politics, the weaving of familial history to place history and both of these to claims of legitimacy, and their totalizing, at times racialized, counterhegemonic stance vis-à-vis Anglo-American hegemony.

Though debates about the borderlands are often conducted on highly metaphorized grounds, it is wise to keep at the center of our explorations the fact that the lived terrain of border zone surrounding Mexico and the United States is under fierce contestation today. The nation-state has not withered away. Indeed, we appear in many ways to be *regressing*, rather than *progressing*, beyond the nation-state along the U.S.-Mexico border. This particularly dark tale emphasizes violence, intolerance, and a growing rigidity of the geopolitical boundary. In this narrative, the nation-state and in particular its boundaries are reaffirmed rather than denied. The space of the border zone, both literally and figuratively, is characterized by a strengthening of boundaries and borders alike. A rising tide of racialized Anglo-nationalism in the United States has, of late, shaped conservative political campaigns, paved the way for the widespread legal-institutional rollback of decades of civil rights gains, and led to a hardening of the very infrastructure of the border itself. Do-it-yourself border vigilantism is on the rise by property owners on the U.S. side of the line, while thieves of all stripes prey on migrants on the Mexican side. From Operation Gatekeeper in San Diego to Operation Hold the Line in El Paso, fortified urban borders have diverted immigrants, particularly families on the move, into desert areas where hundreds die each year from thirst, heat exhaustion, and exposure.

The sense of dislocation that those working within the borderlands perspective find so liberatory has, for others, provoked a sense of disorientation, of loss, of being under attack. Borders and boundaries are viewed by nativists as our last and best bulwark in an increasingly hostile world where social and spatial transgression is an ongoing threat rather than a productively positive event. The stark division now in place is seen as the best of possible worlds, given the horror-story reality of border-transgressing terrorists, ecological disasters, and rising levels of human displacement that have blurred space in discomfiting ways. Contra Burke's assertion of ease, pleasure, and consensuality, smoothness can sometimes be disorienting, vertiginously frightening, parochial, repressive, or reactionary in very real ways.

I want to suggest that literal and figurative spaces on and around the boundary line between the United States and Mexico constitute, in Gillian Rose's characterization, a "paradoxical" sort of place, one where our usual coordinates of navigation no longer work.[14] It is a condition I approach in terms of spatial schizophrenia. This condition has been at once highly productive and highly unsettling. The borderlands perspective, for example, has given birth to a body of intellectual and aesthetic production that, it is hoped, can open doors to exciting critiques of modernity, critiques that have the potential to forge paths beyond modernity's more oppressive features. The discourse of globalization, for its part, has offered many an optimistic outlook toward the future. Both perspectives, however, have produced scripts of the future that, when rehearsed, have given rise to their own deep contradictions, paradoxes, and exclusions. In addition, and despite the aesthetic and legal-institutional rhetoric from both globalizationists and proponents of mainstream border theory and practice, the lived space of the border between Mexico and the United States has witnessed a profoundly disturbing tightening, characterized by physical fortification, legal-institutional rollbacks, and rising racialized intolerance and violence. Some of our dreams-beyond-the-nation are recurring nightmares, wherein our national boundaries rise up in the desert and ensnare us in tangled scrolls of concertina wire.

Global Visions

Images of the earth seen from space are often used by proponents of globalization in corporate logos and advertising campaigns. Denis Cosgrove notes that the image of the earth seen from space, associated with the 1972 Apollo flight, is also used by environmentalists and human rights activists.[15] In all instances, the image is used to convey a sense, sometimes apocalyptic and sometimes hopeful, of a common destiny. Viewing the earth from space drives home the story that geopolitical boundaries are a fiction, and if this is true, then our activities need not be restrained by them. The images suggest that the world is literally and figuratively graspable as a whole. We are all naturally connected and our progress, as well as our responsibility, knows no real bounds.

The European Union is often touted as the shining example of regional integration, a real move in the direction of a borderless world, blazing a trail for other groups of nation-states who wish to exchange the borders between them for common policies regarding trade, monetary system, population mobility, governmental structure, and the military. North America is not far behind and has embarked on the path of regional integration through a series of legal and institutional reforms, culminating in the North American Free Trade Agreement (NAFTA) in 1994 and a proposed Free Trade Area of the Americas (FTAA) that would reach from pole to pole. Not only have trade barriers begun to fall but cultural barriers as well, leading *Time* magazine to proclaim, in a special issue dated 11 June 2001, that "the border [between the United States and Mexico] is vanishing before our eyes, creating a new world for all of us."[16] "How much," *Time* writer Nancy Gibbs asks, "has to cross the border before it might not be there at all? There is no Customs station for customs—for ideas and tastes, stories and songs, values, instincts, attitudes, and none of those stop in El Paso, Texas, or San Diego, Calif., anymore. The old world fades away . . . and the border is everywhere."[17]

And it is not just geopolitical boundaries that are dissolving; more importantly, it is the nation-states of which they are emblematic that are naturally, thankfully, seen to be on the decline.[18] For the nation-state itself is conceptualized, by advocates of globalization, to function as a sort of border—understood in this instance as a barrier—to achieving a new level of growth. In order to maximize profits and streamline production and consumption, territory must be allowed to aggregate at scales that make sense, into "natural business units" based on "the four I's"—investment, industry, information technology, and individual consumers—that join people and activities into appropriate combinations.[19] Nation-states, however, according to globalizationist spokesman Kenichi Ohmae, frequently operate at an inappropriate level of aggregation:

> The nation state has become an unnatural—even a dysfunctional—organizational unit for thinking about economic activity. It combines things at the wrong level of aggregation. . . . in a borderless economy, the nation-focused maps we typically use to make sense of economic activity are

woefully misleading. We must, managers and policymakers alike, face up at last to the awkward and uncomfortable truth: the old cartography no longer works. It has become no more than an illusion.[20]

In the globalized vision, social relations of production and consumption lateralize and are allowed to flow freely and quickly across space for the benefit of all: producers, consumers, and citizens alike. The useful role of the streamlined state is that of watchdog, on guard to make sure that the (inherently fair) rules of the market are followed. Eventually, the forces of equalization at work in the market will pull other aspects of social, political, and cultural life forward with it, for the good of all. Politics will provide a vehicle for coordination, cooperation, and increased efficiency, rather than a mechanism for endlessly mediating conflict. Social differences will level out. Culturally, an appreciation of difference will develop, nurturing the culture of democracy, and easing the task of governance.

However, as Denis Cosgrove has so correctly pointed out in regard to the corporate use of images of the earth as seen from space: "In using these 'cartographic' images for corporate promotional purposes, the *idea* of 'being global' is far more important than the actual ways in which a company operates across the world."[21] Globalization, it is suggested, is a marketing strategy, not an ethical blueprint. Simon Dalby interprets this tension within a framework of "globalization or global apartheid?" In this schema, Dalby notes the divergent morals of different accounts of the new world order. On one hand we have, according to Dalby, the globalization approach, wherein geopolitical borders are vanishing "fossils of an earlier age" replaced by the fast-flowing and unfettered information superhighway, transnational corporations replacing the state as the key decision-makers, economic and cultural wealth being created on a massive scale, and where, ultimately, "the international free market is supposedly the route to prosperity for all."[22] On the other hand is an assessment of the emerging world order as one of global apartheid, one that Dalby understands via an analogy between the former South African government's policy of racialized sociospatial segregation of black and white South Africans and the increasingly stark sociospatial contours of the global economy: "Apartheid, as formerly practiced in South Africa, offers a microcosmic model of the current global polity. . . . They add a racial dimension to the geopolitical categories [developed and underdeveloped], emphasising the affluence of the white races and the relative poverty of most of the rest."[23]

The evidence here is readily apparent to even the mildest of critical eyes, and it reveals the simplistic script that gives rise to the fable of globalization. What, for example, of the irony of Bill Gates, computer software mogul, multi-gazillionare, and screechy defendant of "free trade" in his ongoing antitrust battles, referring to "a frictionless capitalism. . . . In the great planetary marketplace, we as social creatures will sell, negotiate, invest, bargain, choose, discuss, stroll, meet"?[24] Does he honestly expect that we will all participate equally in this borderless free trade zone? What of the hundreds of thousands of people actually employed in constructing the circuitry through which this smooth space of informatics, trade, and investment flows? Do these new patterns of productions not follow lines on maps, older lines of colonialism and newer lines of imperialist expansion, all of which are tied to ongoing geographies of exploitation? Are these particular references to borderlessness not reminiscent of the wavelike patterns of spread that characterized nineteenth-century Anglo American expansionism? Who could truly stand at the border checkpoint between Tijuana and San Ysidro, take in the stadium floodlights, triple-layered fence, surveillance cameras, motion sensors, and the endless binary processing of human beings and truthfully claim that the border is "vanishing"?[25] Such questions quickly disrupt even the smoothness of the narrative itself, not to mention the lived spaces of the future its authors envision.

In a more nuanced treatment, Michael Hardt and Antonio Negri discuss the ever more encompassing space of the globalizing world within the framework of "Empire," wherein the anachronistic divisions between first, second, and third worlds have all but vanished, as have the cumbersome borders of nation-states, and "capital seems to be faced with a smooth world."[26] In drawing on the critical social theory of

Foucault, Deleuze and Guattari, and others, Hardt and Negri elaborate a theory of power in *Empire* wherein the concept of smooth and striated space is central and well worked.

> The striated space of modernity constructed *places* that were continually engaged in and founded on a dialectical play with their outsides. The space of imperial sovereignty, in contrast, is smooth. It might appear to be free of the binary divisions or striation of modern boundaries but really it is crisscrossed by so many fault lines that it only appears as a continuous, uniform space. In this sense, the clearly defined crisis of modernity gives way to an omni-crisis in the imperial world. In this smooth space of Empire, there is no *place* of power—it is both everywhere and nowhere. Empire is an *ou-topia*, or really a *non-place*.[27]

Yet for all their use of critical social theory, their provocative discussions of the changing spatiality of resistance, and their observation that Empire fosters social and economic divisions that are in many ways deeper than those lived under colonialism, imperialism, or socialism, Hardt and Negri's assessment of Empire is at the end of the day a largely positive one. Curiously enough, their assessment is positive in the decidedly linear worldview characteristic of the old left, inasmuch as Empire's real usefulness is seen to reside in its advance beyond modernity and its anachronistic appurtenances.

> We insist on asserting that the construction of Empire is a step forward in order to do away with any nostalgia for the power structures that preceded it and refused any political strategy that involves returning to that old arrangement, such as trying to resurrect the nation-state to protect against global capital. We claim that Empire is better in the same way that Marx insists that capitalism is better than the forms of society and modes of production that came before it.[28]

Perhaps so, but does Hardt and Negri's understanding, which they admit is elaborated at a primarily theoretical level, overlook the lived reality of so many caught amid the quiet striations of Empire at its peril? *Empire's* most valuable contributions, at least with regard to the concerns of *Dry Place*, involve its authors' recognition that the apparently smooth surface of the global world is, in fact, a highly striated one, though the striations may operate in spatially novel fashions. Even in their questionable assertion that Empire represents a progression beyond modernity, Hardt and Negri challenge us to push beyond the nation-state. This challenge is also advanced by proponents of the borderlands, albeit in strikingly different ways.

Moving to the Borderlands

Aztlán, as with modern nationalisms everywhere, relied on the clear definition of external boundaries and the setting and policing of strict internal borders, particularly regarding gender and sexuality. The silencing and exclusion of the many Chicanas and Chicanos banished to the margins of Aztlán ultimately undermined it as a unifying concept. As Smadar Lavie and Ted Swedenburg have noted, resistance *by* the margins often results in a transformation *of* the margins, involving a deep-reaching internal critique of homogenization-in-resistance, and resulting in a wide-scale paradigm shift away from dichotomous understandings of struggle as self-versus-other and toward "historically grounded multiple subject positions."[29] As I observed in the previous chapter, the Chicano movement and the nationalist sentiment symbolized by Aztlán have, like many counterhegemonic nationalist struggles worldwide, undergone just this sort of deeply transformative questioning. As a result of the process of internal critique worked around Chicano nationalism and its primary symbolization in Aztlán, the notion of "the borderlands" has emerged as a predominant paradigm, holding great aesthetic, intellectual, and political currency.[30] For many Chicanas/os, the borderlands have replaced the Aztlán of the Chicano nationalist period.

At one level, the borderlands can be seen as that zone of physical exchange between the United States and Mexico, the territory that straddles the geopolitical boundary between these two countries. As globalizationists have suggested, because goods, services, and information move ever more fluidly between the two countries, there is a progressive blurring of differences on both sides of the border, and the emergence of a culturally, economically, environmentally, and politically distinct region that the popular press has dubbed "Mexamerica." The notion of the borderlands, as contemporary Chicana/o, and other, scholars, artists, and writers have used the term, is broader and differently motivated. The borderlands, for these proponents and practitioners, open up all that was fixed in Aztlán. Where Aztlán was bounded and closed to difference, the borderlands are by definition deterritorialized, a crossroads defined by the fluid traversal, and acceptance, of difference.[31] Gloria Anzaldúa, a founding mother of the borderlands perspective, describes the borderlands as a place where "the prohibited and forbidden are its inhabitants. *Los atravesados* live here: the squint-eyed, the perverse, the queer, the troublesome, the mongrel, the mulato, the half-breed, the half dead; in short, those who cross over, pass over, or go through the confines of the 'normal.'"[32] The uncertainty that for some looms so threateningly unsettled is embraced.

The U.S.-Mexico border area provides a literal grounding for the work of border scholars, activists, writers, poets, performance artists, musicians, and painters. At a metaphorical level, as well, the fluid space of the borderlands provides an anchor of sorts for their identity and their work. Pat Mora and Gloria Anzaldúa have both suggested that the slippery space of the U.S.-Mexico border may best be understood as *nepantla* (middle land).[33] In their writing, they argue that the liminal space of *nepantla* and the disorientation it entails is not to be lamented. Rather, by its very fluidity, the border constitutes a potential-laden space where old power relations can be reworked and perhaps made less oppressive. Anzaldúa writes: "To be disoriented in space is to be in *nepantla*, to experience bouts of disassociation of identity, identity breakdowns and buildups. The border is in a constant *nepantla* state, and it is an analog of the planet."[34] Similarly, the performance artist Guillermo Gómez-Peña has lived displacement with great pleasure:

> When I am on the East Coast of the United States, I am also in Europe, Africa, and the Caribbean. There, I like to visit Nuyo Rico, Cuba York,

and other micro-republics. When I return to the U.S. Southwest, I am suddenly back in Mexamerica, a vast conceptual nation that also includes the northern states of Mexico, and overlaps with various Indian nations. When I visit Los Angeles or San Francisco, I am at the same time in Latin America and Asia. Los Angeles, like Mexico City, Tijuana, Miami, Chicago, and New York, is practically a hybrid nation/city in itself.[35]

The emergence in the mid-1980s of Gómez-Peña's borderlands-focused performance art coincides with Anzaldúa's publication of *Borderlands/La Frontera*, and the timing is not incidental. In the previous chapter, I elaborated on the specific scholarly critiques arising from feminist and queer Chicanas/os in response to the nationalist—and thus patriarchal and homophobic—understandings of the Chicano movement in the late 1960s and 1970s. This incubator of the borderlands approach was consistent with other critiques of leftist political praxis: gender blindness and heteronormalization were understood as limiting the anticolonial possibilities of Chicano nationalism to, at best, an inversion of the Anglocentric version, one that continued to reproduce the gendered and sexualized exclusions of the Anglo model. These critiques led to an internal fragmentation of Chicana/o cultural production.

By the early 1980s, Chicano cultural production had reached a low point.[36] But this lull, when the sweeping, grandly transformative visions of the late 1960s and 1970s began to give way to the self-absorption and individualism of the early 1980s, was in fact a crucible of change. Confronted by fresh waves of racialized intolerance and legal-institutional rollbacks in the Reagan years, the influx of migrants escaping Central America's war zones, and a massive sea change in the production and practice of knowledge in U.S. universities, Chicana/o scholarly, literary, cultural, and artistic production flowered forth in response in the mid-1980s. This new era emphasized building bridges with other minority U.S. groups, particularly blacks, Asian Americans, feminists, and queers. Rather than producing for a Chicano-only audience, sights were turned outward, toward mainstream United States, Europe, South America, and the Caribbean. Blurring boundaries through mixing genres and experimenting with new media also became important. The epic focus of the

1960s and 1970s gave way to the personal voice of the artist, individual experience, and finding the complex and significant in the seemingly simple and mundane. Processes of destabilization, questioning, searching, and opening-up in the mid-1980s through the 1990s can be viewed as involving a reworking of the very spatiality of Chicana/o cultural production. "The objective seems to be a greater introspection—*more vertical than horizontal*—into a wide array of manifestations that document Chicano social spheres."[37]

For a number of scholars, the borderlands have provided a place of departure, both literally and metaphorically speaking, that emphasizes interdisciplinarity, openness to feminist, queer, and an array of American ethnic studies scholarly critiques, and significant contributions to the emergence of non-Anglo, at times non-Western, perspectives for theory and practice in the academy. The borderlands move the margins—and not just the margins of Chicano nationalism, but the racialized and sexualized margins within the imaginary and practice of Americanness— to the center. Such a shift signifies nothing less than a revolution in American studies, whereby the constitutive outside is reconceptualized as inside:

> Where the frontier implies a model of center and periphery, which confront one another in a one-way imposition of power, the borderlands are seen as multidimensional and transterritorial; they not only lie at the geographic and political margins of national identity but as often traverse the center of the metropolis. . . . At these borders, foreign relations do not take place outside the boundaries of America, but instead constitute American nationality.[38]

In this, borderlands scholars share much with, and have contributed much to, larger contemporary interventions in Western knowledge production from feminist, queer, and postcolonial perspectives. What is perhaps most distinct about borderlands scholars is their concentration on the physical space of the U.S.-Mexico border zone. Most productively, the borderlands are approached by scholars, activists, and artists as a space in-between: not just in-between nations, peoples, and identities but also in-between metaphorical and physical understandings of place in ways that highlight the productive ties between these two levels of existence. The very plasticity of the borderlands, both as a physical reality that has become quite porous to all sorts of flows, and as a metaphorical space that allows transgression and reworking of myriad divisions in social space, is recognized as a useful dimension of critique and is utilized as such. Whether the borderlands perspective constitutes a truly "postmodern" paradigm is a difficult issue, but if the borderlands do indeed signal a shift beyond the modern, the question of what social collectives "beyond the nation" might look like, not to mention possible forms of postmodern political practice, can perhaps be approached via the borderlands.

The optimism of mainstream borderlands scholars has been deeply questioned of late, and I will explore these challenges further in this chapter. Here, however, I wish to recognize four distinct, but interrelated, strands of borderlands work that are illustrative (though certainly not exhaustive) of scholarly and artistic work conducted from a mainstream borderlands perspective: borderlands scholarship largely resident in U.S. academic institutions, literature and poetry, contemporary popular cultural production (particularly music), and performance art broadly understood to encompass literal performance as well as large-scale art installations.[39] In particular, all four arenas display a strategic use of a notion of in-betweenness in the metaphorical (and at times, the literal) borderlands.[40]

With its publication in 1987, Gloria Anzaldúa's *Borderlands/La Frontera* quickly became a foundational text of the mainstream borderlands perspective in the U.S. academy. Anzaldúa begins her book by directly engaging with the silences and exclusions of Chicano nationalism as signaled by Aztlán. She, like many borderlands writers, scholars, and artists, sought to uncover voices that had been silenced, and to revisit pre-Columbian and Mexican myths and symbols for different, more inclusive, ways of retelling stories that have already been told. Central to Anzaldúa's, and subsequent, theorizing of the borderlands is the experience, both literal and metaphorical, of border crossing. Yet the sort of "crossing" invoked by Anzaldúa is not the onetime migration of an individual from point A (Mexico) to point B (the United States). Rather, the notion of border crossing is expanded to constitute a to-and-fro movement over time (repeated crossings of the geopolitical boundary), and across a variety of borders not limited to the physical boundary between nations but including sexual, linguistic, and racialized borders as well. In these repeated acts of crossing, a hybridized terrain is spun, and, from this, identities that are by definition betwixt and between: not Mexican, but not fully "American" either, neither "straight" nor "gay," "here" nor "there." Anzaldúa uses the term *mestizaje* to refer to this sort of hybridization. The "mestiza" state is an outsider-within stance that, according to many borderlands scholars, lends unique critical insights into questions of social, political, and economic justice in the physical space of the borderlands. Anzaldúa signals the borderlands as a critical space where outsiders-within are welcomed and recognized for their particular, powerful insights.

Guillermo Gómez-Peña has also produced some of the mainstream U.S. borderlands perspective's key texts, in particular his *Warrior for Gringostroika* (1993) and *The New World Border* (1996). Gómez-Peña is one of the most widely recognized border performance artists, and his written work, in the form of creative essays, song lyrics, play scripts, performance pieces, and poetry, has reached a large readership. Gómez-Peña intervenes directly in the paradoxical space of the supposed "opening of borders" so touted by NAFTA-inspired rhetoric, and the harsh realities of increasing regulation of the physical space of the Mexico-U.S. boundary, as well as the hardened institutional and ideological stance within the United States regarding the funding and production of artistic work, and sets this alongside the difficult, at times intensely productive, reality of border crossing in his own life and creative undertakings. He (along with collaborators Coco Fusco, Roberto Cifuentes, Roger Bartra, Emily Hicks, David Avalos, and Sara-Jo Berman, among others) invites, provokes, and compels his audience to reconsider their comfortable racialized, sexualized, and geographic categorizations and the work that such categorizations do in perpetuating borders both literal and metaphorical.

Gómez-Peña has described his own border trajectory as a Mexican-born, California-dwelling, bicultural, bilingual individual in terms of a Möbius strip, along which he is uncertain of being inside, outside, neither, or both.[41] Yet rather than succumb to desperation at this uncertainty, he positions it at the center of his highly politicized performance art. For example, in the BAW/TAF (Border Arts Workshop/*Taller de Arte Fronterizo*), the line between California and Mexico was explicitly mocked by setting up a picnic table straddling the border. Participants in this critical border performance shared food and held hands across the table, even turning it around 180 degrees at one point, so that performers were "illegally" in each other's countries for a few seconds.[42]

Both Anzaldúa and Gómez-Peña frequently utilize original poetry as a textual strategy of border crossing. The visual parsimony of their poetic imagery complements, extends, and enriches their academic prose. Rather than attempting to purify their writing by bordering according to genre, Anzaldúa and Gómez-Peña instead incorporate poetry, performance, and academic prose in their intellectual production. Thus their writing itself is hybrid in conceptualization and execution.

Rafael Pérez-Torres has analyzed the shifting foci of Chicana/o poetry in rich depth in his *Movements in Chicano Poetry: Against Myths, Against Margins*. Pérez-Torres understands the principal movement in Chicano poetry to involve just this transition from fixed notions of homeland embodied in Aztlán to the less sure, more inclusive, deterritorialized notion of the borderlands. Drawing on comparative analysis of the poetry of Chicano nationalists like Alurista (poet and coauthor of the *Plan Espiritual de Aztlán*, discussed in the previous chapter) and Rodolfo "Corky" Gonzales (activist and author of the epic Chicano nationalist poem *Yo Soy Joaquín/I am Joaquín*)[43] and the poetry of Jimmy Santiago Baca, collected in *Black Mesa Poems*,[44] Pérez-Torres makes this observation:

> Certainly between Gonzales's early portrait of the intersection of history and land in 1967 and Baca's meditations some twenty years later, the

terrain of Aztlán can be seen to buckle and break in a number of different and divergent ways. Within this span of time, the nationalism—literal
or symbolic—implicit in Gonzales's configuration of Aztlán gives way
to a more subtle and complex vision of the interaction between land and
history in Baca's poetry. . . . This poetic vision conceives of the land as a
text telling a story not so much about a return to home as about a nomadic
passage.[45]

As I have noted of the work of Anzaldúa and Gómez-Peña, Pérez-
Torres also highlights the importance of the theme of migration across
four decades of Chicano poetry. Yet he elaborates upon the changing
uses of this thematic in the two periods under consideration here.
Pérez-Torres views this principally as a shift from the fixed territory
symbolized by Aztlán and migration as involving a determined, one-way
trajectory with a known destination, which has given way to the wan-
derings of immanently mobile subjects who inhabit the unfixed metaphorical terrain of the borderlands, "a ceaseless engagement between
Self and Other."[46] Yet these "ceaseless engagements" are not aimless;
rather, they have produced a profound and ongoing interrogation of
one's identity and place in society, a new respect for the complexity and
subtlety of life in the contemporary borderlands, and a constructive
opening-up to difference.

Popular culture, too, has experienced a similar shift in focus. Music
produced in the literal borderlands, in particular, has strongly emphasized the theme of crossing over literal and figurative borders. Scan the
radio stations of most locations across the U.S. Southwest and you will
come across hybridized forms of music that draw on traditional regional
styles blended with each other, as well as with contemporary modes
of musical production and distribution. The departed diva of Tejano
music, Selena, provides one of the best illustrations of the crossover
nature of much contemporary borderlands music.[47] Selena sang covers
of Donna Summer's disco-era ballads alongside contemporary pop music,
ballads, and traditional songs sung in Spanish, performed them in the
United States and in Mexico, executed Latin dance steps impeccably

in her sequined bustiers, had major hits in Spanish-speaking, English-speaking, and bilingual audiences, and was on the cusp of releasing her wildly successful crossover album, *Dreaming of You*. The album was released posthumously in July of 1995, just four months after her assassination at the hands of her longtime groupie, fan club manager, and consultant, Yolanda Saldívar. Selena was not yet twenty-four years old.[48]

Shifting U.S. demographics, rising purchasing power of Latino music consumers, and the success in making and marketing music on the part of Latino groups, record labels, and promoters has led to a boom in Latino and Latino-inspired music production: Tejano, Latin rap and hip-hop, technobanda, and tropical music (salsa, cumbia, Afro-Caribbean, *norteño*), among others.[49] One of the latest genres of music to emerge from the borderlands is nortec, an innovative fusion of traditional northern Mexican music, *música norteña*, and the high-tech mixing, dubbing, echoing, and looping common to European and American techno music genres such as trance, jungle, and rave. According to the promotional flyer that accompanies a currently popular CD sampler of nortec music, *The Tijuana Sessions Vol. 1*, nortec is "the sound of the First World in the Third and the Third World in the First. . . . A sound like this only could have been dreamed up in a place like Tijuana."[50] Nortec music thus deliberately draws on and fuses a transborder sonic landscape to create a distinct flavor that appeals to audiences on both sides of the line. It also attempts to bridge generations along the border, where parents raised on traditional Mexican sounds often have next to nothing in common with the musical tastes of their children, who are hungry for the latest dance beats from the United States and European urban centers. Nortec attempts to "transform the strangeness of Tijuana into art,"[51] to mediate the gaps created by a constant human traffic from both the United States and the interior of Mexico and Central America, an economy of contrasts where extreme poverty exists cheek by jowl with the fabulous excesses of the drug trade, the high tech drudgery of the maquiladoras rests alongside the stunningly beautiful blue California coastline, and most Tijuanenses utilize their particular *rasquache* creativity to get by.

The visual arts, too, have experienced a *nueva onda*,[52] or new wave, away from the rather hermetic outlook of Chicano art and artists in the 1960s and 1970s, with their backward-looking iconography, realist style, and collectivist ideology. By contrast, the mid-1980s through the 1990s saw a reaching out and opening up of Chicana/o art and artists:

> Chicano artists tore down the stereotypical images of Chicano separatist rhetoric of the Movimiento in order to create space for new cultural images of Chicanos as Americans alive with new attitudes about themselves and their struggles. . . . Chicano art also became connected with a healthy trend toward pluralism/multiculturalism in American art. Chicano artists began a dialogue with other American artists of color and immigrants from Latin America and Asia.[53]

Vargas notes that some of the nationalist-inspired artists of the late 1960s and 1970s have simply faded away, while others matured and became more experimental with medium, subject, and audience, and still others have crossed over into the mainstream graphic arts and advertising industries, giving Chicana/o art and artists a wider and more mainstream American audience.[54]

Perhaps the most explicit examples of crossover in the visual arts involve large-scale installations that simultaneously span the literal and figurative border between Mexico and the United States. The development of three successive inSITE installation projects, in 1992, 1994, and 1997, illustrates this tendency well.[55] Based in San Diego, inSITE92 did have several works located in Tijuana, yet its emphasis was on the San Diego area and its artists. For inSITE94, the border between Tijuana and San Diego became a central theme, and artists from San Diego, Baja California, and Mexico City participated. By inSITE97, the border was potentially everywhere, although the primary focus on the border between the United States and Mexico had not been lost. As Néstor García Canclini underscores, the forty-two participating artists, arriving from Canada to Argentina, were required to spend several weeks in Tijuana and San Diego, touring the region and mingling with the populations in the places that they had chosen for their installations.[56] Yet inSITE97 attempted to highlight the fact that even in the seemingly most binary expression of space and society—the geopolitical boundary between the United States and Mexico—there was, increasingly, a multiplicity of flows, identities, and lived experiences.

One of the best examples of this tension between dichotomy and multiplicity was artist Marcos Ramírez ERRE's two-headed Trojan Horse, installed to physically straddle the geopolitical border, with one head looking into Mexico and the other facing the United States. Yet, unlike the nationalist monuments that typify major border crossing points along the Mexico-U.S. line (statues of national heroes, pre-Columbian figures, huge flags, maps), which signal clearly what country the traveler is in, or the ubiquitous billboards raining the same, deterritorialized messages of capitalist consumption down on passers-by regardless of which side they're on, the Trojan Horse was designed to provide a *universal* symbol with a binary twist. Symmetrical about its midsection, it gives equal weight to both sides of the border. Items could be passed back and forth through the two-headed, openworked body of the horse. ERRE remarked:

> A closed Trojan horse is no longer possible, this is a transparent Trojan horse. The whole idea of the piece (ideologically and technologically) is based on transparency, because a solid horse would have been blown over by the wind. It's about a double invasion, who's invading whom and how and are hamburgers stronger than tacos, or mariachis better than rock groups, it's a "pollution" that doesn't seem so polluting to me.[57]

Its visibility to all crossing the border was intended to underscore that many people with a wide array of purposes cross the bridge at Tijuana-San Ysidro. The artist focuses on this aspect of border crossings in the fictive testimony of John Doe, Emigrant, a border crosser who lives in Tijuana and works in San Diego, who like so many "travel cocooned in their cars and in their thoughts," and whose only problem crossing is the long traffic delays on the bridge. The horse appears one day, gigantic, imposing, causing John Doe great curiosity and a measure of comfort with its daily presence. When the piece is removed at the end of the installation, "Suddenly, the horse was no longer there. Its absence felt strange. It had become a part of my personal journey. So went my thoughts until my turn came at the border port. I showed the official my work permit and he waved me on. Only then did I realize that the horse remains in its place."[58]

Trouble in Paradise? Rebordering the Borderlands

With such a backdrop, the borderlands perspective appears creative, optimistic, and progressive. In the words of one of its preeminent spokespeople, Guillermo Gómez-Peña, creative production in the borderlands emphasizes "the brave acceptance of our trans-borderized and de-nationalized condition; the *ars poetica* of vertigo; the metaphysics of fragmentation; and the total collapse of linear logic, dramatic time, and narrative aesthetics."[59] Contemporary creative endeavors on and about the geopolitical border have opened up binary understandings of landscape—of peoples' ties to places, and of the legitimacy of such ties—to profound rethinking. Does the fact that these contestations are occurring on the geopolitical border go beyond the symbolic? Could the reworking of oppositionality in representations of the border constitute a first step towards unraveling the nation itself, a construct so dependent on inside and outside? Can the nation, and the bordering upon which it rests, finally be got beyond? Proponents of the borderlands suggest this may be happening already.

Yet dangers lurk in these borderlands, too. To begin with, there are important connections between the globalizationist fable of a borderless world and the grim reality of how that world is lived for so many along the Mexico-U.S. border. As I have already discussed at length, and as many other border-based scholars have also underscored, we must recall that the creative outpouring of borderlands writing, art, song, and scholarship is occurring in a context of legal-institutional hardening, of profound border anxiety, of violence along the border proper. To acknowledge that nothing is ever "just cultural" or "merely symbolic," that culture is political and politics is cultural, is not to gloss the fact that the border zone is in a state of profound crisis. The seemingly unitary optimism of the borderlands approach may, in fact, obfuscate some of these connections. Katharyn Mitchell has written that an emphasis on liminal, deterritorialized, borderless spaces and their partial, hybrid, and decentered subjects can be used strategically for the purposes of capital accumulation because of their tendency to obscure, blur, and deny the sort of specificity required of careful critique.[60] The decentered smoothness of globalization, which is in key ways akin to the rhizomic lateralization of the borderlands perspective, can hinder accountability. What, in fact, does accountability look like in a global world, in the borderlands, and on the border? Beyond their similarly, optimistically glossy surfaces, do the globalization and the borderlands narratives in fact underwrite the performance of these dark tales? I turn now to a deeper critical analysis of the borderlands approach.

Dwelling in the ever-decentered metaphorical borderlands can mean losing touch with located communities and place-specific concerns of real people. The deterritorialization that is the borderlands can perhaps lead to a dangerous lack of specificity regarding the sites, literally and figuratively, of oppression. Ignacio García, for example, decries the decline of major political activism on the part of Chicana/o studies scholars since the 1970s, which he sees as a betrayal of their founding disciplinary commitment to engage in action-oriented scholarship in close engagement with community groups:

> Scholarly ties to the community have declined as scholars concentrate on gaining tenure and promotion, or on building networks with politicians and educational lobby groups who are politically correct and who offer opportunities for professional enhancement. The former propensity by Chicano Studies faculty to invite people from the community to the university, or to take students to the barrio to get them involved in issues affecting Mexican Americans, has been almost forgotten.[61]

In her analysis of contemporary border visual imagery, Claire Fox traces a similar movement in some border art and theory, where "the border" functions increasingly as a deterritorialized metaphor, yet because of its very site-*un*specificity, these projects lack the power to locate and critique asymmetrical relations of power as these play out in specific places.[62] For example, Fox explores the intriguing stance of Guillermo Gómez-Peña, who on the one hand has centralized an increasingly non-site-specific "border" in his work, yet has, on the other hand, been quite critical of the mainstreaming of the border theme in advertising, national art museums, galleries, and funding for artists— which, in his view, has pulled the border back from the avant-garde and ignored the artists who had worked so hard to bring the border to national attention. Yet, as Fox notes, these criticisms came at precisely the time when Gómez-Peña was moving away from his association with San Diego–based BAW/TAF and toward a solo career based in New York.[63]

In addition, U.S.-based borderlands scholarly, artistic, and cultural production is often undertaken without collaboration with (or at times even awareness of) parallel scholarly, artistic, and cultural endeavors underway in Northern Mexico. This constitutes an important lacuna in the U.S.-based mainstream borderlands perspective and can lead to a literally and figuratively one-sided depiction of the border, or to an ascendance of the border solely to the realm of metaphor, in ways that actively forget the ongoing regressions, exclusions, and repressions along both sides of the border. As Debra Castillo and María Socorro Tabuenca Córdoba have insisted, it is just this persistent desire for centeredness on the part of metropolitan theory, a desire haunted by the persistent decenteredness of the lived border—what Castillo and Tabuenca Córdoba call, after Balibar, the "missing letter"—that makes the border such a seductive and dangerous site of theorizing. For, they assert, "it is simply too easy for us intellectuals to read the metaphorical potential of the missing letter without taking into account the very real material conditions of a closed border/barrier. . . . Far too often, as for the Pátzcuaro fisherman [cited in Balibar's essay], the geopolitical border looms as a puzzling barrier against which Mexican nationals' dreams are dashed and broken."[64]

Pablo Vila has also discussed the silences within U.S.-based borderlands scholarship at length. He reiterates the need to balance metaphorical and literal approaches to the U.S.-Mexico border, as well as the tendency to exclude the scholarship, perspectives, and experiences of those living and working south of the boundary. In addition, Vila notes the dangerous tendency of many mainstream borderlands scholars and artists to romanticize the figure of the "border crosser":

> The migrant of mainstream border studies, the exemplary "border crosser," is one who is completely bilingual (in order to take full advantage of being "in between"), while many Mexican immigrants are Spanish monolingual or have low English proficiency. People like Gómez-Peña, the "hybrid" par excellence, want to stay in the United States, while many Mexican immigrants want to return to their homeland. Migrants like Gómez-Peña, the celebrated artist, have highly marketable skills, unlike many Mexican immigrants. The list of differences goes on and on.[65]

This romanticism extends to the racialized privileging of the mestizo in much of mainstream borderlands scholarship, a privileging that acts to construct and marginalize equally racialized others. Both Anzaldúa and Gómez-Peña, for example, privilege a mestizo subject in their work, a subject whose *mestizaje* is constructed not solely at a metaphorical level but at a rather literally racialized level as well. To be fair, at some point all identities are constructed relationally, within a framework that excludes as well as includes, and the perception of racialized difference is a long-standing axis of identity. David Johnson and Scott Michaelsen, for example, note this in their edited collection, *Border Theory*, in an introduction appropriately titled "Border Secrets": "We begin with an understanding that for all of border studies' attempts to produce a cultural politics of diversity and inclusion, this work literally can be produced only by means of—can be founded only upon—exclusions."[66] Yet I find the title "border secrets" to be so appropriate because it resonates strongly with my own experiences as a racialized outsider in mainstream borderlands studies. I have experienced a pervasive Chicana/o supremacy in the peer review process, in scholarly exchanges at conferences and symposia, and in personal interactions with colleagues. This stance arises from a presumption that because I am Anglo-American I will not, indeed cannot, move beyond what is assumed to be a unitary, hegemonic, and ultimately imperialist subject position to contribute in meaningful ways to critical scholarship from and about the borderlands. Such presumptions are often, but not always, unspoken and thus kept secret, but they provide a persistent subtext in mainstream borderlands scholarship in the United States. Johnson and Michaelsen go a bit further and assert that there exists an active anti-Anglo bias in mainstream borderlands scholarship in the United States: "In other words, for every bare multiculturalist gesture in these texts, there is another gesture toward the demonization and repression of a presumed white or Anglo culture."[67] Pablo Vila's sociological research in El Paso, Texas, has painstakingly documented that not all Anglo-Americans are nativists, and not all mestizos want to cross borders. For example, some mestizos are in fact ardent "border-reinforcers"; they are employed in the U.S. border patrol as well as local police forces and do engage in, as well as ideologically support, the often violent repression of real-life border crossers.[68] Thus Vila concludes that

> At some point in their writings, it seems that it is Gloria Anzaldúa in particular, and Chicanos in general, who are historical hybrids and border crossers (between nationalities, cultures, ethnicities, and the like) and thus possess the possibility of intellectual creativity and morality—but when it comes to the borderite or Fronterizo in general, none of these possibilities exist. When one reads the border literature, one sometimes feels that Chicanos are the only people capable of taking full advantage of the border and its opportunities, leaving out not only Anglos, blacks, American Indians, and Asians who also "experience" the border, but also Mexicans who are not Chicanos and therefore cannot fully be "border crossers" or "hybrids."[69]

Thus far from smoothing a utopian space for study and artistic production, the borderlands have instead presented scholars and artists with a differently bordered, or rebordered, terrain. Even in the border lands, place and identity are still constructed in relational terms that exclude as well as include. Others continue to inhabit the borderlands.

Tales from the Dark Side

Both the globalizationists and the denizens of the borderlands ultimately narrate tales of hope. Theirs are stories of *progressing* beyond the nation-state, of the arts blazing a trail for intercultural understanding, or of a global boom in trade and investment leading to lasting prosperity and democracy for all. Yet in many ways these narratives conceal—and in important ways they also enable—a far darker script. The smoothness that the globalizationists and the borderlands proponents so differently imagine is, in both cases, reminiscent of Anthony Burke's assertion that smoothness is characterized by ease, consensuality, and pleasure. All three dimensions characterize the wishful narratives of both contingents.

Along the contemporary U.S.-Mexican boundary, a geopolitical reality lived by millions of individuals, another story is told. In this plotline, the boundary between the United States and Mexico is becoming etched more and more firmly onto the physical landscape, in the national imaginary of the United States, and in its official legal-institutional practice. This is a story of *regressing* beyond the nation-state. The narrative it presents is predicated on the border's continued existence, rather than its erasure. It is a storyline that has become all too familiar of late. It centralizes a vehemently anti-immigrant posture, one which views immigration as something to be "reformed" as "we" attempt to "regain control" through "taking back the border." Leo Chávez and Rebecca Martínez simply call it neoracism.[70] This anti-immigrant backlash constructs purifying rhetoric of belonging and exclusion, wherein "aliens" and "illegals" are rendered radically Other, unlike Us in any way, as "dirty," "amoral," and "disease-ridden."[71] It has played out in recent legislation that quietly targets Hispanics by swapping an ethnic category, "Latino," for a category of nonbelonging, "illegal." Chávez and Martínez detail recent legislative revisions in California that signal all Latinos as potentially illegal: regulating hiring practices around establishing legality (particularly for those "foreign-looking" workers), attacking bilingualism in education and the workplace, and limiting the acceptable occupational density of housing.[72] The 1986 Simpson and Rodino Immigration Reform and Control Act, former California governor Pete Wilson's Proposition 187, and Florida governor Jeb Bush's "One Florida" rollback on affirmative action in hiring and education are further examples of swift, sweeping erasures of the civil rights gains so painstakingly won over the past thirty years.

Though the debates over who belongs in the United States are old ones, the contemporary nativist rhetoric highlights the particular centrality of Mexico as the focus de jour of this long-standing threat:

> Chief among these new arguments is that "we've lost control of our borders," and chief among the borders in question is the one with Mexico. [An article in the series] documents growing incidents of racist hatred along the US-Mexico border, and the transformation of the borderlands into a "war zone," as a multi-agency US task force engages in daily combat against the flow of immigrants, weapons, drugs and currency.[73]

Various political campaigns of the 1990s explicitly singled out Mexico and Mexicans as a prime focus for border anxiety. In his book *The Great Betrayal*, for example, former presidential hopeful Pat Buchanan used profoundly fearful phrasing when he described "the crowds of Mexicans forming up to dash into the United States," "illegal aliens . . . pouring across the US border in record numbers to take jobs and get welfare benefits," and "the militant few whose number is growing" and "who have designs on the American Southwest."[74]

Mike Davis has written that neoracism, in the context of Los Angeles, has produced a "fragmented, paranoid spatiality" in that city.[75] Neoracism has further fractured the border landscape between Mexico and the United States as well. The deserts are being deeply striated in response to the anti-immigrant hysteria, in a desperate attempt to bulwark Us against Them. In a fascinating example of U.S. military might redeployed, fiberglass panels left over from the Gulf War were upended to form a wall along the boundary at Nogales, while landing mat material "from Guam to Guantanamo"[76] was recycled to build a similar wall at El Paso. Thermal-imaging cameras, night-vision scopes, aerostat balloons stationed along the border, and state-of-the-art computer processing of entrants at border checkpoints have erected an ephemeral fence, a high tech silicon border to buttress the physical walls already in place.[77]

Deterrence has become the primary ethos of the U.S. government's stance toward the boundary with Mexico, and the mid- to late 1990s saw the institutional scaffolding arise to reinforce the infrastructural build-up. This ranges from San Diego's Gatekeeper Operation to Nogales, Arizona's Operation Safeguard and El Paso, Texas's Operation Hold the Line (formerly Operation Blockade), and numerous similar initiatives in cities between. Fixed border patrol agents spend hot, boring afternoons under insufficient awnings, "sitting on an X," hoping their very presence will convince those wanting to make a dash for it to try elsewhere.[78] Concerned citizens, too, are doing their part. In San Diego in the mid-1990s, for example, residents parked their cars along the line at night and turned on their headlights to "light up the border" in a symbolic display of solidarity with the deterrence approach advanced both by the U.S. government and some nativist border-based citizen groups.

And this strategy ostensibly has worked: apprehensions of illegal crossers are down in all major urban areas.[79] Understandably, a growing number of illicit border crossings attempt to avoid the brightened, muscle-bound border at traditional urban checkpoint areas. Rather, a growing number of would-be migrants prefer to risk the long trek through the desert and arid mountains of south central California through to rural Arizona, or cross the Rio Grande and hike for miles through the desolate South Texas brush land.[80] Small towns like El Centro, California, and Douglas, Arizona, as well as rural border areas in Arizona, New Mexico, and southeastern Texas, have become the high-traffic areas for undocumented crossers, particularly those who come in family groups.[81] A recent University of Houston report found that from 1993 to 1997, an estimated 1,185 people drowned, died of exposure or dehydration, or were hit by cars while trying to jump the wire away from traditional crossing points.[82] Néstor Rodríguez, one of the report's authors, said, "It's the equivalent of a large plane load of people crashing every year."[83]

In this paranoid landscape resulting from repeated attempts to pile more border onto the border, it is no surprise that tales of everyday violence, hate, and death abound. Local anti-immigrant activism, do-it-yourself justice, and rising gun-ownership levels have been the response on the part of many U.S. ranchers and property owners.[84] As Larry Vance, a Douglas, Arizona, homeowner who lives within shouting distance of the border and is cochairman of the newly founded Cochise County Concerned Citizens group, was being interviewed for a story on border ranchers' responses to illegal immigration, the following incident occurred. It illustrates a growing rage:

> As if on cue, a dozen migrants dash across Vance's property about 50 yards away in the twilight. At first, Vance just stares at them. Finally he says, "Those people right there, I don't know nothing about them. All I know is they're human beings from somewhere else, and they have no loyalty to the country, and they're moving into my home."[85]

Geopolitical boundaries are spoken of by nativists as if they were fundamentally constitutive of a slippery something known as "our way of life." Failure to stabilize place through failing to stabilizing borders would, it seems, lead to a threatening and ultimately uncontrollable placelessness, and along with this, a loss of identity. In a *Frontline* report, a San Diego boat repairer expressed his anxiety over California's porous border with Mexico in precisely such terms:

> There are whole portions of Los Angeles city . . . if you don't know where you're at you'd swear you're in Tijuana. You cannot tell the difference. *You cannot tell the difference.* The barrio that exists in Tijuana looks exactly the same as the one in Los Angeles. As an American, I'm offended by that![86]

The boat repairer's fears center on geographic disorientation and cultural homogenization, which he views as tainting and debasing his Anglo-Angeleno cityscape. Another interviewee in the same program, an unemployed roofer, expressed his regrets over immigration in terms of personal loss equated with theft and annihilation:

> They're stealing, and they're not stealing from the government, they're stealing from me. 'Coz I'm the clown that gets unemployed when they're taking my job. They're stealing. They're coming over here to get my job. Y'know, it's just . . . you might as well come over here and get my house! You might as well just come over here and starve my family! Y'know, kill my dog, whatever![87]

As we have seen, for some, the idea that borders have come unhinged from the map provides a new sense of freedom, holding forth the potential for a new cartography of identity and a new terrain of politics. For others, however, all of this debordering and rebordering bespeaks the crisis of place with which I began this chapter. Its resolution has involved an urgent need to solidify borders in order to keep from being overrun. It seems that in this version of events the terrain between the United States and Mexico is becoming more and more starkly bounded. Increasing impoverishment, violence, hatred, tighter restrictions, and critical levels of anti-immigrant sentiment have, of late, combined to make the fence between Mexico and the United States larger than life itself.

Schizophrenia, Borders, and the Rubble of Place

By some accounts, the late-modern world order should be a truly borderless one, smoothed of old anachronisms like nation-states and their boundaries. Apparently, however, old boundaries are becoming ever more sharply etched on the late-modern landscape, and new cleavages spring up unexpectedly, evidencing the refusal of borders to disappear altogether and thus their durable function in the human imaginary. As we saw in the previous section, the desire for smoothness, whether it is benignly or malevolently enacted, is always countered by the jagged realities of striation, bordering, difference that cannot be suppressed.

Most of our critical tools in the social sciences, borrowed from the left or some reworking of the left, view power as layered along the relatively aporetic levels of global, regional, national, and local. Our traditional views of geopolitical boundaries have been conceptualized in precisely this way, as delimiting fixed demarcations of one country from another. This definition of a geopolitical boundary, as that line (or zone) where one nation abuts another, requires spatial contiguity. Yet I propose that spatial contiguity is no longer the only criterion of border ontology. Borders no longer function solely laterally, to cordon off states from one another and constitute them as discrete geographic entities. Borders can also be discontinuous, fragmented, refracted across space and scale. Julie Murphy Erfani, for example, has argued that Mexico City represents, in its chaos of urban spaces and meanings, a borderland. Of course, Mexico City lies smack in the middle of the country, so literal ideas of border are not invoked. Rather, argues Murphy Erfani, "It is not that the U.S.-Mexico border . . . has been relocated to the capital, but, instead, that yet another borderland has sprung right up in the heart of the country."[88] Similarly, Kathleen Staudt and David Spener suggest understanding the U.S.-Mexican border "as an ongoing, dialectical process that generates multiple borderland spaces, some of which are not located very close to the official international boundary itself."[89] They are following Roger Rouse's lead, who sensed what he called "a proliferation of border zones . . . miniature borders are erupting throughout the two countries."[90]

What I am suggesting is that the very nature of borders and their function in late modernity deserves reexamination. I will argue that contemporary borders function in a *transverse* fashion. Borders do not layer out in ways that we expect them to. This may be why borders are seeming to disappear: perhaps we are simply looking for them in the wrong places, or failing to recognize them for what they are when we do run into them. This exceeds a simple expansion of the idea of geographic scale: it involves rethinking the notion of scale entirely. It entails thinking beyond geometric, Euclidean spaces and toward borders as more fluid sorts of spaces, both real and imagined. Rethinking borders in these ways constitutes the beginning of an empirical and theoretical endeavor to forge precisely those sorts of critical tools that work in transverse, scale-defying fashions. Given that "the major component institutions of contemporary society—marriage, the firm, the state—are bordered institutions,"[91] rethinking borders involves nothing less that a rethinking of the conceptual scaffolding of modernity's key institutions.

I suggest that what can be termed "spatial schizophrenia" is manifest in such pervasive contemporary anxieties at being lost and overrun, at the perceived annihilation of national difference in space.[92] This references Fredric Jameson's contention that identity under postmodernism can be understood as schizophrenic.[93] Jameson employs Lacan's account of schizophrenia to make this argument. Lacan views the schizophrenic condition as arising from a fundamental rupture in the logic of our linguistic-based system of meaning and reality. This system posits a one-to-one relationship between signifier and signified, between word and referent: a signifying chain. "When that relationship breaks down, when the links of the signifying chain snap, then we have schizophrenia in the form of a rubble of distinct and unrelated signifiers."[94] Lacan and Jameson interpret schizophrenia in temporal terms. For the schizophrenic, past, present, and future collide in "a series of pure and unrelated presents in time. . . . [The] present suddenly engulfs the subject with undescribable vividness."[95] This implies multiplicity, fracture, and destabilization of identity, whereas the paranoiac modern condition relied on a unitary sense of self.

I propose that we extend these ideas spatially. We can approach contemporary anxieties over placelessness, dislocation, and being lost, and the annihilation of livelihood and way of life that is seen to be allowed by this, as the product of a fundamental rupture of meaning between place and identity. When the linkage between place and meaning is perceived to have ruptured, when this spatial signifying chain snaps, the result is loss (or a shattering) of a stable identity—or at least the illusion of that stability—which is rooted, in part, in a place.

If this is in fact occurring, how, then, do real people in real places go about living their lives? How, in other words, might the rather abstract discussion of spatial schizophrenia be applied to the everyday negotiations of those who dwell in the borderlands? In the next two chapters, I will introduce five contemporary border *personajes*, or characters, who populate the narrative space on and around the geopolitical boundary. I won't suggest that they provide answers to the vexing questions of accountability and exclusion I've raised in this chapter. Rather, these *personajes* literally embody the multiplicity of ways in which people who live along, under, and around the U.S.-Mexico boundary make meaning. They are guides of sorts across a paradoxical space. They return us to narratives, and the characters that populate them, as strategies with which people living in places stake claims, forge identities, and make sense of their roles and their realities. The diverse stories they recount trace new lines of flight in a landscape that simply cannot be leveled for long.

CHAPTER 5

Good and Evil on the Line

The woman in blue delicately lifts her skirts to clear the swirling turgid river rising around her bare ankles. She shades her brow against the early morning sun with one hand, looking left and right, up and down the river. Her name is Guadalupe. She needs no help from a coyote or a lanchero. Lupita has crossed this river so many times, day in and day out, that she could walk on the water itself. Her feet are not wet. She steps over the irrigation canal in a single stride. The barbed wire falls away as if melted. She laughs clear as birdsong as she passes easily through the iron curtain fence. High tech meets holy, and the motion detectors, infrared cameras, and heat sensors fail to register. The dawn wind is scented with roses of Castile. As the sun rises behind her, a golden halo forms about her head, and she makes her way swiftly to El Paso, Houston, Elsa, Pilar, Yuma, Tucson, Douglas, San Diego . . .

The man at the bar glances nervously to his right and left, and taps the rim of his glass to request another drink. The bartender knows him. A regular. His dark suit, well-trimmed goatee, and cultivated manners announce that he is not from around here. Comes and goes quietly, but no one knows where from or where to. Popular with the ladies. Too popular, some would say. They say he dances like a dream, flatters them, whispers promises in their ears. They say he poisons them with his words, his caresses. They say that he has driven women to search desperately for him, traveling beyond the dusty edges of town, out on the highway to Houston, San Antonio, Tucson, San Diego . . . must be from a big city. They never come back. The man's red eyes dart behind sunglasses in the darkened bar. His cloven feet are hidden inside expensive shoes. The two nubs on his head are covered with a stylish hat, but they bother him and he scratches furtively. Only the bartender notices . . .

Hierophany on the Border

The crisis of place described in the previous chapter has given rise to a number of tales that attempt to renarrativize claims to place, and the identities that are fashioned from them, in light of profound contemporary social, political, economic, and cultural transformations. In this space of crisis, of narrative exhaustion and rebirth that has centered on and around the boundary between Mexico and the United States, an enduring plotline persists: the battle between good and evil. In this chapter, I will explore the contentions that apparitions of the Virgin of Guadalupe are on the rise, alongside allegations that the Devil is at work once more. The coincidence of good and evil on and around the geopolitical boundary signifies the magnitude of the struggle to define our place, and ourselves, in these uncertain times.

In providing a stage of sorts upon which the age-old drama between good and evil is set, the space on and around the U.S.-Mexico border becomes sacred. This is true in a literal sense, as with sites where the Virgin of Guadalupe has recently appeared. It is also true in a symbolic sense. Drawing on the foundational work of Mircea Eliade, I will suggest that the border is a space of hierophany, of the manifestation of the sacred in the profane. Itself a border state, hierophany transforms the space of the mundane and the everyday into a space apart, a sacred space. As Eliade elaborates, hierophany involves a rupture or break with homogeneous space, an idea that resonates with Deleuze and Guattari's ideas of smoothness and striation. "If the world is to be lived in, it must be founded—and no world can come to birth in the chaos of the homogeneity and relativity of profane space."[1] The irruption of the sacred in the profane is what, according to Eliade, allows humans to gain a foothold in a chaotic world; it provides an axis mundi, a seam between heaven and earth that gives life its meaning: "Revelation of a sacred space makes it possible to obtain a fixed point and hence to acquire orientation in the chaos of homogeneity, to 'found the world' and to live in a real sense."[2] Though Eliade refers to smooth space as profane, he recognizes that it is not necessarily a formally religious experience that can provoke a rupture, and thus a sanctification and meaningfulness:

> There are, for example, privileged places, qualitatively different from all others—a man's birthplace, or the scenes of his first love, or certain places in the first foreign city he visited in youth. Even for the most frankly non-religious man, all these places still retain an exceptional, a unique quality; they are the "holy places" of his private universe, as if it were in such spots that he had received the revelation of a reality other than that in which he participates through his ordinary daily life.[3]

The apparitions of the Virgin of Guadalupe, as well as those of the Devil, signal a setting apart of the territory on and around the boundary between the United States and Mexico, a sanctification that brings into conversation the essence of faith and the future of the nation-state. The smoothness of national narratives and the boundary that enables them is interrupted, paused, questioned by these events. In referencing a time before the nation-state through invoking timeless struggles, they suggest the contours of places, and identities, outside the nation-state.

The Virgin of Guadalupe Jumps the Wire

Thousands of Guadalupes jump the wire every day, on their way to and from work in U.S. cities. Yet a particular Guadalupe has relentlessly zigzagged the rivers, arroyos, and deserts, north and south, east and west, back and forth, for nearly five centuries. Beloved particularly by poor *mexicanos*, she is called La Morenita, the brown-skinned Virgin, "Little Darkling." On banners and baseball caps, wrapped inside tortillas and tilmas of rough-woven cactus cloth, stamped on Los Angeles phone cards and burnished into the bumpers of cars with Texas license plates, the image of the Virgin of Guadalupe has long moved across borders, held close to the bodies and souls of *mexicanos* on both sides of the line.

The Virgin of Guadalupe provides a long-standing archetypical manifestation of goodness, purity, and protection. Her various apparitions have, from the sixteenth century onward, sutured the sundered halves of Greater Mexico and embroidered a tapestry-in-motion where place and identity have merged on a plane of faith. The restless mobility of the Virgin of Guadalupe has always pushed the limits of static, bounded notions of belonging. She has ridden the crest of battle on banners at crucial moments in the various births and rebirths of the Mexican nation, providing protection and valor simultaneously to the insurgents. She was the leader of Miguel Hidalgo's insurgent army against the Spanish colonizers in 1821, emblazoned on banners and in Hidalgo's battle cry. Emiliano Zapata and his rebel army carried her image aloft in battle during the Mexican Revolution (1910–1917). In the 1960s, she appeared on banners held high by United Farm Workers demonstrating against the oppression of *mexicano* agricultural workers on the farms of the U.S. Southwest. Always light on her feet, the Virgin of Guadalupe is becoming ever more fluid as her image graces automobiles, trucks, mobile bodies, and the very circuitry of a world where borders matter less and less.

She is not only swift, she is strong, too. According to Virgil Elizondo, a renowned Guadalupan scholar, traditional belief holds that La Morenita held the gringo armies at bay along *El Río Bravo del Norte* (the Rio Grande), halting their expansionist advances on Mexico south of today's international border between the two countries. In a similar fashion, Elizondo asserts, "a new tradition maintains that she will find ways of breaking the electronic curtain that keeps the poor of Latin America from migrating into the United States."[4] Some say she has appeared along the U.S.-Mexico border, luring border patrol agents down dead ends while migrants are left free to jump the fence.[5]

Violence and Healing

One of the key issues facing the inhabitants of the Western Hemisphere in the early sixteenth century was how two radically different groups

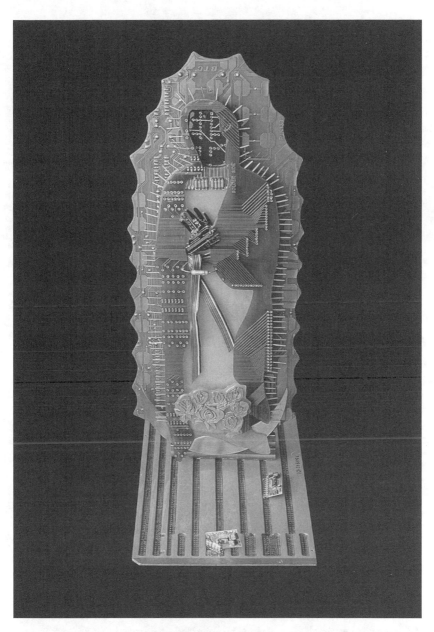

Marion C. Martínez unites elements of modern technology to celebrate Guadalupe as ageless icon. Photograph by Charles Mann from Jacqueline Orsini Dunnington, *Viva Guadalupe! The Virgin in New Mexican Popular Art* (Santa Fe: Museum of New Mexico Press, 1997), 74. Photograph copyright Charles Mann; book copyright 1997 Museum of New Mexico Press. All rights reserved. Reprinted with permission.

of people—Iberian conquerors and American Indians—could come to understand one another well enough to inhabit the same space under a more or less commonly understood set of rules. Indigenous ideas about life and the meaning of life, death and the meaning of death, human relationship to the earth, and the nature of time, the human soul, and the divine could not have been further from European views at the time.[6]

Operating within this discursive space, a space profoundly marked by what appeared to be insurmountable barriers, was the apparition of the Virgin of Guadalupe. In 1521, Spanish conquistadors mounted a second bloody siege and sacked Tenochtitlán, the capital city of the Aztec empire (now Mexico City), in August of that year. A mere ten years later, in December of 1531, the Virgin of Guadalupe appeared four times to a converted peasant in his fifties, a man baptized Juan Diego.[7] The *Nican Mopohua*, the Nahuatl-language account of Guadalupe's apparitions, holds that she first appeared to Juan Diego as he was walking to church early in the morning.[8] Hearing strange and beautiful music emanating from a hillside, Juan Diego sought the source of the song and was confronted with a resplendently beautiful and kind woman. She introduced herself as the Virgin Mary (along with a litany of other names harkening to holy names in Nahuatl theology). She beseeched him to approach the Bishop of Mexico City, a Franciscan friar named Juan de Zumárraga, and tell him that she wished a hermitage to be built to her on the very site where they were standing. Needless to say, Zumárraga had to be convinced that indeed the most Holy Virgin Mary was in fact making such a lofty request of a mere peasant. Several days and two apparitions later, she directed Juan Diego to ascend a barren hill and there gather a bouquet of roses of Castile—impossible blooms for December in Mexico—and to fill his *tilma* (a cape made of rough-woven cactus fiber) with the roses. Arranging the roses in his *tilma*, she bade Juan Diego approach Bishop Zumárraga yet again and offer the roses as the sign that he awaited. Before the bishop's astonished eyes, Juan Diego unfolded his cape and the roses of Castile spilled forth. On his *tilma* was divinely tattooed the image of the most Holy Mother of God, the Virgin Mary, manifest on this occasion as the

Virgin of Guadalupe. This image is enshrined today in the Basilica of Guadalupe in Mexico City.

Some scholars have questioned the authenticity of the accounts, suggesting that the narrative of the Virgin was invented much later, around the middle part of the seventeenth century. The Virgin of Guadalupe could be understood, then, simply as a malleable symbol that has been used to manipulate successive generations of Mexicans to various social, political, and religious ends.[9] Perhaps this is so, yet it is the enduring power of the image and narrative of the Virgin—the epistemology of the Virgin, if you will—that concerns me here. Guadalupe provided a mother figure for Mexico, one of several mother figures modeled on the Virgin Mary that appeared throughout the Americas in colonial times. She constituted a vital component in the cycle of violence and healing that characterizes the process of nation-building in the Americas. Along with other acts of healing—poetry, the visual and performative arts, song, magic, and ritual—the religious faith symbolized in Guadalupe worked, not unproblematically, to salve that which had been rent asunder in the bloody gestures of conquest, colonization, forced labor, illness, torture, and warfare. The story of Juan Diego's transition "from the pain of social non-being to becoming a full, confident, and joyful human person"[10] through the mediation of the Virgin of Guadalupe provided a powerful allegory for the incorporation of indigenous Mexicans into European ideas of collectivity. In the seven years following her apparition to Juan Diego, it is said that eight million Indians were converted to Christianity.[11] Mexico became a largely (though never fully) mestizo nation, a mediation in flesh between European and Amerindian. Guadalupe became the symbol of such a nation, embodying hope, health, protection, salvation, synthesis, and wholeness.[12] In 1945, Pope Pius XII designated her the Empress of the Americas, extending her spatial and spiritual mantle from Alaska to the Tierra del Fuego.

Her image and message resonate with the deepest-held sense of Mexicanness, wherever Mexicans reside. For Mexicans, the image of the Virgin of Guadalupe exceeds its religious signification. Eric Wolf considers her image in terms of a "Mexican master symbol" whose social functioning has every bit as much to do with a profound sense of Mexicanness in a culturally nationalistic sense as it does in a religious, Marian-centered Catholic sense.[13] Thus, for Wolf, the Virgin of Guadalupe distills national and religious collective identities, melding Church and state. Rubén Martínez says, simply, "*La Virgen* is at the center of the Mexican soul."[14]

That she is now—and has been for the last five centuries—jumping borders geopolitical as well as social, racial, and economic points to her role as a mediator par excellence.[15] All religious apparitions are essentially mediations between heaven and earth, between human beings and the divine.[16] Mary generally functions as a relatively approachable mediatrix between the faithful and the heavenly Father and his Son, Jesus. In the case of the Virgin of Guadalupe, the narrative structure and symbology of the *Nican Mopohuah*, considered the definitive relation of the appearances of the Virgin of Guadalupe to Juan Diego in 1531, and the image itself, speak to both Iberians and indigenous Mexicans.[17] She spoke to Juan Diego in Nahuatl, her skin olive-toned and her hair dark; her bearing was humble, yet she spoke of a Christian God and His Son; her rendition was medieval European in style; and her prototype—the Virgin Mary—had never been seen before in the Americas.[18] She worked across difference: language, gender, race, and space. She crossed scales, from the individual level of her mediation between Juan Diego and Bishop Zumárraga, to the eventual formation of a more or less syncretic Mexican nation. Her home is on the border, understood both literally and metaphorically.

Quotidian Apparitions and Everyday Crises

There has been a notable increase in the frequency of apparitions of the Virgin Mary worldwide.[19] For her part, the Virgin of Guadalupe appears to be following suit. Apparitions of the Virgin of Guadalupe coincide with times of crisis, both in the literal sense of the word in contemporary Mexico (the economic crisis occasioned by international debt repayments beginning in 1982), and figuratively, as I have used the term throughout the book, as a turning point offering both closures and openings. Thus while Clarissa Pinkola Estés observes that, in general, "she is often most present when there is most need for order, strength, fierceness, hope, and vitality,"[20] Carlos Monsiváis makes a closer connection between Guadalupan apparitions and Mexico's contemporary economic crisis:

> You favored no other nation like ours, Little Virgin; you accompanied the liberator Miguel Hidalgo and overthrew the foreign Virgin of Remedios; you never left Emiliano Zapata's side; you shine on bare walls and allow us to adore you in shops and garages, on the roads and on coaches, in the slum housing where we live. . . . Lend us a hand—the minimum wage is a mockery, and they've just put up the prices of petrol, tortillas and beans.[21]

Historically, apparitions of the Virgin of Guadalupe have been manifest most frequently in dire periods of rupture and suture in the ongoing process of stabilizing the immanently unstable: conquest, colonization, independence, U.S. expansionism, civil war, and civil rights. Recently, Mexico's debt crisis of the 1980s, financial crises of the mid-1990s, and their aftermath in terms of unemployment, poverty, and violence into this millennium have driven hundreds of thousands of Mexican nationals to the brink of desperation and across the international boundary in search of employment. Los Angeles is now the second largest Mexican city after the Federal District itself. The restructuring of labor arrangements on an international scale in the last thirty or so years, beginning in the case of the United States and Mexico with the Bracero Program in 1964 and the implementation of the Border Industrialization Program, the rise and spread of the border assembly factories (maquiladoras) in the 1970s through the present, and the implementation of the North American Free Trade Agreement (NAFTA) in 1994, has profoundly reworked the spatial and social relations of labor on both sides of the border. The dramatic demise of Mexico's long-ruling political dictatorship, the *Partido Revolucionario Institucional* (PRI), in the 2000 national elections provided another moment of rupture in a longer-range process of political change within Mexico. The demographic shifts in the contemporary United States, wherein Latinos have overtaken all other non-Anglo groups in their rate of growth and now represent 10 percent of the population of the United States and a growing share of popular culture, advertising, and consumption in this country, constitutes yet another moment of crisis in the political, economic, and social profile of Greater Mexico. Writes Rubén Martínez, "It's no coincidence that She's been appearing more often lately. In times of crisis, She's always there. Today, the crisis is on both sides of the border."[22]

All of this is at once invigorating and vertiginously frightening. The spatial schizophrenia I discussed in the previous chapter is not only expressed and lived by those Anglo-Americans who fear the erosion of their culture and their livelihoods. For conditions lived by many in the contemporary diaspora of hundreds of thousands of recent arrivals to the U.S. Southwest—homelessness, continuous residential dislocation through escalating property values and changing rental restrictions, recurring joblessness, ill health, racialized discrimination, violence, the possibility of deportation—all constitute an extended schizophrenic condition. I suggest that the Virgin of Guadalupe provides—as she historically has always provided—a powerful way of making sense of these frightening conditions, of making meaning from chaos, of stabilizing self through symbolically stabilizing space. For many people throughout Greater Mexico, the most important apparitions are those that occur on a local level and involve the reiteration of the familiar in the uncertainties of daily life. "Perhaps it's the yearning to remain rooted in a rootless time where one's address can be changed by twists of fate like the economy or the border patrol."[23]

Sergio Quintero was polishing his Camaro in 1993 when the image of the Virgin of Guadalupe appeared on the car's bumper. A shrine to the Holy Camaro was assembled in the Quinteros' backyard in the South Texas Valley town of Elsa, attracting thousands of pilgrims. In 1997, a humidity stain in the shape of the Virgin of Guadalupe appeared on a Mexico City subway platform. The Virgin of the Metro attracted thousands of the faithful and was later excavated and moved to an above-ground permanent shrine blessed by the Catholic Church.

In 1998 in Douglas, an Arizona border town that brushes against Agua Prieta on the other side, rust stains painted the Virgin's image clearly onto a broken-down water heater. The water heater was to have been taken across the border to have a hole cut in it and be used as a stove, but the man never picked it up, and it sat outside and weathered slowly into the beautiful contours of Our Lady of Guadalupe. The area around Douglas is now the number-one crossing for undocumented arrivals from the south. In early 2000, at a Houston apartment complex, a splash left by melting ice cream dropped in front of a soda machine formed the exact shape and coloration of the Virgin of Guadalupe. The image was covered with glass to preserve it from washing away, and the faithful have visited from as far away as Canada to leave flowers, photographs, and candles.

Assisted apparitions abound, too, images that key kitsch into the information economy, lending a timeless quality to the future and a contemporary aesthetic to tradition. Guadalupe flies down the boulevards and freeways of Greater Mexico on the hoods, doors, and stick shift knobs of low-riders.[24] There are prepaid phone cards with La Morenita's image gracing the plastic laminate. There is a computer mouse pad, too, that bears her likeness. Many throughout Greater Mexico have etched La Virgen directly into their bodies, carrying her image wherever they go in the form of tattoos.[25] A digitally recreated image of Juan Diego's tilma with a precise reproduction of the Virgin's image toured Southern California in 1999, coinciding unfortunately with a rash of defacements of the many Virgin of Guadalupe murals painted on the sides of small businesses and residences in South Central and East Los Angeles.[26] One of my favorite Virgin images can be found along César Chávez Boulevard in Los Angeles, on the side of Julio Martinez's frame shop, Inez. The stylized purple Virgin appears to be breaking through the sidewalk, larger than life and no worse for the wear and tear after her long tunneling from Guadalajara.

Throughout the 1990s, I had interviewed and kept in touch with several families in a peripheral neighborhood in Guadalajara, Mexico's third largest city and a hub of out-migration to Los Angeles.[27] They knew of my interest in the Virgin of Guadalupe, and I knew of the loss of their sons and daughters as these children had grown and gone to Los Angeles in search of jobs by the late 1990s. In 1997, under a freeway overpass that, doubtlessly, many of these young men and women had traveled on their way along the well-worn corridor from Guadalajara to Los Angeles, the Virgin had once more appeared in a stain of humidity during the summer rainy months. As with other apparition sites, an

Virgin of Guadalupe mousepad. Photograph by Jennifer Gebelein.

Virgin of Guadalupe phone card. Photograph by Jennifer Gebelein.

elaborate shrine to *La Virgen del Puente*, the Virgin of the Bridge, had sprung up under the freeway. Along with the usual petitions for restoring health to an ill loved one, many of the notes requesting divine intercession ask for the safety of migrant sons, daughters, fathers, mothers, and other family members. For contemporary *tapatíos*, or residents of Guadalajara, the Virgin of Guadalupe has accreted another facet in her multiple roles as healer and protectress: *la que guía y socorra a los migrantes* (she who guides and assists migrants).

In this example, the image of the Virgin of Guadalupe perceived in a humidity stain under a freeway overpass provides an anchor and a bridge to family members back home. Her mobile image defies geopolitical formalities, connecting people and place despite separation in space and time, and this is as meaningful for those who leave as it is for those who stay. Her multiple apparitions within Mexico proper and Greater Mexico lend a durable sense of the connection between people and their right to inhabit certain places, acclaim that predates—and

Tunneling Virgin in front of Inez Frame Shop, East Los Angeles.

La Virgen del Puente, Guadalajara, Mexico.

will outlast—the modern nation-state, that redraws boundaries between nations, that helps us think of new sorts of regions, landscapes, and identities. Her home is wherever she decides to appear, and her apparitions constitute ephemeral passport photos. "Guadalupe, in the end, proclaims a vast spiritual region that ignores the political demarcations that divide California and Mexico."[28]

The Devil in Juárez: Gender, Work, and Death on the Border

For some unexplained reason, the Devil has always kept a high profile along the Texas portion of the border between Mexico and the United States. Perhaps divine law requires that the many apparitions of the Virgin of Guadalupe be balanced by equally numerous appearances of the Devil. As José Limón explored in his book *Dancing with the Devil*, South Texas dance halls experienced a rash of these devil sightings in the 1970s.[29] Limón's fascinating analysis contextualizes these sightings within the shifting racial and gender negotiations occurring in the South Texas *mexicano* community at the time. The blond, Robert Redford–like Devil who danced like a dream constituted, in Limón's view, a racialized incursion by Anglos into one of the few remaining arenas where *mexicano* men still reigned supreme: the dance hall, with all its sexual, corporeal, cultural, and economic implications and connotations. For *mexicano* men, the Devil was on the one hand just a silly story told by the women they danced with, *un chisme de viejas*. But on the other hand, he was also a threat: handsome and apparently wealthy, he gave women a fantasy that didn't resemble the local *mexicano* men physically or economically in the least. He highlighted their racialized inferiority in a hegemonically Anglo-American cultural arena where blond and tall and well-dressed was seen as desirable, and to be *moreno* (dark-complexioned) and *chaparrito* (short) and shabbily dressed meant low wages and a future of working in agricultural fields or in blue-collar factories. *Mexicana* women knew this, and the Devil, in their view, while dangerous was also *bien chulo*, attractive, seductive, desirable. They were even willing to overlook his goat feet, because they pointed to a way out of South Texas and a known future.

The elderly of both genders, however, interpreted the Devil within a larger moral context. As Sarah Radcliffe and Sallie Westwood have observed, this is common to the Devil stories that have long circulated throughout Latin America. In these stories, which according to Radcliffe and Westwood serve to express disaffection from the Catholic faith, the Devil represents the corruption, greed, and selfishness brought by capitalism. Priests, in these stories, are typically portrayed as inept, corrupt, and lacking in the skills that people need to negotiate these changes: "Figurative priests have no knowledge and wisdom to impart, no compassion or strategy. By contrast the latter attributes are embodied in old women or local men who have a folk wisdom which usually saves the day; clearly juxtaposed is the popular 'really useful knowledge' in contrast to Catholic dogma and the power of prayer."[30]

Thus Devil stories provide a widespread and durable narrative framework within which tradition and change, intergenerational exchange, and socioeconomic transformations are negotiated. In these moral tales, the wisdom of the elders prevails, while the social and economic changes set in motion by capitalism are likened to the evil distilled in the figure of the Devil himself. In the view of the elderly interviewed by Limón in South Texas, young women of the 1970s had become far too free to come and go as they pleased. Gender roles were changing, and these elderly interlocutors perceived a relaxation of the rules of decorum that they found discomfiting: "The devil, they say, comes because today things are out of hand. Girls go out to dances by themselves. En nuestro tiempo, no se via [*sic*] eso (In our time, you didn't see that). There is too much drinking. Outside the dances and even inside, you see *marijuanos* (marijuana smokers)."[31]

The Devil is on the loose again in Texas. Only this time, he's moved west, to the Ciudad Juárez area, just across the line from El Paso in the corner of Texas, tucked under New Mexico. This is peculiar, because people on both sides of the line here consider themselves to be highly secular, and not terribly susceptible to religious apparitions of any sort. Perhaps this is why the Devil has manifested himself in such a vicious way here. In any event, as of the close of 2003, over 400 women had been murdered in Ciudad Juárez since 1993. According to a series in the *El Paso Times* written by Diana Washington Valdez, as many as 90 of these victims were raped, mutilated, and murdered in what appears to be the work of a serial killer or killers.[32] Many of their corpses were found in the enormous underdeveloped plot of land known as Lote Bravo, thrown away and left to mummify along with the other garbage of Juárez: worn-out furniture, tires, animal parts, wrecked cars. By the summer of 2001, when I visited Lote Bravo, the maquiladoras, or foreign assembly plants (many of them U.S. owned), had solidified a new phase of development in the Lote Bravo area, with their sprawling, fortresslike, ultramodern installations built right next to a huge labor force housed in ramshackle huts or tiny, government-subsidized *unidades habitacionales* (habitation units) the size of toolsheds. Cast-off U.S. school buses, painted green, plied the dusty trails between factory and shack, growling like an army of desert caterpillars when shifts changed at the plants. Many, though certainly not all, of the murdered women worked in these factories.

Lote Bravo, Ciudad Juárez, Mexico.

A great deal of speculation has swirled around the Juárez killings.[33] One storyline holds that the murders were performed by a serial killer, maybe a plant manager from *el otro lado*, definitely someone charming, good-looking, driving a nice car. He approaches women leaving the factory after their shift, offers them a ride . . . who could resist, given that the alternative involved being packed onto a hot, jolting school bus with dozens of your sweating coworkers? He reportedly chooses women of a certain physical type: short, slender women with cinnamon complexions and straight, shoulder-length hair. Once in the car, it is already too late when the young woman realizes she is being driven beyond her house, beyond her street, beyond her *colonia*, out into the dusty wasteland of Lote Bravo. He rapes his victims *por las dos vías*, in both ends, humiliating them in the deepest way before strangling them and leaving them to mummify in the desert or bloat in irrigation canals. He then flees back to *el otro lado*, to the United States, using the border as a sort of finish line that offers him a measure of anonymity. Robert K. Ressler, a former FBI agent who specialized in serial murder cases, warned that investigators should remain alert to the possibility that a psychopath is traveling to Juárez from the United States. "You could have a guy in the U.S. who goes down there periodically to do these things."[34] After reviewing the Juárez police files and touring areas where bodies had been dumped, Ressler concluded that an El Pasoan was the likely murder suspect: "My leading theory is that there's a person living in El Paso who is going over to Mexico to take advantage of these less-sophisticated women."[35]

A second storyline holds that grisly coverage given to the crimes by the local media may have inspired more than one murderer. Instead of being committed by one killer, then, the Juárez murders may in fact constitute a string of copycat killings. Other speculations include the possibility that some of the victims were ritually murdered by members of a satanic cult, that their entrails may have been harvested by international organ traffickers, that their deaths were filmed as key scenes in clandestine "snuff" films, that Central American gangs or *maras* have organized the killings, or that women who attended a chain of computer schools have been targeted for death.

Of course, there is always the possibility that straightforward investigative incompetence may be behind the chain of unsuccessful arrests. In the autumn of 2003, for example, the Fiscalía Especial para la Investigación de Homicidios de Mujeres (Special Task Force for the Investigation of Women's Killings) admitted it may have lost the tissue samples taken from the murder victims between 1993 and 1998. Repeatedly, bodies that have been delivered to families for identification and burial, or exhumed for examination, have been discovered to be those of individuals other than the victim in question. On a number of occasions, a body has been dressed in clothing from one of the victims, to make it appear as if it were in fact the woman in question. Understandably, many have speculated about the use of incompetence to mask a cover-up on the part of police or perhaps of local government officials.

About the only thing that is clear is that suspect after suspect has been jailed, yet the murders have continued. In 1995, an Egyptian chemist, Sharif Abdel Latif Sharif, was booked and jailed for the Juárez crimes. Sharif had a history of sexual battery in the United States, having been convicted twice of sexual assault in Florida. Now incommunicado in a maximum-security prison in Ciudad Juárez, he is still under suspicion, but the bodies keep turning up. Some speculate that before his transfer, Sharif worked from prison, using a cell phone, to coordinate further killings that would make himself appear innocent. He is said to have paid as much as $100 per victim, demanding their underwear as proof of a successful rape-murder. Sharif might have recruited from the Rebels, a gang of about twenty-five young men who hung around clubs in downtown Juárez. Members of the Rebels were jailed for these crimes in 1996 but apparently were not the culprits either, because a gang of fourteen- to sixteen-year-olds, who reportedly held raffles among themselves to see who would get to kill women, were subsequently jailed in 1998. One of the latest gangs, Los Ruteros, dating from spring of 1999, was composed of maquiladora-personnel bus drivers who might have captured their victims as they drove them home. Or perhaps it was just one driver, who had kept one young woman on the bus as she returned home late at night, saying the bus had broken down. He left her for dead, but she wasn't. She made her way to a gas station, filed a complaint, and identified the driver from police photographs. He was pursued and captured in another city.

Far more common in the lives of Juárez women than potential workplace-related victimization at the hands of a serial killer, however, is the everyday violence of the beatings, stabbings, and rapes at home. As Debbie Nathan has noted, levels of reported domestic violence in Ciudad Juárez are higher than anywhere else in Mexico. And, as Nathan has noted, there tends to be a familiar moral edge to the official profile of the victims: they were potentially "loose" women, women who may have "asked for it." They worked outside their homes for wages at jobs that, while not great by any standard, at least provided a steady income and some benefits. This was more than many Mexican men could say, particularly since the last peso devaluation in 1995 and the ensuing skyrocketing unemployment levels. Some of the women frequented Chippendale-style dance halls after work. They came and went unaccompanied by male family members, sometimes in the dark. They wore miniskirts. Perhaps, as Nathan has argued, the assembly-line nature of the killings is but a chilling, yet somehow logical, counterpart to the violently sexualized work and home lives of women in the new global (dis)order, distilled so purely in border electro-boom towns.

Still others have suggested that the popular serial understanding of the killings is inaccurate. Not all of the victims worked in maquiladoras, they were not all similar physically, and they were abducted as well as dumped in various areas of the city.[36] Additionally, as researchers at El Colegio de la Frontera Norte in Ciudad Juárez have emphasized, killings of men rose during the same time period far more precipitously than those of women, yet these killings have remained largely unremarked.[37] The local and federal government's slow response to the concerns of victims' families, their insensitivity, and the widespread perception of persistent official mismanagement of the cases point to a deeper disregard for women as citizens.

As with the interpretations by elderly *mexicanos* in Limón's account of dance-hall Devil appearances in the 1970s, the slippery identity of the killer(s) in Juárez may also, then, be symptomatic of larger, unsettling changes occurring here. And this is precisely the point of setting the Juárez slayings in the framework of Devil stories more generally. As with other Devil stories, the narrative elaboration of the Juárez murders expresses in part the frustration, fear, and uncertainty over larger changes underway in border cities of Northern Mexico.[38] Over the 1990s, the population of Ciudad Juárez swelled to around two million, making this Mexico's fifth-largest urban area. It is estimated that the city grows, per day, by two blocks and 600 in-migrants from the Mexican interior and Central America.[39] As in Tijuana, many of these people quickly move on to seek their fortunes in the United States, while some stay to find work in border assembly factories or other local venues. Workers come and go daily from both sides of the border, some in the fast lane of the bridges, zapping their *visa laser* as they cross, others with their clothes in a bundle as they swim across the Rio Grande. Tourists from the United States find curios, good burritos, and "boys town" to be inviting attractions, while Mexicans drive across to shop for inexpensive gas and dirt-cheap Chinese imports in El Paso on the weekends. People come and go.

People come and go over the Santa Fe Bridge from Ciudad Juárez, Mexico, to El Paso, Texas.

Drug violence has also changed the profile of this city through the 1990s to the present, as bloody *ajustes de cuentas* (settling of accounts) among rival groups resulted in the ascendance of the infamous Juárez Cartel and its kingpin, Amado Carrillo Fuentes. Another, particularly violent, series of *ajustes* followed Carrillo Fuentes's death in 1997. Chilling execution-style killings and drive-by shootings in public areas became daily affairs. In late November 1999, FBI and DEA agents moved in just southwest of Ciudad Juárez in search of clandestine graves reputed to hold the bodies of nearly 200 victims of drug lords, murdered since 1995. Eighteen of the victims were thought to be U.S. nationals. Though agents dug relentlessly through the winter and the frozen dirt of four ranches located along a desolate stretch of highway heading to Casas Grandes, Chihuahua, only eight cadavers were ever exhumed. Others may have been disintegrated beyond recognition as human bodies by acid and lime thrown into the graves with the victims.[40] Most recently, in July of 2001, the forensic investigator who had examined the exhumed bodies from Casas Grandes and some remains of missing women in Juárez, Irma Rodríguez, heard that her most of her family had been executed at her home in Ciudad Juárez while she was away at a conference. Early in the previous year, Rodríguez herself had advanced the idea that larger sociological forces, not a single, deranged man or group of men, were responsible for the homicides in Juárez:

> There exists a rivalry, professionally and economically, between men and women. Women don't stay at home anymore. They have more liberty now, liberty that puts them at risk. I'm sure that the FBI, as experts, will come to the conclusion that this is not the work of a serial killer but of a social criminological phenomena—a product of a loss of values and influence of drugs and alcohol.[41]

Perhaps to stereotype the victims as certain physical types of women who frequented specific sites constitutes, in the collective unconscious of Ciudad Juárez, a way to render the killings less frightening through systematizing them. At least this way you (think you) know what the parameters of victimhood are. People come and go, and Juárez is "ruled by a mysterious alchemy. Things disappear. Cars, money and people dissolve as if they were never there."[42] The Devil is in the details. The Devil is in Juárez. Indeed.

Wounding, Healing, and Getting By

The fullness sought by the nation-state, the shading-in of neatly bordered areas by the bright colors of culture, is disrupted in profoundly different ways by the Virgin and the Devil, archetypes of good and evil, pounding out the future along the ropes of the narrative boxing ring that the border zone between Mexico and the United States has become. Their apparitions work at the fraying edges of the nation-state and its exhausted narratives (which are, in fact, its heart, as the nativist reprisal discussed in the previous chapter illustrates). The stories work within a master narrative, good versus evil, an enduring plotline that echoes back to ties between people and land that predate the nation-state, and that will surely outlast it.

But the figures—the Devil and the Virgin—are perhaps not so clear as we might like them to be. They both blur boundaries geographic and metaphoric. They cross lines. These archetypes are notable for their mobility; they gain their meaning through passage rather than stasis. The Virgin works both horizontally—across space, across oceans and rivers and deserts—and vertically, spanning heaven and earth, divine and profane, believer and infidel, god and man. The Devil plays on our fears, both real and imagined, about what living in a borderless world really means. He inhabits shadowy areas, those profound borders between life and death, the free fall between chaos and order in space and time, the vertiginous sense of having come unhinged. They even blur boundaries between themselves, between good and evil: the Devil is a fallen angel, while the Virgin is a single mother ascended to purity both corporeal and spiritual.

Yet, at a deeper level, both of these archetypes lend a sense of stability and permanence in the midst of what many perceive to be an overwhelming degree of flux. They draw on familiar storylines. They can be viewed as providing comfortable, if not always comforting, ways of coping with the pervasive sense of spatial dislocation described in the previous chapter. Religions have always done this, and the Virgin of Guadalupe is a fascinating contemporary illustration of the slippage between national identification and older, perhaps more durable, forms of collective identity. The Devil, too, provides a familiar, if unwelcome, component of collective identity, that serpent who skirts the boundaries and attacks from time to time. Or who lives with us, within us. The Virgin heals wounds both old and new, while the Devil works constantly to draw fresh blood. The Virgin and the Devil, in their own ways, mark paths that regress—in a temporal rather than the normative sense of regress as used in the previous chapter—to a time before the nation-state.

In the next chapter, I turn to an examination of less-extreme characters. Far from archetypical figures embodying good and evil, Jesús Malverde, Juan Soldado, and Elián González are everyday sorts who have been elevated to popular sainthood. As with the Virgin and the Devil, they provide narrative structures that help people living on and around the Mexico-U.S. boundary make sense of their lives in a context of profound and dramatic change. Yet their themes are not timeless and universal; rather they foreground storylines—drug trafficking and undocumented immigration—that are emblematic of contemporary existence along the border, and that are actively working to reshape both the border and the identities forged on and around it.

CHAPTER 6

Everyday Border Heroes

The making of new frontier tales has traditionally begun by marking
out a new hero. Typically, a new field or tale begins by identifying itself
with an outsider, a subaltern hero. . . . The story initially looks tragic;
the hero roams the margins, subordinated by the dominant culture. . . .
The next turn is romantic; the subaltern has been tragically oppressed
but heroically surmounts these barriers and emerges triumphant,
autonomous, and independent. . . . Finally, the story may turn ironic.
All of these figures are imaginative instruments of the narrative will
to power, and they cannot be reconciled without epistemic and
political violence.

— Kerwin Lee Klein, *Frontiers of Historical Imagination:*
Narrating the European Conquest of Native America, 1890–1990

Saints and Tricksters

In the emerging new world (dis)order, it seems that borders are at once
everywhere and nowhere at all. As Luis Urrea writes, "The border is
nowhere. It's a no-man's land. I was born there."[1] In a manner reminiscent of quantum physics, contemporary borders seem to signal presence
and absence simultaneously. The paradoxical character of contemporary
borders of all sorts reflects a crisis in the arbitration of power and, perhaps more importantly, of our very identities and the places to which
they are rooted. Borders are at once the most palpable delimiters of
the state and as such saturate the landscape itself with the power of the
state. Yet they also constitute the receding horizon of the state as it
is imagined and practiced. Borders are those places where the power of
the state becomes most tenuous, most dissipated, most challenged. The
U.S.-Mexico border has become a space of both fear (of confronting an
uncertain future without the nation-state as we knew it) and of possibility (of crafting human collectives that exceed the neat union of nation

147

and state and that may be less oppressive). The line itself signals this uncertainty: do we choose violence when our fears cannot be resolved, or do we jump the wire, and our fears, to search for new alternatives?

How do we go about finding our bearings, negotiating our identities at all scales, in this uncertain terrain? In this chapter, I will explore the popular narratives surrounding three ex officio border saints: Jesús Malverde, patron saint of narcotraffickers; Juan Soldado, patron saint of undocumented border crossers; and Elián González, the unofficial patron saint of some Cuban exiles in Miami.[2] These three lay saints, though not formally recognized by the Catholic Church, constitute important points of reference on and around the southern borderlands of the United States. All three hail from elsewhere—Malverde from Mexico's mid-Pacific region, Soldado from Northwestern Mexico, and Elián from Cuba—and as such illustrate Americo Paredes's ideas of Greater Mexico (and Ana López's parallel notion of Greater Cuba)[3] in action. Their peregrinations mimic those of contemporary workers and migrants. This perpetual motion has lent the landscape a transverse quality; in the words of Thom Kuehls, "a beyond, an outside, that exists within the geopolitical walls of the sovereign state."[4] New regions are emerging. Stories such as these are helping them to be born.

These figures lend a measure of dignity and protection to the activities of so many (particularly drug smuggling and undocumented border crossing), activities that, like the saints themselves, are deemed ex officio, off the record, unrecognized by official bodies. The everyday realities of the drug trade and labor flows in the lives of so many within Greater Mexico and Greater Cuba are lent a degree of sanctity, a connection to history, and a legitimacy in the land. These three border saints provide hope and fixity in turbulent times. They keep families together. They care about the working class and even reward some of them handsomely, certainly more so than any officially sanctioned venue does. They are narrative characters that populate the contemporary borderlands, guides across an uncertain terrain, stable referents in unstable times.

In more general terms, I will suggest that these lay saints can be understood within the motif of the trickster. The trickster provides an

example of a character who, by definition, navigates uncertain topog-
raphies, and whose knowledge can be extended to the shifting matrix
of space and power on the U.S.-Mexico border, on the South Florida
shoreline, or anywhere else that differences come together. Trickster
figures are prevalent characters in many cultures and across time. Tricksters appear in premodern and classical mythology, Chinese street theater, Hindu festivals celebrating Krishna the Butter Thief, and West
African diasporic storytelling, music, and ceremonial practices. The
trickster's typical guise is as an animal. For example, Raven is a stock
trickster of Pacific Coast Native Americans, while Coyote and Hare
are more common to the South; Ananse the Spider and Brer Rabbit are
both West African, and Europeans had Reynard the Fox. Bugs Bunny, a
contemporary television-based cartoon figure, is a widely known trickster of United States popular culture.[5] Their behavior and manners are
frequently anthropomorphized: they wear clothing, establish hierarchical social structures, and enact essential human traits. As Margaret Baker
notes, tricksters tend to defy authority, show humans our own foibles
and failings, exhibit foolishness and greed, and often act violently in
their dealings with others. More often than not, the trickster's antics
and schemes are intended to benefit himself alone, yet at times, and at
times unintentionally, they benefit humankind at large.

Tricksters are wanderers, messengers, liars, and thieves. Not
human, tricksters nevertheless perform the human margins through
their duplicity, mischief, and transgression. Tricksters inhabit the liminal shadows, and in doing so, they are essential for delimiting a center
for self and community. "In short," writes Lewis Hyde, "trickster is a
boundary crosser. . . . and the best way to describe trickster is to say
simply that the boundary is where he will be found—sometimes drawing the line, sometimes crossing it, sometimes erasing or moving it,
but always there, the god of the threshold in all its forms."[6] Trickster is
literally *tricky*, a master of deceit, one who slips across boundaries nor-
mally not crossed. Yet trickster is not simply evil—not another manifestation of the Devil, for example. For the trickster ultimately releases
needed goods—fire, the arts of agriculture, souls—from the gods in

order that humans may survive in the world. The trickster may also be a healer, as in the Coyote stories of the winter storytelling tradition of the Navajo. The telling of the story of Coyote as Eye-Juggler, used in Navajo rituals involving healing of the eyes, illustrates how trickster tales do not always simply entertain, or teach people how to behave. They can also "knit things together again after disorder has left a wound."[7]

One day, Coyote was out walking.[8] He came across a man who was doing something so curious that Coyote just had to stop and watch. The man removed his eyes, threw them up into a cottonwood tree, and after a while, the eyes flew back to him and he replaced them in their sockets. Coyote came near the man and begged him to tell what he was doing. The man explained that he tossed his eyes into the tree in order to see for long distances. Coyote thought that sounded fascinating, and pleaded with the man to show him the secret behind this magic. He begged the man so mercilessly that, finally, the man said, "All right. Here is what you must do. Pluck out your eyes and throw them up into the cottonwood tree. When you want them back, just shout, 'eyes come back!' Remember, though, that you can only do this four times in one day, no more."

The man went on his way and Coyote did as he said. He tossed his eyes high into the branches of the cottonwood tree. He could see beyond the hills and trees to streams and fields that lay beyond. When he called, "eyes come back!" back they flew to him, and he replaced them in his head. Coyote had a marvelous time tossing his eyes as high as possible and seeing for great distances, further than he had ever traveled before on foot.

But you know Coyote and how greedy he is. He couldn't stop after just four tries. He thought to himself, this is my land, not his, and I can do as I please. Coyote tossed his eyes into the tree a fifth time. But when he called "eyes come back!" they wouldn't come to him. Coyote wailed and cried, stumbling about blindly. Finally, he lay down on the ground and was very still, having exhausted himself.

After a while, a group of mice came upon him and, thinking him dead, began to snip, snip, snip his hairs for their nest. Coyote, of course, was not dead. He waited patiently until one of the mice got close to his snout to clip his whiskers, and quick! grabbed the mouse by the tail. The mouse, terrified, asked him what he could do to be set free. "See my eyes up there in the cottonwood tree?" said Coyote to the mouse. "Yes," replied the mouse. "Scamper up into the tree and bring them down for me," said Coyote, "and I will set you free." So the mouse climbed high into the branches, retrieved the pair of eyes, and dashed back down to Coyote. "Here are your eyes," said the mouse, "but they are covered with flies and oozing after being in the sun all day long." So Coyote thought for a while and said to the mouse, "Give me your eyes instead, and then I will set you free." So the mouse plucked out his own eyes and gave them to Coyote, then ran quickly away. Coyote placed the mouse eyes in his own sockets, where they were, of course, far too small. They rolled around in his head and he couldn't see very well, only those things that were close to the ground.

All sorts of other animals came along, and Coyote begged or tricked each one to trade their eyes for the pair of eyes he had. Finally, Buffalo came lumbering along, and Coyote convinced him to trade eyes too. Though the Buffalo's eyes were a bit too big and bulged out of his head a little, Coyote kept them.

By seeing through the eyes of other animals, Coyote gained an appreciation for many different ways of seeing the world. And so did the animals with whom he had traded eyes.

The geopolitical boundary between the United States and Mexico itself might well be viewed as a trickster figure. Both the historical record and the flexible geoimaginaries of different groups reveal that this boundary is a shape-shifter that firmly refuses to stay put. Of course, the boundary line itself has moved inexorably south and west, most violently and durably in the U.S.-Mexican War of 1846–1848, which fixed the contemporary coordinates of the U.S.-Mexican border by lopping off approximately half of Mexico's national territory at the time. But even the definitive-sounding language of the Treaty of Guadalupe Hidalgo was mocked when the Rio Grande (or Río Bravo del Norte, as it is known in Mexico), refused to stay its course, preferring instead to wander with each rainy season. As Paula Rebert has observed in her account of the difficult, dangerous, and contested circumstances surrounding the establishment of the geopolitical boundary between Mexico and the United States:

> The principles were based on precedents from western Europe and the eastern United States and had been formed in response to the behavior of rivers in humid regions of the world. The actions of arid-zone rivers, commonly involving rapid and violent erosion as well as gradual avulsion processes that produce new channels, were inexplicable in terms of the classical law of fluvial boundaries. One after another case of disputed sovereignty or land ownership was produced by continual change in the course of the Rio Grande, and the legal status of river processes that did not fit the classical definitions of accretion and avulsion were argued extensively. One authority commented, "It is probable that no other international boundary represents such a tangle of accretion and avulsion cases."[9]

A particular piece of land, El Chamizal, which was indicated in 1848 as belonging to the United States, was in effect stranded on the Mexican side at the El Paso–Ciudad Juárez boundary when the river strayed northward of its 1848 channel. A bitter struggle between Mexico and the United States ensued over the scrubby bit of land. It was over a century later, in 1963, that the two nations agreed to the Chamizal Treaty, which declared the Chamizal National Memorial. This binational park now nurtures the visual and performing arts and is dedicated (according to its theme statement) to celebrating cultures and the possibilities of cooperation between nations that share a common boundary.

The dual nature of the boundary line, its shape-shifting qualities, and its fluid transversality all point to a profound disruption in the geoimaginary status quo. Thus, like trickster figures, the border may wreak a great deal of havoc, but it also has the potential to teach, to heal, and to open doors to new futures. As Lewis Hyde writes of Coyote, so too of the border: "When he lies and steals, it isn't so much to get away with something or get rich as to disturb the established categories of truth and property and, by so doing, open the road to possible new worlds."[10] Coyote learned to see with others' eyes. Maybe that's what the border is forcing us to do, too, albeit in a very painful way, not unlike the self-inflicted trials of Coyote Eye-Juggler.

Though the *personajes* I will discuss in the balance of this chapter—Jesús Malverde, Juan Soldado, and Elián González—share some important trickster qualities, they are most certainly human, and their odysseys do not necessarily arise from mythic quests to obtain necessary items from the gods. Rather, they are mundane fellows born of contemporary circumstances. They have been elevated to extraofficial sainthood only because the need is there. Yet in their ability to navigate uncertainty, to see the obvious that others somehow fail to (or will not) see, and to provide a mirror on the contemporary world and its ironies, contradictions, and injustices, they are certainly tricksterlike. Their actions, juxtaposed with their sanctification, ask us to question our notions of what is legitimate and what is illegitimate, what is sacred and what is profane. As with the Virgin and the Devil of the previous chapter, their peregrinations enact the shape-shifting quality of the border. For the many devoted to them, they offer the tools needed to cope and survive in an often hostile, uncertain world.

From Culiacán to Los Angeles: Jesús Malverde, Patron Saint of Narcotraffickers

> *The True Prayer to the Spirit of Malverde*[11]
> Today, prostrated before your cross,
> Oh! Malverde my Lord,
> I ask for your mercy
> And that you alleviate my pain.

You, who live in heaven
And are so close to God
Listen to the sufferings
Of this humble sinner.

Oh! Miraculous Malverde
Oh! Malverde my Lord
Grant me this favor
And fill my heart with joy.

Give me health, Lord
Give me rest
Give me well-being
And I shall be blessed.

(immediately make your personal request and pray three Our Fathers
and three Hail Marys. End by lighting two candles)

Few people on either side of the Mexico-U.S. boundary know
anything at all about Jesús Malverde, unless they happen to live in the
vicinity of the infamous Pacific Coast corridor that runs from deep in
the heart of the Mexican state of Sinaloa[12] north through Tijuana and
on to Los Angeles. Here, Jesús Malverde is the king of ex officio saints.
He has shrines in all of these cities, and others in towns and villages
along the way.[13] Here, everyone knows of him, and many have come to
him for help in times of trouble. The few journalists who have written
about Malverde have labeled him *el narcosantón*, or the main patron saint
of the narcotraffickers, who use the Sinaloa-Tijuana-Los Angeles corridor to move the marijuana and poppy paste grown in the Sinaloa coun-
tryside up and out to the thriving dope markets of the United States.[14]
That narcotraffickers request Malverde's protection and return his favors
in splendorous kind is apparent. One has only to visit Malverde's principal chapel in Culiacán, the capital of Sinaloa, to witness the elaborate
plaques thanking him for his favors, the marijuana leaves that festoon

Shrine to Jesús Malverde, Culiacán, Mexico.

hats and key chains on sale there, and to hear the raucous strains of costly *bandas* and *conjuntos norteños* brought in at all hours, day and night, by thankful men in dark glasses. The neon-lit chapel is always open.

But, as Efraín Benítez Ayala, who helps care for the Culiacán chapel, was at pains to point out to me, it is not only the narcotraffickers who come to Malverde with requests.[15] "You see people of all social classes, with all sorts of problems, coming and going from this chapel." Farmers and shrimp fishermen come to request bountiful harvests.[16] That Malverde is generous to all agricultural producers is evidenced by a jar of garbanzo beans, the first of an evidently successful harvest, that rests on a shelf in the shrine. Next to it, a gargantuan shrimp floats in another jar. The sick come here, too. Indeed, Malverde's image is frequently juxtaposed with that of the Virgin of Guadalupe, because the two together are thought to pack a double whammy of healing power. In one version of his death, Malverde's legs are cut off, thus he is said to have a particular affinity for the one-legged and wheelchair-bound. Jesús Malverde was also a railroad worker, carpenter, and thief. He watches over all in these occupational categories, as well as prostitutes, another ex officio occupational category. Efraín asserted that most of the alms collected at the Culiacán chapel are devoted to buying wheelchairs and providing medicine, funerals, and food for the needy. Elegio González, the shrine's builder and main caretaker, claims to have won the lottery twelve times and to have devoted those winnings to purchases for the poor.[17]

Born Jesús Juárez Mazo in 1870, Malverde lived in a world of great social divisions. Mexico's long-lived dictator, Porfirio Díaz, had sent his crony, Francisco Cañedo, to the Sinaloa governorship in 1877, where he remained for seven terms, until the year of his death—and the death of Malverde—in 1909. Sugar and henequen plantations concentrated agricultural wealth in the hands of their owners, while the majority of Sinaloenses lived miserably. It is said that Malverde's own parents died of hunger or of curable illness. Their deaths galvanized Malverde into action, and he became a Robin Hood figure. It is said that he would steal from the rich and throw their gold coins in the doorways of the poor at night. In one version of his story, he acquired his nickname *mal verde* (bad green) because the rich thought of him as a green devil, green being associated with misfortune.[18]

In any event, Cañedo finally challenged Malverde, saying that if Malverde could steal his sword, he would grant Malverde a pardon. Being a carpenter, Malverde was familiar with the layout of the homes of the rich, and successfully stole Governor Cañedo's sword or, in another version, his daughter. Either way, his manhood severely compromised, Cañedo ordered Malverde hunted down, offering a sizable reward for him, dead or alive.

Malverde died on May 3, the Day of the Holy Cross (also the day of carpenters), 1909. Many say that his own *compadre* killed him for the reward money. Perhaps the *compadre* cut off his legs as they ate. Perhaps government goons hanged him from a mesquite tree, or shot him and he crawled into a bread oven to hide and die. Perhaps he simply died of a contagious illness. All versions say, however, that Malverde's corpse was denied a proper burial; rather it was left to hang from a mesquite tree as an example of what happened to those who defied Cañedo. The poor, who had loved and protected him, began to throw stones at his bones in an attempt to cover them. Upon throwing a stone, they made petitions for the return of lost things, mostly agricultural animals like the cows and mules that were so vital for the incomes and diets of the poor. When their animals returned, the spirit of Malverde gained a reputation as miraculous, more stones were thrown, and his fame grew. As for Cañedo, he died thirty-three days later, of pneumonia.

The final resting place of Malverde's bones is unclear. Some say he was surreptitiously buried in the municipal cemetery as thanks from a grateful old woman, while others say his bones lie where they fell from the mesquite tree nearly a century ago. There is still a pile of stones here, a few hundred feet across Insurgentes Avenue from his main shrine in Culiacán. It is located in a used-car lot, with a plaster bust of Malverde enshrined in a cast-off birdcage. People say that, since Malverde was himself a thief, one must "steal" a stone from this pile and return it only upon the fulfillment of his or her request.

Being a thief, Malverde has the power to make things disappear. Not only do Sinaloenses involved in the narco business request bountiful harvests, they also seek invisibility in passage of the sort that enabled Malverde to steal from Governor Cañedo. They pray for a safe crossing if on foot, or "that their Cessna—that winged horse—becomes invisible on the radar"[19] if delivering their cargo by air. A story told by Efraín illustrated the flip side of this power, the ability to make the lost reappear. In keeping with the petitions of desperate farmers early last century for the return of lost animals, he tells a story of a contemporary Culiacán couple who had recently had their first child, a baby girl. The girl was stolen from her mother, but her father had already crossed *al otro lado*, to the other side, the United States. The baby's grandmother prayed to Jesús Malverde that she would be returned. A few days later, the father saw the baby on the border, recognized her in the arms of her captors, and recovered her. Efraín recounts seeing the grandmother arrive at the shrine, in tears of happiness for this miracle.

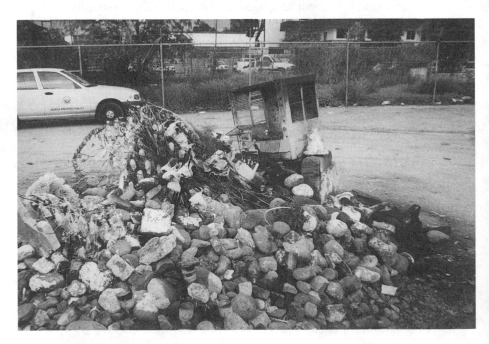

Malverde's final resting place? Culiacán, Mexico.

The veracity of such accounts is not at issue, nor is determining the precise manner of Malverde's martyrdom or whether or not Malverde per se even existed. Rather, it is the widespread belief in Malverde's powers of posthumous intervention that are important. In other words, it is the epistemological function of the image and story of Jesús Malverde that makes him significant. Jesús Malverde stabilizes what has become characterized by its fluid nature, by flows of commodities out of Sinaloa in the form of winter vegetables and drugs, circular flows of human beings who labor in Arizona, and by inflows of remittances and narcodollars and the latest electronics back across the border to Mexico. He keeps families together in times that break them apart and spread them out. Malverde's shrines—reportedly stretching from Columbia to Guatemala to Culiacán to Tijuana to Los Angeles—mark points of inflection along the route of these flows. Such sites allow for pause and reflection in ceaseless journeys back and forth along the Pacific coast.

Narcotraffickers have strategically used Malverde's legend and image as a "generous bandit" to spin their own images as Robin Hoods of sorts, merely stealing from rich, drug-addicted gringos and giving some of their wealth back to their Sinaloa hometowns in the form of schools, road improvement, community celebrations. Faith in Malverde lends a religious familiarity and a developmental public presence to what is not sanctioned by the Catholic Church or government officials. Reviled by the Culiacán diocese (his shrine is thought to divert huge amounts of local funds and faith), and laying shame to the shabby community investment efforts on the part of government officials, Malverde and his followers work outside the box in many ways. Malverde reinvents communities in ways that jump borders and collapse distances. Faith in him allows for permanence, connections to the past, a sort of sanctity, and a measure of power around the activities that shape the lives of so many people in this fluid space.

The Unknown Soldier: Juan Soldado, Patron Saint of Undocumented Border Crossers

A woman in tears has arrived at Tijuana's *Panteón Número 1* (Municiple Cemetery Number 1). Another, younger, woman follows her, looking concerned. The two women make a beeline for the back, passing markers that date from the late nineteenth and early twentieth centuries. The cemetery is crowded with crumbling headstones, cracked crypts, faded plastic flowers, and a light but persistent scent of decay that floats on the hot breeze. It is also packed with very alive pilgrims on this particular Saint John's day. Hundreds press toward the back of the graveyard, bringing petitions, prayers, offerings, or, like these two women, only their tears of thanks.

All have come to honor Juan Soldado, Tijuana's Unknown Soldier, whose reputed place of assassination at the back of *Panteón Número 1* houses his tomb, while another shrine to him is located near the middle of the cemetery. Like Jesús Malverde, Juan Soldado is a lay saint with posthumous powers to divinely intercede on behalf of his faithful petitioners in a wide variety of problems. Along with the usual curing of illness and help in finding love or employment, Juan Soldado—since he was a soldier himself—accompanies other soldiers in combat. His legend, as we will explore shortly, also holds that Juan Soldado was unjustly executed; therefore, he watches over those who feel persecuted without reason. He is said to help people avoid prison. He is also, and most importantly for our purposes here, the patron saint of undocumented border crossers, those hundreds of thousands from Mexico and Central America, and, increasingly, South America, the Caribbean, Asia, Africa, and Eastern Europe, who have for years made the Tijuana–San Ysidro (San Diego) border checkpoint one of the most transited ports of entry anywhere in the world, and who doubtlessly feel unjustly persecuted much as Juan Soldado must have felt.

The identity of the "Unknown Soldier" is not really unknown. Born Juan Castillo Morales in 1914, he was accused in 1938 of raping and strangling an eight-year-old girl, Olga Camacho. What is unclear are the exact circumstances of his death, and how he became such an important local figure. Some say that Juan was framed. In this version, he was given a mysterious bag by his military superior (alternately a sergeant, captain, colonel, or general) and told not to open it, rather to leave it in the cemetery. Meanwhile, the superior told the townspeople

Shrine to Juan Soldado, Tijuana, Mexico.

what was really in the bag, and, thinking Juan Castillo Morales the guilty party, they shot Morales as he tried to exit over the back wall of the cemetery.

Historical records of Tijuana from that period do indicate that a common soldier by the name of Juan Castillo Morales was indeed shot to death in February of 1938. José Manuel Valenzuela Arce, in one of the few pieces written on Juan Soldado, sets this event in the context of powerful socioeconomic transformations occurring in Tijuana at the time.[20] Valenzuela Arce argues that Juan Soldado functioned as a socio-cultural lightning rod, an unfortunate scapegoat who channeled the deeper frustrations of Tijuana's population. Valenzuela Arce describes how Tijuana, along with the rest of Mexican border towns, was experiencing a rapid rise in population growth due to an influx of nearly half a million Mexicans from the United States, deported from 1930 to 1935 because of the economic depression and unemployment in *El Norte*. In the midst of this influx, Tijuana, having built its reputation as a purveyor of vice during Prohibition years in the United States, saw an enormous drop in business—and employment—as gringo clients stayed at home to drink with the repeal of the Volstead Act in 1933. In 1935, Mexican president Lázaro Cárdenas decreed games of chance illegal, and Tijuana's infamous Agua Caliente Casino closed permanently in 1937. Unionized casino, and other, workers protested and struck, becoming violent.

This sequence of upheavals coincided with the kidnapping of Olga Camacho on 13 February 1938. Her violated body was found the next day. The Delegation of the Government of Tijuana took suspect Juan Castillo Morales into custody, while rival union-provoked mobs grew outside the municipal prison, fighting one another, demanding the prisoner, and ultimately setting fire to the municipal headquarters. The Tijuana firetrucks were blocked and disabled, and the crowd moved on to the government palace, setting fire to the municipal archives. Federal agents and soldiers moved in, shots were fired, and forty-four ultimately died in *el día sangriento de Tijuana* (Tijuana's bloody day), 16 February 1938. Declaring themselves incompetent to try Castillo

Morales, federal police handed his case over to the military, who formed a war council and quickly determined that he was guilty. On 17 February 1938, he was shot.

Not all Tijuanenses, however, believed Castillo Morales to be guilty. Perhaps his purported framing by his superior resonated with some who, like Castillo Morales, felt themselves unjustly persecuted at the hands of larger forces. Olga Vicenta Díaz Castro speculates that Castillo Morales ran away, blaspheming his accusers, and, as he was shot, cursed those who had accused him.[21] Perhaps, she continues, the only way for Tijuanenses who didn't agree that Castillo Morales was guilty to show their condolences was to cover his tomb with flowers and pray for his soul. Someone may have gone so far as to declare him a martyr, to ask his soul for help, and when their problem was resolved, to declare him miraculous. Valenzuela Arce suggests that a certain Señora García may have placed a stone on the site where Castillo Morales was slain, with a note saying, "All who pass by here place a stone and pray an Our Father."[22] Ralph Rugoff, who has written a brief descriptive piece on Juan Soldado in English, asserts that as Castillo Morales faced the military firing squad that fateful day, his commanding officer urged him to run for the border (only a few blocks away). As he turned to flee, he was shot in the back. According to Rugoff, "A group of outraged witnesses buried Soldado in an adjacent cemetery, but when they tried to clean up the murder site, they found that his bloodstains could not be washed away. That day a martyr was born: Juan Soldado, deliverer of border miracles."[23]

Whatever the circumstances of his death, the fame of Juan Soldado has grown. Notes asking for divine intercession, and giving thanks, are left in his Tijuana shrine by pilgrims from the interior of Mexico and by the faithful who have traveled south from the United States to pay homage for miracles performed. Many pray to Juan Soldado as they pass through Tijuana on their way to the United States, asking for a safe passage, for protection once in the United States, for the arrangement of a false passport, the provision of resident alien cards, or the scheduling of a migration hearing. The two women who arrived in tears at the cemetery were in fact mother and daughter. The daughter had crossed over to San Diego, losing touch with her mother who, inconsolable, prayed to Juan Soldado to find her daughter and bring her back. A San Diego news station filmed her testimony and it was aired on the other side, where the daughter saw her tearful mother and rejoined her immediately. They had come to give their thanks to the Unknown Soldier who had reunited them.[24]

Much like Jesús Malverde, the image of Juan Soldado functions to stabilize social relations in a place: Tijuana. Though shrines to Juan Soldado are not strung along a corridor, as are those to Jesús Malverde, Tijuana itself is characterized by its enormous levels of human mobility.[25] For many, Tijuana is an open pore, rather than a fixed point. It has historically been the single site of heaviest human transit funneled from the South—specifically Mexico and Central America—into the United States across the border with Mexico.[26] And though only one tower of the formerly glorious Agua Caliente casino stands today in Tijuana, there are many who still come down from the North: to work as managers in Tijuana's assembly plants, to shop for groceries and liquor as these are less expensive in Mexico, and to sightsee, party, and whore. Amidst such relentless coming and going, it is nice to have a quiet point of arrival to which one returns, time and again. It is also nice to have an ally in these tough times of border anxiety. As Rugoff writes, "Now that California's voters have passed Prop. 187, which denies state services to undocumented immigrants, business could turn brisk as pilgrims find themselves praying for new forms of assistance such as help in obtaining schooling for their children and access to public healthcare."[27]

Monster-Boy

I write these pages from the shores of another borderland, South Florida, gazing from time to time across the luminescent sea toward the Caribbean islands sparkling like a handful of stones skipped across the waves by some unwittingly poetic giant. Though I have researched, and written here at length of, the U.S.-Mexican border, far to the west of Miami, the cryptic new world border is here, too. South Florida does not share a land border with the Caribbean or South America, yet we experience high levels of "border transgressions" and their attendant controversies. Well-heeled Brazilians overstay their visas for the latest innovation in plastic surgery and snap up beachfront condos far out of range of the latest samba-effect of Brazil's gigantic, wobbling economy, while their well-to-do Colombian neighbors flee almost unimaginable political and social deterioration to buy their stately South Florida dream mansions with suitcases full of cash. On the other end of the social scene, desperate Caribbean islanders set float across the Florida Straits, praying that the wire and rope patching their ersatz watercraft together will hold until they reach the United States. Every week brings another tale of tens, at times hundreds, who set off on this wrenching voyage.[28] If they are lucky, the Cubans set foot on shore before they are intercepted at sea by the Coast Guard, and will have a chance to remain in the United States under the Clinton-era "wet foot–dry foot" policy. If they do, family members in Miami will pick them up and welcome them with the full knowledge that the next group might not be so lucky. If they are unlucky—intercepted before making landfall, or guilty simply of being Haitian—their severely dehydrated, and usually black, bodies will be on the next boat south. Many, of course, don't make it at all. The nightly newsreels in South Florida do not lack for footage of bloated corpses fished off the Keys, or baking in boats meandering aimlessly in the currents.

Such was the odyssey of Elián González, an almost-six-year-old Cuban boy plucked from the sea on Thanksgiving Day, 1999. Clinging to an inner tube for three days, he innocently slipped past sharks, thirst, and precisely one hundred and one years of imperialism. He and two other survivors were far outweighed by the eleven casualties caused when their patchworked vessel capsized. Among the dead were Elián's mother and stepfather. Treated for shock at a Miami hospital, he was released to local relatives until more could be known about his situation. The Miami Gonzálezes, related to Elián's father but devoutly anti-Castro, decided that the boy had no future in Cuba and that, since his mother had died, he should rightfully stay with them and grow up "free" in the United States. Marysleysis, his twenty-one-year-old cousin, developed strong maternal feelings toward Elián and saw herself as taking the place of the boy's mother. She quit her job as an assistant loan processor in a bank to devote herself to his care. Her father and Elián's great-uncle, Lázaro, became the boy's father figures in an Electral plot twist. The Cuban government, for its part, considered the González family's unwillingness to release Elián into the custody of his father, Juan Miguel González, to be tantamount to kidnapping.

For some months the national news (and certainly our local news) was dominated by the Elián saga. At least one local news station posted an "Elián-cam" outside the family's Little Havana home and ran continuous live video feed for a while. Another claimed to be "the only station where Elián speaks for himself," yet I wonder who really believed that the much-televised videotape in which a puppetlike Elián recited a painfully rehearsed denunciation of the Castro regime constituted speaking for himself. Even God was on his side, according to the González family, claiming that the Virgin Mary had appeared in a bluish reflection in a mirror in their home. Others insisted that the Virgin

Common ex-voto style depiction of the odyssey of Elián González.

Mary had also appeared in the window of a nearby Total Bank, buttressing the family's claims that the boy was blessed and that God did not want Elián to be returned to Cuba. Tales were told of how Elián had been escorted by dolphins during his three days at sea, the animals protecting him from sharks and pushing his inner tube shoreward. He was dubbed "the Dolphin Boy" and parallels to Moses were swiftly drawn. The family's Little Havana home became a virtual shrine where hundreds of Cuban exiles, and the news media, congregated daily in an ongoing vigil to keep Elián in the United States.

On 28 June 2000, Elián and his father returned to Cuba. The Miami González family has since moved on, their home in Little Havana turned into a museum, with Elián's bed, clothing, and toys on display for the streams of pilgrims who have not forgotten him. A seventh-birthday party was held in absentia in the González's yard in December 2000, despite the fact that Elián had returned to Cuba several months earlier. Exuberant supporters of Elián considered him to be there in spirit, and feasted on *lechón* (roast pig) and *pastel* (cake) in his honor. There is still talk among some about how Elián might be brought back

Elián's house in Miami shortly after his departure.

to Miami, despite reports that he has adjusted well to his renewed life in Cuba with his father. Miami is, more than three years after Elián, still awash with Elián bumper stickers and posters. A made-for-TV movie aired on the Fox Network in September of 2000. Reviews of *The Elián González Story* claimed that it didn't come close to the circuslike hype that really surrounded the boy during his stay in Miami.

The extended González family itself, part living in Miami and the other part in Cuba, seems to be irrevocably divided by political lines that, apparently, do run thicker than blood. The freezing of time and space around Elián is a microcosm of the more than forty-year paralysis of some of Miami's Cuban community, whose eyes and hearts forever gaze steadily backward in time to before 1959, and south, across the Florida Straits. Vitriolic debates over Elián's right, indeed his desire, to float across an invisible line and remain in the United States highlighted larger class and ethnic divisions as well, tensions that were already at a high pitch in South Florida and that went beyond the González family and the small, but powerful, contingent of Miami's Cuban population that vocally denounces Fidel Castro at every opportunity. Elián's case did not simply involve the *right to be* on one side or another of the boundary line, this Euclidean legalism buried deep in the Florida Straits. It distilled other borders, as well. The battle over Elián revealed lines of division, as well as solidarity, among Cubans and Cuban Americans in the United States, Miami's Cubano population, and Miami's wider Latino population. Miami Anglo and African Americans, who hardly ever agree about anything, largely concurred that Elián should be on the next boat south. Miami's Haitian community was outraged at the special treatment accorded to nonblack Cubans, when their own countrymen are routinely and swiftly deported (if they are lucky enough to avoid washing ashore, drowned, on Key Biscayne first).

In the end, Elián had become something quite other than a six-year-old boy. He became kaleidoscopic, shot through with multiple borders, fractured along many fault lines, and crudely glued back together for us by a media with a penchant for coherent narratives. Elián González emerged a horrifyingly lovely composite child, taken apart and put back together at all geographical scales by the desiring machines of families, cities, countries, and an emergent world order that is inexorably gelling around incidents like t/his. Elián seldom spoke (despite the claims made by the television station), yet he clearly articulated the collapsing borders between the old global order and the new, left and right, home and away, life and death, kin and stranger. Elián became a monster.

Who really knows, of course, what became of Elián-the-Boy, for he was seldom allowed to speak. Relatives, neighbors, opinion polls, congressmen, presidents, and news anchors spoke loudly for him. Deafeningly. Only time will tell how this multiscaled tug of war, at once so about him yet so profoundly not about him, will be resolved, and how the dust of all this will swirl and settle around his psyche. But we can, indeed we must, begin to speak of Elián-the-Monster. For Elián is not much different at all from Ilena, or from Ramón, Guadalupe, Juan, and María, all fully monsters in their own right. The bordered sea reluctantly spit this small monster forth on Thanksgiving Day, yet the bordered desert births them by the thousands every night. It just so happens that this was South Florida, Elián is Cuban (and white, and male, and motherless), and 2000 was an election year.

In labeling Elián a monster I do not mean to insult or belittle him, or to make light of the battle over his future that, to this day, deeply divides Miami. Certainly some of the displays on all sides of the opinion spectrum were monstrous in a rather immediate sense. In using the term "monster," however, I am invoking Donna Haraway, who reminds us that monsters hold forth promises.[29] In her journey to produce a modest theory, or "sighting device," concerning struggles over what may count as nature, Haraway wrote of the necessity of producing "a patterned vision of how to move and what to fear in the topography of an impossible but all-too-real present, in order to find an absent, but perhaps possible, other present."[30] Elián's story, as with the stories of the millions of other monsters afoot in the global landscape, challenges us to find other possible presents.

CHAPTER 7

Hatred and Beautiful Things

Rather, the phrase "poetically man dwells" says: poetry first causes
dwelling to be dwelling. Poetry is what really lets us dwell. But through
what do we attain a dwelling place? Through building. Poetic creation,
which lets us dwell, is a kind of building.

—Martin Heidegger, *Poetry, Language, Thought*

I think construction deserves more respect; it cannot be name-called
out of (or into) existence, ridiculed and shamed into yielding up its
powers. And if its very nature seems to prevent us—for are we not also
socially constructed?—from peering deeply therein, that very same
nature also cries out for something other than analysis as this is usually
practiced in reports to our Academy. For in construction's place—what?
No more invention, or more invention? And if the latter, as is assuredly
the case, why don't we start inventing? Is it because at this point the
critic fumbles the pass and the "literary turn" in the social sciences and
historical studies yields naught else but more meta-commentary in
place of poesis, little by way of making anew?

—Michael Taussig, *Mimesis and Alterity*

This is the last chapter, and by all rights it should be a conclusion. But I
don't claim to know a way out of the current situation of rising violence
on and about the boundary between Mexico and the United States,
beyond the reassertion of racist nationalism, and the increasingly chilly
legal-institutional climate of the United States. I want to believe that
tricksters have the potential to disrupt the present gloomy tale of self,
nation, and globe as it is told today in Northern Mexico and the desert
Southwestern United States. Perhaps in their variously personified dis-
ruptions, tricksters can teach us how to slip the trap of bifurcated narratives, where one version of the future turns on radical otherness, and

the other turns on the impossibly romantic serial-dreaming of nations focusing on the same piece of arid land. At least alterity, though it turns on difference, presupposes a holistic tension, a mutuality wherein the Other performs the role of constitutive outside for the Self. Alterity lets us live together, and that is a starting place. But alienation (alien-nation) moves away from the mutuality of alterity and toward a radical separation, the "foreignness" described here by Georges Benko: "Today, we think of the other in terms of foreignness, not of alterity. To think in terms of alterity is also to think in terms of identity, relation, bond. We are creating categories for exclusion, yet we are made to live together."[1] The results can be frightening.

The illegal alien, however, is a profoundly scrambled, or "illegally alienated," self.[2] And to a degree we have all become aliens, inasmuch as none of us is really at home everywhere, and some are not fully at home anywhere. Many of us are unsure what home even means anymore. We are all alientated, to varying degrees. Yet it is in this very scrambling, disruption, and shattering of old categories across geographic scales that a germ of hope for something beyond the same old stories resides. It is in places like Los Angeles, Tijuana, Miami, Las Vegas, and Juárez that, for all their dark underside, this potential emerges most readily. Like Elián González, these scrambled cities are monsters of sorts, monsters that, for all their terribleness, hold forth promises. It is up to us to search for these promises and recognize them as such when we come across them. This is no easy task, for as Kerwin Klein reminds us, "Modern science has traditionally legitimated its often brilliant instrumental success by contrasting its factual and logical language with 'other' figurative languages. It has associated 'soft', 'poetic' forms with savages (myths), women (old wives' tales), and children (fairy tales)."[3]

The guiding spirit of this book is humanist, wherein the redemptive power of human creativity is front and center. I have suggested throughout that stories, storytelling, and storytellers can be agentic. At the very least, they are at the heart of how humans, both individually and collectively, make meaning and as such help to provide paths that allow us to go on living our lives. At best, they can help to provide alternate visions of places and peoples' places in them, visions that, little by little, might help to reshape power relations in less oppressive ways. Of course, I do not pretend that stories can do this single-handedly and do not mean to suggest that they can. Rather, as Crispin Sartwell has suggested in another context, "New and inconceivable hatreds will spring up and yield beautiful things."[4] Perhaps Sartwell's suggestion of a relationship between hatred and beauty provides a way to think about the contemporary border and interconnections between a hopeful aesthetic and a grim materiality, between monsters and the promises they make. Indeed this is where humanists, myself included, assert that the arts—narrative, visual, performing, aural, poetic—can play a vital role. As the epigraphs to this chapter suggest, it is the generative poesis found, not just in poetry but across the arts in their distillative, abstract, and at times oblique conveyance of meaning, that is particularly important. Through the arts, we might speak our fears more directly, voice our dissent in more concise and broad terms at once, attempt (as Taussig suggests) to make anew. Perhaps, like the Navajo tale of Coyote as Eyejuggler, our contemporary borderrama of despair, violence, and hatred forms an essential part of a collective healing ritual. Perhaps the soft language of savages, women, and children emerging from this collision of place visions will suggest a new storyline, a more inclusive place vision, a poesis of place that weaves connections between peoples and places rather than stringing another fence.

Borderlining

I could be

patrolling the line in a stiff green uniform and

a dog with alert ears, night-vision eyes, a nose for death

and a Blazer like an agile beetle to scuttle the sand

or

Cutting for sign in soft moccasins

with my notebook and tape recorder

and a set of 24 pastels

or

Slinking shadowing waiting for the chance to break over and out
alone

I expect a chain link fence
chicken wire?
A cheap string of Christmas lights would do the trick
or a faint line scratched with a stick in the rusty dirt
Something, anything, to stake those long miles
Holding hands, spanning the howling space to
force meaning like a green lawn out of the arid land
Us
Them

Texaco
Motel 6
Denny's
Those, I suppose, are the chains that hold hands
back-to-back to
stretch a twinkling fence
underlining the fact that
there really is no border on the border
Only borderlining

This smooth space from which so much is conjured
and into which so much has been distilled
Embroidered by patient hands, surgical minds, blessed hearts, sacred feet
Colored and flavored with blood, sweat, tears, hopes, dreams, fears
Ground into dry sand
Pulverized and dribbled
A shaman's scribbles
A Kool-Aid trail
Nazca lines in the shape of a snail
A chain of stories
A silver lining
Borderlining

Angel

The Angel of History is
a ninety-year-old woman in Tijuana
Picking over the junk heap of modernity
Looking for something to recycle

Grace

(for my grandparents, Grace and Shorty Price)
I promise myself that today I will drive to Pecos
Sweep the graves clean,
pass by their old house, and try to picture Grace
behind the counter at the five-and-dime, Grace
picking cotton and knowing all about that thorn, Grace
with the Most Beautiful Baby of 1939.
But
Mars rotates slowly overhead, an orange toy blinking in the night as
the wind blows a fierce gritty curtain across Interstate 10 and
I cannot see but drive blindly
Away.

Twin Cities

From the mirador
they are inseparable.
Undulating strings of sodium vapor
pool ghost pink along the river and
stretch eager fingers for hills all around.

Shared blood circulates
as people and cars, wires and bars
cross bridges and streets and railways.
Cut the veins and they bleed out into the thirsty land,
turning the water red,
painting the desert sand.

We know.
We have tried.

Because connecting capillaries
conjoin the brothers
who, back to back
have sealed their pacts
with a stitch in time,
a hairline fracture,
and a delicate scroll of barbed wire.

Field Trip to Enchanted Rock

It has rained for weeks. Renewing and fatiguing at the same time.
Yet the field trips have drummed steadily on.

Enchanted Rock is a bubble of ancient pink granite that rises
like the hump of a colossal camel frozen into the landscape. Four limbs
stuck solid in the Triassic, hooves grazing the beginning and end of
time, flanks barely clearing the Cretaceous. I climb to the top of the
world and see the granite shearing below me in slow motion into
smooth rosy onion layers. Even as the batholith rises through the
surrounding strata it peels steadily down and away. Erosion cancels
its own forces and drives everything inexorably toward a common
ground. I watch the camel slowly stumble and die, crashing into
the future.

Indians feared and respected the place and would not shoot
arrows in its direction, for spirits dwelt in caves networked into the
flesh of the beast. Yet as the sun sets, fantastic arrows of color fly forth
unprovoked, and if the night coming on is a cool one the spirits howl
and rail against their pink prison. A white woman spent years of her life
on the rock in utter madness, at one with the spirits, moaning and
wailing and rattling her chains with them at night. But then they too
were all driven down and crumbled into the past: the spirits, the
Indians, the madwoman, all peeling down and away, feeding the
erosional jumble below, an offering laid at the base of time.

Today, the rain sheets steadily earthward, pelting the beating heart of Texas. I lay down and put my ear gently to the skin of this animal. And if it wasn't for the wind I would have heard the water seeping through the layers of calcite and oolite and limestone all around, trickling delightfully through the tissues of rock toward the voices, and the aquifer, cradled deep within. Renewing.

No te vayas, Elián
Elián, alien
You for dinner again
What will it be? Plátano frito y frijolitos, or Pollo Tropical drive-
    through?
We've had you already for breakfast, and lunch too
But just can't seem to get enough of you

Llévanos contigo, Elián
Miami is colder now that you've gone
The glare from the spotlights long dimmed
Only Castro's tired ghost left to shake weary fists at
You're so close and yet so far away

Compañerito,
Take us with you if you must go
We'll touch fingers across the Straits
Play dodge-the-raft, wet-foot dry-foot, and Cold War draw
Stop traffic on the Dolphin, make prank phone calls to Janet Reno

No te vayas, Elián

MV Coho
It is difficult to imagine Spaniards
this far north.
Their breastplates and helmets not sweltering but
chilled to the bone,

grey light glinting and bouncing hard
like cold bright bullets
across the Straits

They left their names scattered stones across the land:
Juan de Fuca
Quadra
Flores
Garibaldi
Texada
But disappointed, the men
turned their horses,
tightened slack ropes,
and left.
"Acá no hay nada"
Canada

Blinded by a feverish golden haze to
the silver flash of salmon,
emerald firs suddenly shedding diamonds of snow,
sapphire seas swallowing it all.
Gems pulsating before their hallucinatory eyes.

I shade my brow aboard the MV Coho
This light blinds me too.
And just then a line is crossed.
Deep, vegetable, silent.
A liquid totem snaking far below the surface.

Pitch up: robin's egg skies
Roll down: cerulean night
Pitch up: Spanish blue eyes
Roll down: dark water streaked with crisp white

Some remain on deck,
screaming into the breeze with raised fists
and words carried backward, or
vomiting bitterly into the mist.
Inside the rest of us are silent and
gently warmed by the sun
we are cradled and rocked and
we hold each other and dream together

of god-men wrought from furious red-gold desire
of blood and soil and warm shades of brown
of fantastic languages and odd-shaped roots
of being born anew from the land
and surfacing in a dry port.

Notes

Introduction

1. In earlier, ethnographic work I have explored these relations more closely. See Patricia L. Price, "The Three Malinches: Betrayal and the Death of an Urban Popular Movement," *International Feminist Journal of Politics* 3, no. 2 (2001): 237–61. Pablo Vila explores questions of race, gender, and power in ethnographic practice in his edited collection, *Ethnography at the Border* (Minneapolis: University of Minnesota Press, 2003), particularly in his introductory chapter, "Introduction: Border Ethnographies" (ix–xxxv). Here, Vila provocatively suggests that the racialized, gendered, and sexualized (among others) silencings at work in the writing of some border scholars who use ethnographic methods are in fact the result of the unequal power relations within academia. For a different perspective on similar questions, see Ruth Behar, *Translated Woman: Crossing the Border with Esperanza's Story* (Boston: Beacon, 1993). The bibliographies of the three works cited here provide fairly comprehensive coverage of recent debates surrounding ethnographic representation, power, and practice in the social sciences, which are far too numerous to address in this footnote.

2. Nancy Scheper-Hughes, *Death without Weeping: The Violence of Everyday Life in Brazil* (Berkeley: University of California Press, 1992), 28.

3. Doreen Massey, *Space, Place, and Gender* (Minneapolis: University of Minnesota Press, 1994), 156.

4. There is no verbatim transcript of Chief Seattle's 1854 speech, and there exists much controversy over later rewritings of the speech. This quotation is taken from H. A. Smith, "Early Reminiscences, Number Ten. Scraps from a

Diary: Chief Seattle—A Gentleman by Instinct—His Native Eloquence, Etc., Etc.," *Seattle Sunday Star*, 29 October 1887 (no page number discernible on microfiche copy). The full text of Smith's version can be accessed online at http://www.halcyon.com/arborhts/chiefsea.html (4 November 2002). Smith is reported to have heard, and transcribed from memory, Chief Seattle's spoken speech. This online version and the microfiche copy of Smith's article do not match precisely. Portions of the first two sentences of this quote are obliterated in the microfiche copy, and I have relied on the online text to fill them in.

5. Quoted in Edie Lau, "Who Really Were the First Americans?," Scripps-McClatchy Western Service, *Kennewick Man Virtual Interpretive Center*, 12 December 1997, http://www.kennewick-man.com/news/121297.html (4 November 2002).

6. I am fully cognizant of the perils of pursuing such a classic narrative strategy of absolution, truth seeking, and authorial purification in anthropology. In the context of United States history, however, the two places I write of in this introduction—the Pacific Northwest and the arid Southwest—have long been narratively claimed by their Native American inhabitants. Thus a dialogue with dead Indians is at some point inevitable.

7. Smith, "Early Reminiscences." All text in this quote taken from microfiche copy.

8. Brian Jarvis, *Postmodern Cartographies: The Geographical Imagination in Contemporary American Culture* (New York: St. Martin's, 1998), 191.

9. Paula Gunn Allen, "*Cuentos de la Tierra Encantada*: Magic and Realism in the Southwest Borderlands," in David M. Wrobel and Michael C. Steiner, eds., *Many Wests: Place, Culture, and Regional Identity* (Lawrence: University Press of Kansas, 1997), 357.

10. I use the term "Anglo" in the way it is commonly used along the contemporary southern borderlands of the United States, to denote an English-speaking white person of European descent.

11. Roland Bleiker, "Editor's Introduction," *Alternatives* 25, no. 3 (2000): 271.

1. Place Visions

1. Regarding the long-standing difficulty of defining the Southwest, see Scott Slovic, "Introduction," xv–xxviii in Scott Slovic, ed., *Getting Over the Color Green: Contemporary Environmental Literature of the Southwest* (Tucson: University of Arizona Press, 2001), and Eric Gary Anderson, *American Indian Literature and*

the Southwest: Contexts and Dispositions (Austin: University of Texas Press, 1999), esp. 1–16.

2. "Mimetic" and "performative" are two additional terms that could be on this list. Because my focus here is the closely related idea of narrative, however, I have simply included this term alone. Furthermore, to list mimesis and performance is necessarily to invoke vast literatures that I do not review here in sufficient detail.

3. Edward S. Casey, "How to Get from Space to Place in a Fairly Short Stretch of Time: Phenomenological Prolegomena," in Steven Feld and Keith H. Basso, eds., *Senses of Place* (Santa Fe: School of American Research, 1996), 13–52. For an extended discussion, see Edward S. Casey, *Getting Back into Place: Toward a Renewed Understanding of the Place-World* (Bloomington: Indiana University Press, 1993).

4. Judith Butler, *Bodies That Matter: On the Discursive Limits of "Sex"* (New York: Routledge, 1993).

5. Michael Taussig, *Mimesis and Alterity: A Particular History of the Senses* (New York: Routledge, 1993), xvii.

6. This phrase is Clifford Geertz's; see *The Interpretation of Cultures* (New York: Basic Books, 1973), 28–29.

7. Taussig, *Mimesis and Alterity*, xvii.

8. Michael Taussig, *Shamanism, Colonialism, and the Wild Man: A Study in Terror and Healing* (Chicago: University of Chicago Press, 1987), 10. Emphasis in original.

9. Butler, *Bodies That Matter*, 10. Emphasis in original.

10. Paul C. Adams, Steven Hoelscher, and Karen E. Till, "Place in Context: Rethinking Humanist Geographies," in Adams, Hoelscher, and Till, eds., *Textures of Place: Exploring Humanist Geographies* (Minneapolis: University of Minnesota Press, 2001), xiii–xxxiii.

11. For general overviews, see essays in Charles Reagan Wilson, ed., *The New Regionalism* (Jackson: University Press of Mississippi, 1998), and Edward L. Ayers, Patricia Nelson Limerick, Stephen Nissenbaum, and Peter S. Onuf, eds., *All Over the Map: Rethinking American Regions* (Baltimore: Johns Hopkins University Press, 1996). For an interesting edited illustration of the large and growing body of New West scholarship, see Valerie J. Matsumoto and Blake Allmendiger, eds., *Over the Edge: Remapping the American West* (Berkeley: University of California Press, 1999).

12. The notion of rounds of accumulation is introduced by Doreen Massey, *Spatial Divisions of Labour: Social Structures and the Geography of Production* (Basingstoke: Macmillan, 1984).

13. Patricia Nelson Limerick, "The Realization of the American West," in Wilson, ed., *The New Regionalism*, 73.

14. Chris Park, *Sacred Worlds: An Introduction to Geography and Religion* (London: Routledge, 1994), 198. See also Daniel Cooper Alarcón, "The Aztec Palimpsest: Toward a New Understanding of Aztlán," *Aztlán: A Journal of Chicano Studies* 19, no. 2 (1992): 33–68.

15. Adams et al., "Place in Context," xiii.

16. Lillian Hellman, *Pentimento: A Book of Portraits* (Boston: Little, Brown, 1973), frontispiece.

17. Belden C. Lane, *Landscapes of the Sacred: Geography and Narrative in American Spirituality*, expanded edition (Baltimore: Johns Hopkins University Press, 2002 [1988]).

18. Though they bring out the layered qualities of place well, both palimpsest and pentimento are of limited usefulness as metaphors describing place making, for they retain the notion of privileged authorship (particularly pentimento) and suggest that there is a base stratum of place that can be uncovered by the critical observer.

19. Akhil Gupta and James Ferguson, "Culture, Power, Place: Ethnography at the End of an Era," in Gupta and Ferguson, eds., *Culture, Power, Place: Explorations in Critical Anthropology* (Durham: Duke University Press, 1997), 1–29.

20. And the terms themselves cue deep differences among geographers; see David Newman, "Boundaries, Border, and Barriers: Changing Geographic Perspectives on Territorial Lines," in Mathias Albert, David Jacobson, and Yosef Lapid, eds., *Identities, Borders, Orders: Rethinking International Relations Theory* (Minneapolis: University of Minnesota Press, 2001), 137–51.

21. Randall Bass, *Border Texts: Cultural Readings for Contemporary Writers* (Boston: Houghton Mifflin, 1999), 1. Emphasis in original.

22. For a thoughtful discussion by geographers of broadening the notion of borders and the implications for research and thought in political geography, see David Newman and Anssi Paasi, "Fences and Neighbors in the Postmodern World: Boundary Narratives in Political Geography," *Progress in Human Geography* 22, no. 2 (1998): 186–207.

23. See, for example, Mary Douglas, *Purity and Danger: An Analysis of Concepts of Pollution and Taboo* (Baltimore: Penguin, 1970 [1966]); Julia Kristeva, *Powers of Horror: An Essay on Abjection*, trans. L. Roudiez (New York: Columbia University Press, 1982 [1980]); David Sibley, *Geographies of Exclusion: Society and Difference in the West* (London: Routledge, 1995).

24. Martin Heidegger, *Poetry, Language, Thought*, trans. and intro. Albert Hofstadter (New York: Perennial Classics, HarperCollins, 1971), 154. Emphasis in original.

25. Michael Billig, *Banal Nationalism* (London: Sage, 1995).

26. Benedict Anderson, *Imagined Communities: Reflections on the Origin and Spread of Nationalism*, rev. ed. (London: Verso, 1991), 7.

27. Casey, "How to Get from Space to Place," 15–16.

28. Ibid., 43.

29. Robert D. Sack, "Place, Power, and the Good," in Paul C. Adams et al., eds., *Textures of Place*, 233. For a criticism of Sack's conceptualization of the relationship between space and place, see Edward S. Casey, "Body, Self, and Landscape: A Geophilosophical Inquiry into the Place-World," in Adams et al., eds., *Textures of Place*, 403–25.

30. Casey, "How to Get from Space to Place," 20.

31. Ibid., 44, 46.

32. Ibid., 24.

33. Anne Buttimer, "Home, Reach, and the Sense of Place," in Anne Buttimer and David Seamon, eds., *The Human Experience of Space and Place* (New York: St. Martin's, 1980), 171. In turn, both Buttimer's and Casey's focus on gathering can be traced to Heidegger; see *Poetry, Language, Thought*, esp. 152–53.

34. Ibid. Other scholars sharing Casey's, and Buttimer's, phenomenological understanding of place reiterate the insistence of place as an experiential, subjective construct. For an extended discussion, see J. Nicholas Entriken, *The Betweenness of Place: Towards a Geography of Modernity* (Baltimore: Johns Hopkins University Press, 1991).

35. John Brinckerhoff Jackson, "The World Itself," in John Brinckerhoff Jackson, *Landscape in Sight: Looking at America*, ed. Helen Lefkowitz Horowitz (New Haven: Yale University Press, 1997), 299.

36. See W. J. T. Mitchell, "Introduction," W. J. T. Mitchell, ed., *Landscape and Power* (Chicago: University of Chicago Press, 1994), 1–4.

37. D. W. Meinig, "The Beholding Eye: Ten Versions of the Same Scene," in

Douglas W. Meinig, ed., *The Interpretation of Ordinary Landscapes: Geographical Essays* (New York: Oxford University Press, 1979), 37.

38. Denis Cosgrove discusses this history at length in *Social Formation and Symbolic Landscape* (Totowa, N.J.: Barnes and Noble Books, 1985 [1984]). Cosgrove locates the beginnings of landscape painting as a genre in Flanders and northern Italy in the fifteenth century, with its apogee in the Dutch and Italian schools of the seventeenth century and the English and French schools in the eighteenth and nineteenth centuries. For other extended discussions of the evolution of the landscape concept, see Edward Relph, *Rational Landscapes and Humanistic Geography* (London: Croom Helm, 1981), and John Brinckerhoff Jackson, "The Word Itself."

39. Yi-Fu Tuan, *Topophilia: A Study of Environmental Perception, Attitudes, and Values* (Englewood Cliffs, N.J.: Prentice Hall, 1974), esp. 129–49.

40. The gender specification is intentional; for feminist readings of the landscape tradition, see Gillian Rose, *Feminism and Geography: The Limits of Geographical Knowledge* (Minneapolis: University of Minnesota Press, 1993).

41. See also John Berger, *Ways of Seeing* (London: British Broadcasting Corporation and Penguin Books, 1972).

42. Cosgrove, *Social Formation and Symbolic Landscape*, 25.

43. Don Mitchell, *The Lie of the Land: Migrant Workers and the California Landscape* (Minneapolis: University of Minnesota Press, 1996), 2.

44. W. J. T. Mitchell, "Imperial Landscape," in Mitchell, *Landscape and Power*, 6.

45. Ibid., 10.

46. Pierce Lewis, "Axioms for Reading the Landscape: Some Guides to the American Scene," in D. W. Meinig, *The Interpretation of Ordinary Landscapes*, 12.

47. Trevor J. Barnes and James S. Duncan, "Introduction: Writing Worlds," in Barnes and Duncan, eds., *Writing Worlds: Discourse, Text, and Metaphor in the Representation of Landscape* (London: Routledge, 1992), 1–17.

48. Hayden White, *Tropics of Discourse: Essays in Cultural Criticism* (Baltimore: Johns Hopkins University Press, 1987), 2, quoted in Barnes and Duncan, "Introduction," 4.

49. This approach has also shaped the work of some cultural anthropologists in similar ways; see particularly George E. Marcus and Michael M. J. Fischer, *Anthropology as Cultural Critique: An Experimental Moment in the Human Sciences* (Chicago: University of Chicago Press, 1986).

50. James S. Duncan, *The City as Text: The Politics of Landscape Interpretation in the Kandyan Kingdom* (Cambridge: Cambridge University Press, 1990), 19.

51. Ibid., 20.

52. Ibid., 182.

53. Ibid., 182–83.

54. An excellent example of just such an approach is found in Melissa Wright, "From Protest to Politics: Sex Work, Women's Worth, and Ciudad Juárez Modernity," manuscript in progress. In this piece, Wright examines the production and circulation of value through the strategic disappearance of women from specific urban spaces.

55. Mitchell, *The Lie of the Land*, 27.

56. For a broad, critical discussion of the evolving positionalities of cultural geography within human geography, and cultural geography's growing interdisciplinarity, see Clive Barnett, "The Cultural Turn: Fashion or Progress in Human Geography?," *Antipode* 30, no. 4 (1998): 379–94.

57. Mitchell, *The Lie of the Land*, 27.

58. Ibid., 4.

59. Richard Walker, "Unseen and Disbelieved: A Political Economist among Cultural Geographers," in Paul Groth and Todd W. Bressi, eds., *Understanding Ordinary Landscapes* (New Haven: Yale University Press, 1997), 170–72.

60. Ibid., 169.

61. Mitchell, *The Lie of the Land*, 8. Mitchell alludes here to the work of Stephen Daniels and Denis Cosgrove, "Iconography and Landscape," in Cosgrove and Daniels, eds., *The Iconography of Landscape: Essays on the Symbolic Representation, Design, and Use of Past Environments* (Cambridge: Cambridge University Press, 1988), 1–11.

62. "A Good Day to Die: Kill the Indian, Save the Man," vol. 3 in video series *How the West Was Lost*, executive producer Jim Berger, director Chris Wheeler (Bethesda, Md.: Discovery Enterprise Group and 9K-USA, 1993).

63. Gunn Allen, "*Cuentos de la Tierra Encantada*," 351.

64. Ibid., 352. Some accounts of Native American ties to the land quickly verge into impossibly romantic terrain, yet it must be remembered that the land, for many Native Americans, was that which was continually taken from them and destroyed, becoming a space of exile and death rather than rootedness and life.

65. Robert Layton, "Relating to the Country in the Western Desert," in Eric

Hirsch and Michael O'Hanlon, eds., *The Anthropology of Landscape: Perspectives on Place and Space* (Oxford: Clarendon, 1995), 210–31.

66. Roland Barthes, *Image—Music—Text*, trans. Stephen Heath (New York: Hill and Wang, 1977), 79.

67. Clifford Geertz, *Local Knowledge: Further Essays in Interpretive Anthropology* (New York: Basic Books, 1983), 31.

68. Kenneth Fote, *Shadowed Ground: America's Landscapes of Violence and Tragedy* (Austin: University of Texas Press, 1997), 33.

69. Keith Basso, *Wisdom Sits in Places: Landscape and Language among the Western Apache* (Albuquerque: University of New Mexico Press, 1996), 23–27.

70. Ibid., 59.

71. Casey, "Getting Back into Place," 34.

72. Heidegger, *Poetry, Language, Thought*, 145–61.

73. Simone Weil, *The Need for Roots: Prelude to a Declaration of Duties toward Mankind*, trans. Arthur Wills (New York: Harper Colophon, 1971 [1952]), 43.

74. Barbara Bender, "Introduction," in Barbara Bender and Margot Winer, eds., *Contested Landscapes: Movement, Exile, and Place* (Oxford: Berg, 2001), 5.

75. Tuan, *Topophilia*, 93. Gaston Bachelard, too, writes of topophilia in a much earlier volume that resonates quite closely with Tuan's, in both structure and spirit. See Gaston Bachelard, *The Poetics of Space*, trans. Maria Jolas (Boston: Beacon, 1969 [1958]), esp. xxxi–xxxii.

76. And, as Davis reminds us, the emergence of a sanctioned story can also close off other stories, other possible arrangements of things and events. See Joseph E. Davis, "Narrative and Social Movements: The Power of Stories," in Joseph E. Davis, ed., *Stories of Change: Narrative and Social Movements* (Albany: State University of New York Press, 2002), esp. 25.

77. Christopher Tilley, *A Phenomenology of Landscape: Places, Paths, and Monuments* (Oxford: Berg, 1994), 33.

78. Matthew Potteiger and Jamie Purinton, *Landscape Narratives: Design Practices for Telling Stories* (New York: John Wiley, 1998), 5–6.

79. Simon Schama, *Landscape and Memory* (New York: Knopf, 1995), 25.

80. A notable exception is J. Nicholas Entriken's *The Betweenness of Place*.

81. Catherine Nash, "Irish Placenames: Post-Colonial Locations," *Transactions of the Institute of British Geographers* 24 (1999): 457–80.

82. Tim Edensor, "National Identity and the Politics of Memory: Remembering Bruce and Wallace in Symbolic Space," *Environment and Planning D: Society and Space* 29 (1997): 175–94.

83. Kenneth Foote, *Shadowed Ground*.

84. David Chidester and Edward T. Linenthal, "Introduction," in David Chidester and Edward T. Linenthal, eds., *American Sacred Space* (Bloomington: Indiana University Press, 1995), 19.

85. Ibid., 18–19. For a fuller discussion of the political implications of empty signifiers, see Ernesto Laclau, "What Do Empty Signifiers Mean to Politics?," in Ernesto Laclau, *Emancipation(s)* (London: Verso, 1996), 36–46.

2. A Blank White Page

1. Whether or not the nation per se is an inherently modern social formation is the subject of much debate, but not a debate I will spend time on here as my approach is of a more epistemological nature, regarding the function of the nation in modernity rather than the precise definition of the nation. For a thorough overview of contending positions on the "modernity" of the nation, see Anthony D. Smith, *Nationalism and Modernism: A Critical Survey of Recent Theories of Nations and Nationalism* (London: Routledge, 1998).

2. See, for example, Michael Taussig, *The Magic of the State* (New York: Routledge, 1997).

3. Homi K. Bhabha, "DissemiNation: Time, Narrative, and the Margins of the Modern Nation," in Homi K. Bhabha, ed., *Nation and Narration* (London: Routledge, 1990), 311.

4. Anne McClintock, "No Longer a Future Heaven: Gender, Race, and Nationalism," in Anne McClintock, Aamir Mufti, and Ella Shohat, eds., *Dangerous Liaisons: Gender, Nation, and Postcolonial Perspectives* (Minneapolis: University of Minnesota Press, 1997), 89.

5. For an interesting exploration of pervasiveness of such work, see Michael Billig, *Banal Nationalism* (London: Sage, 1995).

6. Sarah Radcliffe and Sallie Westwood, *Remaking the Nation: Place, Identity, and Politics in Latin America* (London: Routledge, 1996), 25. This is also the focus of Taussig's *Magic of the State*, though it is not stated as directly as in Radcliffe and Westwood's book.

7. See Víctor Zúñiga, "Nations and Borders: Romantic Nationalism and

the Project of Modernity," in Kathleen Staudt and David Spener, eds., *The U.S.-Mexico Border: Transcending Divisions, Contesting Identities* (Boulder: Lynne Rienner, 1998), 35–55.

8. Bhabha, "DissemiNation," 300.

9. Gilles Deleuze and Félix Guattari, *A Thousand Plateaus: Capitalism and Schizophrenia*, trans. Brian Massumi (Minneapolis: University of Minnesota Press, 1987 [1980]), 474.

10. Zúñiga, "Nations and Borders," 35.

11. Ibid., 35, 51.

12. Anthony Burke, "Poetry Outside Security," *Alternatives* 25, no. 3 (2000): 307–21.

13. Ibid., 314.

14. Ibid., 316.

15. John Joss, *Strike: U.S. Naval Strike Warfare Center* (Novato, Cal.: Presidio Press, 1989), 2.

16. Patricia Nelson Limerick, *Desert Passages: Encounters with the American Deserts* (Niwot: University Press of Colorado, 1989), 174.

17. Frederick J. Turner, "The Significance of the Frontier in American History," reprinted in Frederick Jackson Turner, *The Frontier in American History* (New York: Holt, Rinehart and Winston, 1962 [1920]), published originally in the *Proceedings of the State Historical Society of Wisconsin*, 14 December 1893.

18. Throughout, I use the term "American" to refer to the United States of America rather than to the lands of North, Central, and South America together, as the term properly applies. Unfortunately, there exists no elegant adjective with which to distinguish peoples and culture of the United States from those of the Americas more broadly. Additionally, the term "Anglo," which I use to describe the nationalism of white, English-speaking peoples in the United States, is a form of shorthand that is not tremendously accurate. "Anglo" properly refers to only a segment of the English national population, and using it to denote all of the white, English-speaking population of the United States leaves out other important groups such as the Scots. On the other hand, "white" does not encompass the same groups today as it did in the nineteenth century, so using that term was also potentially misleading. The variable social and historical construction of racialized identity is, of course, at the heart of my dilemma. I settled on using "white" and "Anglo" interchangeably for lack of a clearly more accurate term.

19. William Cronon, *Nature's Metropolis: Chicago and the Great West* (New York: Norton, 1991), 51.

20. Anders Stephanson, *Manifest Destiny: American Expansionism and the Empire of Right* (New York: Hill and Wang, 1995), 4.

21. Ibid., esp. 5–12.

22. Reginald Horsman, *Race and Manifest Destiny: The Origins of American Racial Anglo-Saxonism* (Cambridge: Harvard University Press, 1981).

23. Quoted in ibid., 90. Emphasis in original.

24. Joseph Conrad, *Heart of Darkness and Other Tales*, ed. Cedric Watts (Oxford: Oxford University Press, 1990), 142.

25. Ibid., 142.

26. For a fascinating discussion of reason and madness in the accounts of European colonizers in Central Africa, see Johann Fabian, *Out of Our Minds: Reason and Madness in the Exploration of Central Africa* (Berkeley: University of California Press, 2000).

27. Annie Dillard, *Teaching a Stone to Talk: Expeditions and Encounters* (New York: Harper Perennial, 1982), 59.

28. Ibid., 40. My emphasis.

29. See John Muir, *The Cruise of the Corwin: Journal of the Arctic Expedition of 1881 in Search of De Long and the Jeannette*, ed. William Frederic Bade (Boston: Houghton Mifflin, 2000 [1917]).

30. Stephen Leacock, "Introduction," *Unsolved Mysteries of the Arctic* (Freeport, N.Y.: Books for Libraries Press, 1938), viii. For a discussion of arctic exploration and U.S. expansionism, see Nancy Fogelson, *Arctic Exploration and International Relations, 1900–1932* (Fairbanks: University of Alaska Press, 1992).

31. The Gadsden Territory, purchased through the Gadsden Treaty (signed in 1853, ratified in 1854), transferred additional territories from Mexico at a cost of $10 million dollars.

32. And even more, if the arid portions of the Oregon Country, acquired in 1846, are added to those arid lands comprising the vast majority of the Texas Annexation and Mexican Cession (and the relatively small, but decidedly dry, Gadsden Purchase) are considered.

33. This is not to say that there is no variety in the arid Western lands; far from it. There exists a significant diversity of landform types, rainfall levels, vegetation, and wildlife across the four major desert areas found in the contemporary United States: the Mojave, Great Basin, Sonora, and Chihuahua.

34. Limerick, *Desert Passages*, 166.

35. Ibid., 5.

36. Barry Lopez, *Arctic Dreams* (New York: Charles Scribner's Sons, 1986), 260. Yi-Fu Tuan has also analyzed the varied cultural perceptions and language acquisition regarding landscapes at length; see *Topophilia*.

37. David W. Teague, *The Southwest in American Literature and Art: The Rise of a Desert Aesthetic* (Tucson: University of Arizona Press, 1997). A classic in this genre is certainly John C. Van Dyke's *The Desert: Further Studies in Natural Appearances* (Baltimore: Johns Hopkins University Press, 1999 [1901]), though see in this volume Peter Wild's "A Critical Introduction to the 1999 Edition," xxiii–lxiii. Wild provides a fascinating analysis of Van Dyke's book as "a grand fraud" (xxviii), discussing the author and his work's enduring legacy in spite of this contention.

38. Slovic, *Getting Over the Color Green*, xvii.

39. And the term "white" has undergone various reclassifications over time in the United States: race is socially constructed. Additionally, by focusing on white Americans (or at least those who were thought to be white at the time), it is not my intention to imply that nonwhites (the Irish, for example, who were not initially considered white, or certainly black Americans) did not move west.

40. See Patricia Seed's discussion of the evolution and colonial use by the English of "waste land" in *American Pentimento*, esp. 30–56.

41. Stephanson, *Manifest Destiny*, 4. This, of course, in willful ignorance of several centuries of variously successful Spanish attempts to Christianize the native inhabitants of their northern frontier in the New World.

42. See Patrick McGreevy, "Attending to the Void: Geography and Madness," in Paul C. Adams et al., eds., *Textures of Place*, 246–56.

43. Richard Drinnon, *Facing West: The Metaphysics of Indian-Hating and Empire-Building* (Minneapolis: University of Minnesota Press, 1980), xvi.

44. Ibid., xii. Emphasis in original.

45. Potteiger and Purinton, *Landscape Narratives*, 75.

46. The treaty is often referred to simply as the Treaty of Guadalupe Hidalgo. The text of the treaty can be found in Oscar Martínez, ed., *U.S.-Mexico Borderlands: Historical and Contemporary Perspectives* (Wilmington, Del.: Scholarly Resources, 1996), 20–37.

47. For discussions of these conditions, see essays in Martínez, ed., *U.S.-Mexico Borderlands*, esp. 45–84, and David Montejano, *Anglos and Mexicans in the Making of Texas, 1836–1986* (Austin: University of Texas Press, 1987).

48. Quoted in Stephanson, *Manifest Destiny*, 44. For further discussion of Anglo-American racism toward *mexicanos*, and parallels to anti-Indian attitudes, see Thomas R. Hietala, "'This Splendid Juggernaut': Westward a Nation and Its People," in Sam W. Haynes and Christopher Morris, eds., *Manifest Destiny and Empire: American Antebellum Expansionism* (College Station: Texas A&M University Press, 1997), 48–67.

49. Pablo Vila, *Crossing Borders, Reinforcing Borders: Social Categories, Metaphors, and Narrative Identities on the U.S.-Mexico Frontier* (Austin: University of Texas Press, 2000), 87. Emphasis in original.

50. Joseph F. Park, "The Apaches in Mexican-American Relations, 1848–1861," in Martínez, ed., *U.S.-Mexico Borderlands*, 50–57. See also Oscar Martínez, "Border Strife," ibid., 45.

51. See Paula Rebert, *La Gran Línea: Mapping the United States–Mexico Boundary, 1849–1857* (Austin: University of Texas Press, 2001), esp. 184–85, 190. Concerns over Anglos dismantling the monuments for building materials, or moving them to gain control over land or resources, were also expressed, as were fears that irate Mexicans might deface the monuments as expressions of anti-U.S. sentiment.

52. Douglas, *Purity and Danger*, see esp. 137–53.

53. For an interesting account of the often high drama involved in surveying the geopolitical boundary between the United States and Mexico, see Rebert, *La Gran Línea*.

54. Thom Kuehls, *Beyond Sovereign Territory* (Minneapolis: University of Minnesota Press, 1996), 43.

55. For a discussion of landscape and gender, see Rose, *Feminism and Geography*, esp. 86–112.

56. Krista Comer, *Landscapes of the New West: Gender and Geography in Contemporary Women's Writing* (Chapel Hill: University of North Carolina Press, 1999), 203.

57. Seed, *American Pentimento*, 29.

58. Comer, *Landscapes of the New West*, 28. Emphasis in original.

59. See particularly the essays in Vera Norwood and Janice Monk, eds., *The Desert Is No Lady: Southwestern Landscapes in Women's Writing and Art* (New Haven: Yale University Press, 1987).

60. Theodore Roosevelt, "Manhood and Statehood," in Theodore Roosevelt, *The Strenuous Life: Essays and Addresses* (New York: Century Co., 1902), 245–59.

61. John Annerino, *Dead in their Tracks: Crossing America's Desert Borderlands* (New York: Four Walls and Eight Windows, 1999), 104.

62. Annette Kolodny, *The Land Before Her: Fantasy and Experience of the American Frontiers, 1630–1860* (Chapel Hill: University of North Carolina Press, 1984), esp. 3–13.

63. See Roosevelt, *The Strenuous Life*.

64. Charles Bowden, "Leave Something Behind," *Esquire* (December 1999): 92–93, 164.

65. Ibid., 93.

66. Ibid.

67. Charles Bowden, *Blue Desert* (Tucson: University of Arizona Press, 1986), 151–75.

68. Edward Abbey, *Desert Solitaire: A Season in the Wilderness* (Tucson: University of Arizona Press, 1988 [1968]).

69. Bowden, "Leave Something Behind," 164.

70. Ibid.

71. For discussion of the "rape script," see J. K. Gibson-Graham, *The End of Capitalism (as We Knew It): A Feminist Critique of Political Economy* (Cambridge, Mass.: Blackwell, 1996), esp. 120–47.

72. Kolodny, *The Land Before Her*, 7.

73. Gloria Anzaldúa, *Borderlands/La Frontera: The New Mestiza*, intro. Sonia Saldívar Hull, 2nd ed. (San Francisco: Aunt Lute Books, 1999 [1987]), 24–25.

74. Guillermo Gómez-Peña, *Warrior for Gringostroika*, intro. Roger Bartra (Saint Paul: Graywolf, 1993), 37.

75. Carlos Fuentes, *The Crystal Frontier: A Novel in Nine Stories*, trans. Alfred MacAdam (New York: Farrar, Straus, and Giroux, 1995), 342.

76. See particularly Henry Nash Smith, *Virgin Land: The American West as Symbol and Myth* (Cambridge: Harvard University Press, 1950).

77. See in particular Mark Busby, "Texas and the Southwest," in Peter Rollins, ed., *The Columbia Companion to American History on Film* (New York: Columbia University Press, 2004), and Comer, *Landscapes of the New West*.

78. Leonard Engel and John Gourlie, "Introduction: Western Landscape as Narrative," in Leonard Engel, ed., *The Big Empty: Essays on Western Landscapes as Narratives* (Albuquerque: University of New Mexico Press, 1994), xv–xxi.

79. Teague, *The Southwest in American Literature and Art*, 61.

80. Drinnon, *Facing West*, 465.

81. Brian W. Dippie, "Frederic Remington's West: Where History Meets Myth," in Chris Bruce, Brian W. Dippie, Paul Fees, Mark Klett, and Kathleen Murphy, *The Myth of the West* (Seattle: Henry Art Gallery, 1990), 111–19.

82. Michael Wallis, *The Real Wild West: The 101 Ranch and the Creation of the American West* (New York: St. Martin's, 1999), esp. 45–47. See also Smith, *Virgin Land*, esp. 102–11.

83. Richard Francaviglia, "Elusive Land: Changing Geographic Images of the Southwest," in Richard Francaviglia and David Narrett, eds., *Essays on the Changing Images of the Southwest* (College Station: Texas A&M University Press, 1994), 8–39.

84. See, among many other sources, Kathleen Murphy, "Graves and Grails: Mythic Landscape in Western Fictions," in Bruce et al., *The Myth of the West*, 153–67; Albert B. Tucker, "Reel Cowboys: Cowhands and Western Movies," in Paul H. Carlson, ed., *The Cowboy Way: An Exploration of History and Culture* (Lubbock: Texas Tech University Press, 2000), 179–200; and Busby, "Texas and the Southwest."

85. Not coincidentally, the Chicago Exposition was the same venue at which Turner presented his frontier thesis to the American Historical Association.

86. Richard Slotkin, "Buffalo Bill's 'Wild West' and the Mythologization of the American Empire," in Amy Kaplan and Donald E. Pease, eds., *Cultures of United States Imperialism*, 164–81. Wallis (*The Real Wild West*, 174) contends that Wild Bill's show was not an official Exposition participant but was performed twice daily, "rain or shine," just outside the walls of the Exposition in a covered grandstand seating up to 18,000 onlookers.

87. According to David Weber, only Mickey Mouse is a more readily identifiable symbol of Americanness than the cowboy (lecture delivered to the National Endowment for the Humanities Summer Institute, "Traversing Borders," held at the Center for the Study of the Southwest, Southwest Texas State University, San Marcos, Texas, June 2000). For further discussion of cowboys, their origins, and elevation to mythic stature, see essays in Paul H. Carlson, ed., *The Cowboy Way*.

88. Virgil Carrington Jones, *Roosevelt's Rough Riders* (Garden City, N.Y.: Doubleday, Inc., 1971), 34, n. 4.

89. Slotkin, "Buffalo Bill's 'Wild West,'" 165.

90. Wallis, *The Real Wild West*, 47.

91. Slotkin, "Buffalo Bill's 'Wild West,'" 176.

92. Drinnon, *Facing West*, 457.

93. Though this is not to ignore Patricia Limerick's contention that scholars must not lose sight of the West as a real place; see Limerick, "The Realization of the American West."

94. Peter Reyner Bahnam, *Scenes in America Deserta* (Cambridge: MIT Press, 1989), 44.

3. Debordering and Rebordering in Aztlán

1. Luis Leal, "In Search of Aztlán," in Rudolfo A. Anaya and Francisco Lomelí, eds., *Aztlán: Essays on the Chicano Homeland* (Albuquerque: Academia/El Norte Publications, 1989), 13.

2. John R. Chávez, *The Lost Land: The Chicano Image of the Southwest* (Albuquerque: University of New Mexico Press, 1984), 8; Leal, "In Search of Aztlán," 10–11.

3. When I write of the Chicano nationalist period, from the mid-1960s to the mid-1970s, I use the term "Chicano" purposely, as the masculine singularity implied in the term is appropriate for the spirit of this period. Later, I use the term "Chicana/o" to refer to the multiple gender and other subject positions that can be claimed under this broadened term. See "A Note on Ethnic Labels," in Adela de la Torre and Beatríz Pesquera, eds., *Building with Our Hands: New Directions in Chicana Studies* (Berkeley: University of California Press, 1993), xii–xiv, for further discussion and suggested readings.

4. Rudolfo A. Anaya and Francisco Lomelí, "Introduction," in Anaya and Lomelí, *Aztlán*, iv.

5. Paul Routledge, "Geopoetics of Resistance: India's Baliapal Movement," *Alternatives* 25, no. 3 (2000): 375–89.

6. Ibid, 387.

7. Fray Diego Durán, *The History of the Indies of New Spain*, ed. and trans. Doris Heyden (Norman: University of Oklahoma Press, 1994), 12, n. 2; Michael Pina, "The Archaic, Historical, and Mythicized Dimensions of Aztlán," in Anaya and Lomelí, eds., *Aztlán*, 19.

8. Carlos Fuentes, *The Buried Mirror: Reflections on Spain and the New World* (Boston: Houghton Mifflin, 1992), 99.

9. Pina, "The Archaic, Historical, and Mythicized Dimensions of Aztlán," 23–24.

10. Durán, *The History of the Indies of New Spain*, 12, n. 1.

11. Ibid., 24. Durán was convinced that the Aztecs were a chosen people of God because of his belief that they constituted one of the ten lost tribes of Israel.

12. Factions of the original migrants settled and remained along the route. Those who reached the end of the journey changed their name to, variously, "Mexica," "Mexica-Aztecs," or "Mexicans" along their pilgrimage. Ibid., 13, n. 3, also p. 25.

13. Pina, "The Archaic, Historical, and Mythicized Dimensions of Aztlán," 25.

14. Durán, *The History of the Indies of New Spain*, 220.

15. See especially ibid., and Fray Bernardino Sahagún, *General History of the Things of New Spain (Florentine Codex)*, trans. Arthur J. O. Anderson and Charles E. Dibble, 2nd ed. (Santa Fe: School of American Research and the University of Utah, Monographs of the School of American Research, 1978 [1970]).

16. Pina, "The Archaic, Historical, and Mythicized Dimensions of Aztlán," 29–30; Fuentes, *The Buried Mirror*, 102.

17. Chávez, *The Lost Land*, 16.

18. Yet it is important to note that Chicano activism (as well as the broader spectrum of Mexican American activism) has a long history and did not spring forth suddenly in the mid-1960s without antecedents. There were also multiple influences on *El Movimiento* besides African American civil rights struggles, particularly anti–Vietnam War and prorevolutionary Cuba sentiments among (some) Chicanos and sectors of the larger U.S. population at that time. See Rodolfo Acuña, *Occupied America: A History of Chicanos*, 4th ed. (New York: Longman, 2000 [1972]); David Montejano, ed., *Chicano Politics and Society in the Late Twentieth Century* (Austin: University of Texas Press, 1999); Ignacio García, *Chicanismo: The Forging of a Militant Ethos among Mexican Americans* (Tucson: University of Arizona Press, 1997); Francisco A. Rosales, *Chicano! The History of the Mexican American Civil Rights Movement* (Houston: Arte Público Press, 1996).

19. There were diverse strands of Chicano nationalism, ranging from those more focused on cultural issues to those inspired by a more materialist or even Marxist agenda; those who considered themselves more nationalist or even radically separatist to those who were less extreme in their outlook. See Rafael Pérez-Torres, "Refiguring Aztlán," *Aztlán: A Journal of Chicano Studies* 22, no. 2 (1997): 15–41, and J. Jorge Klor de Alva, "Aztlán, Borinquen, and Hispanic

Nationalism in the United States," in Anaya and Lomelí, *Aztlán*, 135–71, for detailed discussions of political as opposed to cultural nationalists.

20. García, *Chicanismo*, 95.

21. See especially ibid.

22. See Rosales, *Chicano!*, and Jack Forbes, *Aztecas del Norte: The Chicanos of Aztlán* (Greenwich, Conn.: Fawcett, 1973).

23. Chávez, *The Lost Land*, 144.

24. For a detailed discussion of this approach, see Ramón Gutiérrez, "Chicano History: Paradigm Shifts and Shifting Boundaries," in Refugio I. Rochín and Dennis N. Valdés, eds., *Voices of a New Chicana/o History* (East Lansing: Michigan State University Press, 2000), 91–114.

25. Pina, "The Archaic, Historical, and Mythicized Dimensions of Aztlán," 36.

26. Quoted in Chávez, *The Lost Land*, 140.

27. The brief text of *El Plan Espiritual de Aztlán* is reproduced in Anaya and Lomelí, *Aztlán*, 1–5.

28. Rudolfo Anaya, "Aztlán: A Homeland without Boundaries," in Anaya and Lomelí, eds., *Aztlán*, 230.

29. Klor de Alva, "Aztlán, Borinquen, and Hispanic Nationalism in the United States," 149.

30. Quoted in Forbes, *Aztecas del Norte*, 307.

31. Rosales, *Chicano!*, 23.

32. García, *Chicanismo*, 18.

33. Quoted in Forbes, *Aztecas del Norte*, 311–12.

34. Cooper Alarcón, "The Aztec Palimpsest," 36.

35. See Gutiérrez, "Chicano History," and Rosa Linda Fregoso and Angie Chabram, "Chicana/o Cultural Representations: Reframing Alternative Critical Discourses," *Cultural Studies* 4 (1990): 203–12.

36. Helen Delpar, *The Enormous Vogue of Things Mexican: Cultural Relations between the United States and Mexico, 1920–1935* (Tuscaloosa: University of Alabama Press, 1992), 90.

37. Pérez-Torres, "Refiguring Aztlán," 30.

38. Alarcón, "Aztec Palimpsest," 57.

39. Forbes, *Aztecas del Norte*, 13.

40. Chávez, *The Lost Land*, 4.

41. Guillermo Lux and Maurelio E. Vigil, "Return to Aztlán: The Chicano Rediscovers His Indian Past," in Anaya and Lomelí, *Aztlán*, 93–110.

42. Alarcón, "Aztec Palimpsest," 59.

43. Pérez-Torres, *Movements in Chicano Poetry*, 183.

44. Taussig, *Shamanism, Colonialism, and the Wild Man*, 100.

45. María Montoya, "Beyond Internal Colonialism: Class, Gender, and Culture as Challenges to Chicano Identity," in Rochín and Valdés, eds., *Voices of a New Chicana/o History*, 187.

46. Sonia Saldívar-Hull, *Feminism on the Border: Chicana Gender Politics and Literature* (Berkeley: University of California Press, 2000), 19.

47. Armando B. Rendón, *The Chicano Manifesto* (New York: Macmillan, 1971), 105.

48. See Gutiérrez, "Chicano History"; Cherríe Moraga, "From a Long Line of Vendidas: Chicanas and Feminism," in Anne C. Hermann and Abigail J. Stewart, eds., *Theorizing Feminism: Parallel Trends in the Humanities and Social Sciences* (Boulder: Westview Press, 1994), 34–48; Beatríz Pesquera and Denise Segura, "There Is No Going Back: Chicanas and Feminism," in Norma Alarcón, Rafaela Castro, Emma Pérez, Beatríz Pesquera, Adaljiza Sosa Riddell, and Patricia Zavella, eds., *Chicana Critical Issues* (Berkeley: Third Woman Press, 1993), 95–115.

49. See Tamar Mayer, "Gender Ironies of Nationalism: Setting the Stage," in Tamar Mayer, ed., *Gender Ironies of Nationalism: Sexing the Nation* (New York: Routledge, 2000), 1–22; Norma Alarcón, Caren Kaplan, and Minoo Moallem, "Introduction: Between Woman and Nation," in Caren Kaplan, Norma Alarcón, and Minoo Moallem, eds., *Between Woman and Nation: Nationalisms, Transnational Feminisms, and the State* (Durham: Duke University Press, 1999), 1–16; Nira Yuval-Davis, *Gender and Nation* (London: Sage, 1997).

50. Moraga, "From a Long Line of Vendidas," 40–41. Emphasis in original.

51. Elizabeth Martínez, "Chingón Politics Die Hard: Reflections on the First Chicano Activist Reunion," in Carla Trujillo, ed., *Living Chicana Theory* (Berkeley: Third Woman Press, 1998), 127.

52. Ibid., 127.

53. Angie Chabram-Dernersesian, "And Yes . . . the Earth Did Part: On the Splitting of Chicana/o Subjectivity," in de la Torre and Pesquera, eds., *Building with Our Hands*, 47.

54. Saldívar-Hull, *Feminism on the Border*, 23.

55. Emma Pérez, "Sexuality and Discourse: Notes from a Chicana Survivor," in Carla Trujillo, ed., *Chicana Lesbians: The Girls Our Mothers Warned Us About* (Berkeley: Third Woman Press, 1991), 159–84.

56. For a recent reiteration of this fear, see Ignacio M. García, "Juncture in the Road: Chicano Studies since 'El Plan de Santa Barbara,'" in David R. Maciel and Isidro D. Ortiz, eds., *Chicanas/Chicanos at the Crossroads: Social, Economic, and Political Change* (Tucson: University of Arizona Press, 1996), 181–203.

57. Moraga, "From a Long Line of Vendidas," 37.

58. See essays in Alma M. García, ed., *Chicana Feminist Thought: The Basic Historical Writings* (New York: Routledge, 1997).

59. Chabram-Dernersesian, "And Yes . . . the Earth Did Part," 40.

60. Martínez, "Chingón Politics Die Hard," 127.

61. Chicana feminists have adopted varied stances toward the family as a source of oppression, of strength, or of both. Cherríe Moraga ("From a Long Line of Vendidas") and Sonia Saldívar-Hull (*Feminism on the Border*), for example, provide quite different personal accounts of their experiences with and views of family. The numerous excerpts of key Chicana essays in Alma García's *Chicana Feminist Thought* provide a rich account of the varied Chicana feminist views of family, the Chicano movement's early years, and diverse stances vis-à-vis mainstream feminism in the United States. See also Beatríz M. Pesquera and Adela de la Torre, "Introduction," in de la Torre and Pesquera, eds., *Building with Our Hands*, 1–11; Beatríz M. Pesquera and Denise Segura, "With Quill and Torch: A Chicana Perspective on the American Women's Movement and Feminist Theories," in Maciel and Ortiz, eds., *Chicanas/Chicanos at the Crossroads*, 231–47; and Pesquera and Segura, "There Is No Going Back."

62. Anzaldúa, *Borderlands/La Frontera*, 41–42.

63. Saldívar-Hull, *Feminism on the Border*, 73.

64. Anzaldúa, *Borderlands/La Frontera*, 42.

65. Ibid.; Carla Trujillo, "Chicana Lesbians: Fear and Loathing in the Chicano Community," in Alarcón et al., eds., *Chicana Critical Issues*, 117–25.

66. Moraga, "From a Long Line of Vendidas," 43. Emphasis in original.

67. Pérez-Torres, "Refiguring Aztlán," 21.

68. Moraga, "From a Long Line of Vendidas," 47.

69. Alarcón, "The Aztec Palimpsest," 39.

70. Chabram-Dernersesian, "And Yes . . . the Earth Did Part," 52. Though see Laura Elisa Pérez, "*El Desorden*, Nationalism, and Chicana/o Aesthetics," in Kaplan, Alarcón, and Moallem, *Between Woman and Nation*, 19–46, who argues that Chicana feminism was present at the birth of Aztlán, and that queer and feminist Chicana/o thought has refigured, not imploded, the notion of Aztlán.

71. Emphasis in original. John Tagg, with Marcos Sanchez-Tranquilino, "The Pachuco's Flayed Hide: Mobility, Identity, and Buenas Garras," in John Tagg, *Grounds of Dispute: Art History, Cultural Politics, and the Discursive Field* (Minneapolis: University of Minnesota Press, 1992), 193.

72. Smadar Lavie and Ted Swedenburg, "Introduction: Displacement, Diaspora, and Geographies of Identity," in Smadar Lavie and Ted Swedenburg, eds., *Displacement, Diaspora, and the Geographies of Identity* (Durham: Duke University Press, 1996), 11. See also Genaro M. Padilla, "Myth and Comparative Cultural Nationalism: The Ideological Uses of Aztlán," in Anaya and Lomelí, eds., *Aztlán*, 111–34 .

73. Pérez-Torres, "Refiguring Aztlán," 37.

4. Alternative Narratives and the Uncertain Cartography of the Present

1. Whether or not this constitutes postmodernity or simply a new phase of modernity is debatable; I do not wish to explore this expansive and hugely vexed question in the brief confines of these observations.

2. Marc Augé, *Non-Places: Introduction to an Anthropology of Supermodernity*, trans. John Howe (London: Verso, 1995 [1992]), 77–78.

3. Lane, *Landscapes of the Sacred*, 7.

4. Philip Sheldrake, *Spaces for the Sacred: Place, Memory, and Identity* (Baltimore: Johns Hopkins University Press, 2001), 8–9.

5. Arjun Appadurai, *Modernity at Large: Cultural Dimensions of Globalization* (Minneapolis: University of Minnesota Press, 1996), 4. Subsequent page references are given in parentheses in the text.

6. Arturo Escobar, "Culture Sits in Places: Reflections on Globalism and Subaltern Strategies of Localization," *Political Geography* 20, no. 2 (2001): 141.

7. Ibid., 157. For similar cautions, see also (among others) Rose, *Feminism and Geography*, Caren Kaplan, *Questions of Travel: Postmodern Discourses of Displacement* (Durham: Duke University Press, 1996), and Arif Dirlik and Roxann Prazniak, "Introduction: Cultural Identity and the Politics of Place," in Roxann Prazniak and Arif Dirlik, eds., *Places and Politics in an Age of Globalization* (Lanham, Md.: Rowman and Littlefield, 2001), 3–13.

8. See Dirlik and Prazniak, "Introduction," for a discussion of this distinction.

9. For extended discussions of the "glocal," see Erik Swyngedouw, "Neither Global nor Local: 'Glocalization' and the Politics of Scale," in Kevin Cox, ed., *Spaces of Globalization: Reasserting the Power of the Local* (New York: Guilford Press, 1997), 136–66, and Arif Dirlik, *The Postcolonial Aura: Third World Criticism in the Age of Global Capitalism* (Boulder: Westview Press, 1997). For an important parallel discussion utilizing the notion of scale-jumping, see Neil Smith, "Homeless/Global: Scaling Places," in Jon Bird, Barry Curtis, Tim Putnam, George Robertson, and Lisa Tickner, eds., *Mapping the Futures: Local Cultures, Global Change* (London: Routledge, 1993), 87–119.

10. Swyngedouw, "Neither Global nor Local," 142.

11. Kathleen Staudt and David Spener, "The View from the Frontier: Theoretical Perspectives Undisciplined," in David Spener and Kathleen Staudt, eds., *The U.S.-Mexico Border: Transcending Divisions, Contesting Identities* (Boulder: Lynne Rienner, 1998), 3–4.

12. Pablo Vila, "Conclusion: The Limits of American Border Theory," in Vila, *Ethnography at the Border*, 306–41.

13. Américo Paredes, *A Texas-Mexico Cancionero: Folksongs of the Lower Border* (Austin: University of Texas Press, 1995 [1976]), xiv.

14. Rose, *Feminism and Geography*, 137–60.

15. Denis Cosgrove, *Apollo's Eye: A Cartographic Genealogy of the Earth in the Western Imagination* (Baltimore: Johns Hopkins University Press, 2001).

16. Cover text, *Time* (11 June 2001).

17. Nancy Gibbs, "The New Frontier/*La Nueva Frontera*: A Whole New World," *Time* (11 June 2001): 39.

18. Though globalizationists tend to use the terms "nation-state," "nation," and "state" interchangeably and loosely, nations seem to be largely associated with anachronistic solidarities (religion, ethnicity, and so on), while states are associated more closely with outmoded and/or inhibitory legal-institutional expressions of these anachronisms.

19. Kenichi Ohmae, *The End of the Nation State: The Rise of Regional Economies* (New York: Free Press, 1995), 2–5.

20. Ibid., 16, 19–20.

21. Cosgrove, *Apollo's Eye*, 264. Emphasis in original.

22. Simon Dalby, "Globalisation or Global Apartheid? Boundaries and Knowledge in Postmodern Times," in David Newman, ed., *Boundaries, Territory, and Postmodernity* (London: Frank Cass, 1999), 132–33.

23. Ibid., 137. Dalby's principal argument is intriguing; he proposes that the more sophisticated accounts of globalization share with nuanced, postapartheid understandings of the world three assumptions: that the state-as-container is an inadequate basis for understanding contemporary power dynamics, an emphasis on flows across boundaries, and a humanistic impulse in the centralization of the creative potential of both for rethinking contemporary identities.

24. Gates is quoted in ibid., 265.

25. For more extensive and fully referenced discussion of the globalization perspective, see essays in Newman, ed., *Boundaries, Territory, and Postmodernity*.

26. Michael Hardt and Antonio Negri, *Empire* (Cambridge: Harvard University Press, 2000), xiii.

27. Ibid., 190. Emphasis in original.

28. Ibid., 43–44.

29. Lavie and Swedenburg, *Displacement, Diaspora, and the Geographies of Identity*, 12.

30. The key initial publication in the borderlands approach is without question Gloria Anzaldúa's *Borderlands/La Frontera*. Guillermo Gómez-Peña's *Warrior for Gringostroika: Essays, Performance Texts, and Poetry* (Saint Paul: Graywolf, 1993) and *The New World Border: Prophecies, Poems, and Loqueras for the End of the Century* (San Francisco: City Lights, 1996) are also important works in this genre. For collections and overviews of borderlands writing, see (among many others) Claire Fox, *The Fence and the River: Culture and Politics at the U.S.-Mexico Border* (Minneapolis: University of Minnesota Press, 1999), Lillian Castillo-Speed, ed., *Latina Women's Voices from the Borderlands* (Collingdale: Diane Publishing Company, 1998), Rafael Pérez-Torres, *Movements in Chicano Poetry: Against Myths, Against Margins* (Cambridge: Cambridge University Press, 1995), and Alfred Arteaga, "An Other Tongue," in Alfred Arteaga, ed., *An Other Tongue: Nation and Ethnicity in the Linguistic Borderlands* (Durham: Duke University Press, 1994). Published as this manuscript went to press was Debra A. Castillo and María Socorro Tabuenca Córdoba, *Border Women: Writing from La Frontera* (Minneapolis: University of Minnesota Press, 2002). This excellent analysis of contemporary writings and writers from the U.S.-Mexico borderlands makes a number of valuable points that could have been more fully incorporated into my book had my timing been better.

31. In their edited collection, David Maciel et al. denote this shift as one from *El Movimiento* of the late 1960s and 1970s to the post-Movement decades

of the 1980s and 1990s. See David R. Maciel, Isidro D. Ortiz, and María Herrera-Sobek, "Introduction" in Maciel, Ortiz, and Herrera-Sobek, eds., *Chicano Renaissance: Contemporary Cultural Trends* (Tucson: University of Arizona Press, 2000), xiii–xxxiii. I approach this same shift as one from Aztlán to the borderlands simply because of the inherent spatiality of these symbols; however, we are all identifying the same sea change in Chicana/o scholarship and political praxis.

32. Anzaldúa, *Borderlands/La Frontera*, 25. Emphasis in original.

33. Pat Mora, *Nepantla: Essays from the Land in the Middle* (Albuquerque: University of New Mexico Press, 1993), and Gloria Anzaldúa, "Chicana Artists: Exploring *Nepantla, el Lugar de la Frontera*," *NACLA Report on the Americas* 27, no. 1 (1993): 37–42.

34. Anzaldúa, "Chicana Artists," 37.

35. Gómez-Peña, *The New World Border*, 6.

36. Francisco A. Lomelí, Teresa Márquez, and María Herrera-Sobek, "Trends and Themes in Chicana/o Writings in Postmodern Times," in Maciel, Ortiz, and Herrera-Sobek, eds., *Chicano Renaissance*, 285–312.

37. Ibid., 286. My emphasis. See also, among others, Tey Diana Rebolledo and Eliana S. Rivero, *Infinite Divisions: An Anthology of Chicana Literature* (Tucson: University of Arizona Press, 1993), esp. 1–33; Renato Rosaldo, *Culture and Truth: The Remaking of Social Analysis* (Boston: Beacon, 1989), esp. 147–67; George Vargas, "A Historical Overview/Update on the State of Chicano Art," in Maciel, Ortiz, and Herrera-Sobek, eds., *Chicano Renaissance*, 191–231; and Edwina Barvosa-Carter, "Breaking the Silence: Developments in the Publication and Politics of Chicana Creative Writing, 1973–1998," in Maciel, Ortiz, and Herrera-Sobek, eds., *Chicano Renaissance*, 261–84.

38. Amy Kaplan, "'Left Alone with America': The Absence of Empire in the Study of American Culture," in Kaplan and Pease, *Cultures of United States Imperialism*, 16–17.

39. These are subjective divisions; certainly other categorizations could be made. In what follows, I will give only brief overviews of much more detailed treatments of Chicana/o borderlands scholarship, literature, popular culture, and artistic production. There are also many, many more overviews, analyses, and collections than those few that I mention here. I urge the interested reader to pursue specific bibliographic references in this chapter, and their bibliographies in turn, for further, more detailed information on each of these topics.

40. Though some scholars who are variously critical of mainstream borderlands scholarship are at pains to note the distinction between what Robert Alvarez, for example, calls "literalist" and "a-literalist" approaches to the borderlands, such a distinction is itself artificial. See Robert R. Alvarez, "The Mexican-U.S. Border: The Making of an Anthropology of the Borderlands," *Annual Review of Anthropology* 24 (1995): 447–70.

41. Gómez-Peña, *Warrior for Gringostroika*.

42. Gómez-Peña, *The New World Border*, 88–89.

43. Rodolfo Gonzales, *Yo Soy Joaquín/I am Joaquín* (New York: Bantam, 1972 [1967]).

44. Jimmy Santiago Baca, *Black Mesa Poems* (New York: New Directions, 1989).

45. Pérez-Torres, *Movements in Chicano Poetry*, 84.

46. Ibid., 85.

47. Because of her wide popularity in the United States and throughout the Spanish-speaking world, Selena is perhaps one of the best-known crossover artists. Just a few of the many others include Mexican balladeer Luis Miguel, U.S. *divas latinas* Jennifer López and Gloria Estefan, folk singer Tish Hinojosa, El Vez ("the Mexican Elvis"), Enrique Iglesias, Jon Secada, and the U.S.-resident *norteño* band, Los Tigres del Norte.

48. See José E. Limón, *American Encounters: Greater Mexico, the United States, and the Erotics of Culture* (Boston: Beacon, 1998), 169–93, and Roberto R. Calderón, "All Over the Map: La Onda Tejana and the Making of Selena," in Maciel, Ortiz, Herrera-Sobek, eds., *Chicano Renaissance*, 1–47. José David Saldívar has pertinent discussions of Los Tigres del Norte, El Vez, and Tish Hinojosa in *Border Matters: Remapping American Cultural Studies* (Berkeley: University of California Press, 1997).

49. Calderón, "All Over the Map." For a discussion of the contemporary Los Angeles Chicano independent music scene, see Yvette C. Doss, "Choosing Chicano in the 1990s: The Underground Music Scene of Los(t) Angeles," in Gustavo Leclerc, Raul Villa, and Michael J. Dear, eds., *La Vida Latina en L.A.: Urban Latino Cultures* (Thousand Oaks, Calif.: Sage, 1999), 143–56.

50. Nortec Collective (various artists), *The Tijuana Sessions Vol. 1* (New York: Palm Pictures, 2001).

51. Josh Tyrangiel, "The New Tijuana Brass," *Time* (11 June 2001): 76–78.

52. Vargas uses this term to discuss Chicana/o art of the 1980s and 1990s, while Calderón uses the same term to describe the emergence of Tejano music.

53. Vargas, "A Historical Overview/Update on the State of Chicano Art," 205–6.

54. Ibid., 207.

55. For overviews of the inSITE projects, see Néstor García Canclini and José Manuel Valenzuela Arce, *Intromisiones compartidas: Arte y sociedad en la frontera México/Estados Unidos*, trans. Sandra del Castillo (San Diego and Tijuana: Programa de Fomento a Proyectos y Coinversiones Culturales del Fondo Nacional para la Cultura y las Artes y la Coedición de inSITE 97, 2000), and Sally Yard, ed., *Private Time in Public Space/Tiempo Privado en Espacio Público: inSITE97* (San Diego: Installation, 1998).

56. Néstor García Canclini, "De-urbanized Art, Border De-installations," trans. Sandra del Castillo, in Yard, ed., *Private Time in Public Space*, 38–49.

57. Marcos Ramírez ERRE, quoted in José Manuel Valenzuela Arce, "Formas de Resistencia, Corredores de Poder: Arte Público en la Frontera México–Estados Unidos," in García Canclini and Valenzuela Arce, *Intromisiones Compartidas*, 39–40. My translation.

58. Marcos Ramírez ERRE, "Toy an Horse," in Yard, ed., *Private Time in Public Space*, 108.

59. Guillermo Gómez-Peña, "1995—Terreno Peligroso/Danger Zone: Cultural Relations between Chicanos and Mexicans at the End of the Century," trans. Clifton Ross, in Frank Bonilla, Edwin Meléndez, Rebecca Morales, and María de los Angeles Torres, eds., *Borderless Borders: U.S. Latinos, Latin Americans, and the Paradox of Interdependence* (Philadelphia: Temple University Press, 1998), 131–37.

60. Katharyn Mitchell, "Different Diasporas and the Hype of Hybridity," *Environment and Planning D: Society and Space* 15 (1997): 533–53.

61. García, *Chicanismo*, 191. In addition, some have noted the ongoing masculinism and homophobia of (powerful) Chicano scholars and within some Chicano studies programs and organizations. See Elizabeth Martínez, "Chingón Politics Die Hard," also Deena J. González, "Speaking Secrets: Living Chicana Theory," in Trujillo, ed., *Living Chicana Theory*, 46–77.

62. Fox, *The Fence and the River*.

63. Ibid., 127.

64. Castillo and Tabuenca Córdoba, *Border Women*, 3–4. Castillo and Tabuenca Córdoba are working with Etienne Balibar's essay "The Borders of Europe," trans. J. Swenson, in Pheng Cheah and Bruce Robbins, eds., *Cosmopolitics: Thinking and Feeling beyond the Nation* (Minneapolis: University of Minnesota Press, 1998), 216–29.

65. Vila, "Conclusion," *Ethnography at the Border*, 310–11.

66. David E. Johnson and Scott Michaelsen, "Border Secrets: An Introduction," in Scott Michaelsen and David E. Johnson, eds., *Border Theory: The Limits of Cultural Politics* (Minneapolis: University of Minnesota Press, 1997), 3.

67. Ibid., 13.

68. See Vila, *Crossing Borders, Reinforcing Borders*.

69. Vila, "Conclusion," 327. Johnson and Michaelson, however, assert that mainstream borderlands scholarship, far from excluding Native Americans, is in fact populated by a romanticized caricature of the Native American as shaman or healer; see "Border Secrets." It is also worth considering Yvonne Yarbro-Bejarano's counterargument that Anzaldúa's "new mestiza" has become deracinated, or racially watered-down, because of the inappropriate universalization of her speaking position among border scholars. See Yvonne Yarbro-Bejarano, "Gloria Anzaldúa's *Borderlands/La Frontera*: Cultural Studies, 'Difference,' and the Non-Unitary Subject," *Cultural Critique* 28 (Fall 1994): 5–28.

70. Leo R. Chávez and Rebecca G. Martínez, "Mexican Immigration in the 1980s and Beyond: Implications for Chicanas/os," in Maciel and Ortiz, eds., *Chicanas/Chicanos at the Crossroads*, 47.

71. Saldívar, *Border Matters*, 96.

72. Chávez and Martínez, "Mexican Immigration in the 1980s and Beyond."

73. "Coming North: Latino and Caribbean Immigration," *Report on the Americas* 26 (1992): 13.

74. Patrick Buchanan, *The Great Betrayal: How American Sovereignty and Social Justice Are Being Sacrificed to the Gods of the Global Economy* (Boston: Little, Brown, 1998), 16, 271, 274.

75. Mike Davis, *City of Quartz: Excavating the Future in Los Angeles* (New York: Vintage, 1990), 238.

76. *Frontline*, "Go Back to Mexico!," produced by Galan Productions, Inc., for *Frontline*, distributed by PBS Video (Boston: WGBH Educational Foundation, 1994).

77. Timothy J. Dunn, *The Militarization of the U.S.-Mexico Border, 1978–1992:*

Low-Intensity Conflict Doctrine Comes Home (Austin: University of Texas, Center for Mexican American Studies, 1996); Verne G. Kopytoff, "A Silicon Wall Rises on the Border," *New York Times*, 14 January 1999, D1, D5; Peter Andreas, *Border Games: Policing the U.S.-Mexico Divide* (Ithaca: Cornell University Press, 2000).

78. El Paso's Operation Blockade was the touchstone in the border-long wave of deterrence operations in the mid-1990s. In 1992, staff and students of El Paso's Bowie High School brought a class action suit against the INS. Living near the Rio Grande in South El Paso's predominantly Mexican American Segundo Barrio neighborhood, legal residents and U.S. citizens resented frequent interrogations by border patrol agents and feared they would result in physical harm or even the accidental deportation of their children. Claimants contended that they were harassed based on border patrol agents' inappropriate association of "Mexican" physiognomy with being illegal. For their part, border patrol agents asserted that illegal border crossers hid among the milling crowd of school children. The case resulted in a court order that prohibited El Paso border patrol agents from pursuit of individuals based on racial profiles. See Jack Miles, "A Bold Proposal on Immigration," *Atlantic Monthly* 273, no. 6 (1994): 32–43, and Debbie Nathan, *The Time Has Come! An Immigrant Community Stands Up to the Border Patrol* (film produced by the El Paso Border Rights Coalition, 1996).

79. Personal interview with Doug Mosier, public affairs officer, border patrol, El Paso sector, 2 August 2001.

80. Verne G. Kopytoff, "In Tijuana, Border Crackdown Hurts," *New York Times*, 28 August 1996, A8; Daniel B. Wood, "Rural Counties on Border Struggle with Surge of Dangerous Crossings," *Christian Science Monitor*, 4 May 1999, 1, 9.

81. Personal interview with Robert Cordero, border patrol agent, El Paso sector, 2 August 2001.

82. Karl Eschbach, Jacqueline Hagan, Néstor Rodríguez, Rubén Hernández-León, and Stanley Bailey, "Death at the Border," working paper WPS 97-2. (Houston: Center for Immigration Research, 1997). John Annerino's book *Dead in Their Tracks* provides graphic descriptions of desert crossings and photographs of dead migrants tortured by thirst and heat exhaustion, and maps historic and contemporary grave locations of these unfortunate border crossers.

83. Quoted in Sam Howe Verhovek, "'Silent Deaths' Climbing Steadily as Migrants Cross Mexican Border," *New York Times*, 24 August 1997, A1, A20. In fact, Kathleen Staudt and David Spener point out that the Houston study

accounted only for deaths in counties that abutted the international border proper. Thus they consider the death toll from the Houston study to be a low-end estimate. See Staudt and Spener, "The View from the Frontier," 27, n. 2.

84. Scott Baldauf, "In a Border Town, Ranchers Face an Immigration Tide on Their Own," *Christian Science Monitor*, 25 May 1999, 1, 10.

85. Ibid., 10.

86. *Frontline*, "Go Back to Mexico!" Emphasis spoken in original.

87. Ibid. Emphasis spoken in original.

88. Julie Murphy Erfani, "Globalizing Tenochtitlán? Feminist Geo-politics: Mexico City as Borderland," in Spener and Staudt, eds., *The U.S.-Mexico Border*, 143–44.

89. Staudt and Spener, "The View from the Frontier," 4.

90. Roger Rouse, "Mexican Migration and the Social Space of Postmodernism," *Diaspora* 1, no. 1 (1991): 17.

91. Staudt and Spener, "The View from the Frontier," 11.

92. In using the term "schizophrenia," I am in no way implying a connection to the clinical usage of the word, nor is it my intention to make light of schizophrenia as a medical condition.

93. Fredric Jameson, "Postmodernism, or the Cultural Logic of Late Capitalism," *New Left Review* 146 (1984): 53–92. See also David Harvey, *The Condition of Postmodernity: An Enquiry into the Origins of Cultural Change* (Oxford: Blackwell, 1989).

94. Jameson, "Postmodernism, or the Cultural Logic of Late Capitalism," 72.

95. Ibid., 72–73.

5. Good and Evil on the Line

1. Mircea Eliade, *The Sacred and the Profane: The Nature of Religion*, trans. Willard R. Trask (New York: Harper and Row, 1959 [1957]), 22. Emphasis in original.

2. Ibid., 23.

3. Ibid., 24. Emphasis in original.

4. Virgil Elizondo, *Guadalupe: Mother of the New Creation* (Maryknoll, N.Y.: Orbis, 1997), 69.

5. Rubén Martínez, "The Undocumented Virgin," in Ana Castillo, ed., *Goddess of the Americas/La Diosa de las Américas: Writings on the Virgin of Guadalupe* (New York: Riverhead, 1996), 102.

6. For further exploration, see Fuentes, *The Buried Mirror*; Miguel León-Portilla, *The Broken Spears: The Aztec Account of the Conquest of Mexico*, trans. Lysander Kemp (Boston: Beacon, 1992 [1962]); and Jeanette Rodriguez, *Our Lady of Guadalupe: Faith and Empowerment among Mexican-American Women* (Austin: University of Texas Press, 1994).

7. Some Guadalupan scholars insist that there were, in fact, five apparitions, because Guadalupe's apparition to Juan Diego's ill uncle, Juan Bernardino, should also be counted.

8. The full text of the *Nican Mopohua* can be found in Elizondo, *Guadalupe*, 5–22, and in Jody Brant Smith, *The Image of Guadalupe* (Macon, Ga.: Mercer University Press, 1994), 83–92.

9. Stafford Poole, in *Our Lady of Guadalupe: The Origins and Sources of a Mexican National Symbol, 1531–1797* (Tucson: University of Arizona Press, 1995), claims that the symbolism of the Virgin of Guadalupe was first deployed in the mid-seventeenth century with its intended audience being Mexican *criollos*, yet it was not until the eighteenth century that the story of Guadalupe began to take root amongst Mexico's indigenous population. Poole's introduction details the varied scholarly analyses of the Guadalupe tradition and their wide-ranging interpretations of its political and secular uses. For a truly exhaustive account of the history and uses of the image of the Virgin of Guadalupe in Mexico, see D. A. Brading, *Mexican Phoenix: Our Lady of Guadalupe: Image and Tradition across Five Centuries* (Cambridge: Cambridge University Press, 2001). For a discussion that touches on the role of the Virgin of Guadalupe in Mexican nationalism and reproduces key images, see Claudio Lomnitz, *Deep Mexico, Silent Mexico: An Anthropology of Nationalism* (Minneapolis: University of Minnesota Press, 2001), esp. 3–34.

10. Elizondo, *Guadalupe*, 88.

11. Smith, *The Image of Guadalupe*, 6.

12. Eric R. Wolf, "The Virgin of Guadalupe: A Mexican National Symbol," *Journal of American Folklore* 71 (1958): 34–39.

13. Ibid.

14. Martínez, "The Undocumented Virgin," 99.

15. See Patricia L. Price, "Postcards from Aztlán," in Cynthia Weber and Francois Debrix, eds., *Rituals of Mediation: International Politics and Social Meaning* (Minneapolis: University of Minnesota Press, 2003), 89–114.

16. Angela K. Martin and Sandra Kryst, "Encountering Mary: Ritualization

and Place Contagion in Postmodernity," in Heidi J. Nast and Steve Pile, eds., *Places through the Body* (London: Routledge, 1998), 207–29.

17. See Elizondo, *Guadalupe*, for a detailed discussion.

18. For detailed discussions, see Rodriguez, *Our Lady of Guadalupe*; Smith, *The Image of Guadalupe*; and F. Gonzalez-Crussi, "The Anatomy of a Virgin," in Castillo, ed., *Goddess of the Americas*, 1–14.

19. Kenneth R. Samples, "Apparitions of the Virgin Mary: A Protestant Look at a Catholic Phenomenon," *Christian Research Journal* (winter 1991): 21–26.

20. Clarissa Pinkola Estés, "Guadalupe: The Path of the Broken Heart," in Castillo, ed., *Goddess of the Americas*, 35.

21. Carlos Monsiváis, *Mexican Postcards*, trans. John Kraniauskas (London: Verso, 1997), 37.

22. Martínez, "The Undocumented Virgin," 102.

23. Ibid., 111.

24. Carmella Padilla (photographs by Jack Parsons), *Low 'n Slow: Lowriding in New Mexico* (Santa Fe: Museum of New Mexico Press, 1999).

25. For a wonderful discussion of Virgin tattoos in New Mexico, see Víctor Alejandro Sorell, "Guadalupe's Emblematic Presence Endures in New Mexico: Investing the Body with the Virgin's Miraculous Image," in Francisco A. Lomelí, Víctor Sorell, and Genaro M. Padilla, eds., *Nuevomexicano Cultural Legacy: Forms, Agencies, and Discourse* (Albuquerque: University of New Mexico Press, 2002), 203–45.

26. For more information on the vandalism, see Todd S. Purdum, "Revered Catholic Icon Becomes Mysterious Target of Vandals in Los Angeles," *New York Times*, 24 October 1999, section 1, p. 20, and Judith Lewis, "Virgin Territory: Who's Defacing Our Lady of South Central?," *Los Angeles Weekly*, 12–18 November 1999, 26–31.

27. See Patricia L. Price, "Bodies, Faith, and Inner Landscapes: Rethinking Change from the Very Local," *Latin American Perspectives* 26, no. 3 (1999): 37–59, and "The Three Malinches."

28. Martínez, "The Undocumented Virgin," 110.

29. José E. Limón, *Dancing with the Devil: Society and Cultural Poetics in Mexican-American South Texas* (Madison: University of Wisconsin Press, 1994).

30. Westwood and Radcliffe, *Remaking the Nation*, 101.

31. Limón, *Dancing with the Devil*, 174.

32. Diana Washington Valdez, "Death Stalks the Border," *El Paso Times*, 23 and 24 June 2002. Available online at http://www.elpasotimes.com/borderdeath/ [19 December 2002].

33. In my recounting, I am referencing conversations with Alfredo Rodríguez and César Fuentes at El Colegio de la Frontera Norte in Ciudad Juárez, Leticia Castillo at IMIP (Instituto Municipal de Información y Planificación) in Ciudad Juárez, and Sarah Hill, who was conducting field research at the same time that I was in the El Paso–Ciudad Juárez area. All of these conversations took place during the summer of 2001. I am also drawing on the *El Paso Times* series, "Death Stalks the Border," and Debbie Nathan, "Work, Sex, and Danger in Ciudad Juárez" *NACLA Report on the Americas* 33, no. 3 (1999): 453–74. For additional information, in English, on the Juárez murders, see Melissa W. Wright, "A Manifesto against Femicide," *Antipode* 33, no. 3 (2001): 550–66. In Spanish, see Rohry Benítez, Adriana Candia, Patricia Cabrera, Guadalupe de la Mora, Josefina Martínez, Isabel Velázquez, and Ramona Ortiz, eds., *El Silencio que la voz de todas quiebra: Mujeres y víctimas de Ciudad Juárez* (Ciudad Juárez: S Taller de Narrativa, and Mexico City: Ediciones del Azar, 1999). An excellent overview of the Juárez murders with interviews and discussion of the many theories of who is behind the killings is found in the film *Señorita Extraviada*, produced and directed by Lourdes Portillo for Xochitl Films in collaboration with the Center for Independent Documentary (New York: Women Make Movies, 2001).

34. Sam Dillon, "Rape and Murder Stalk Women in Northern Mexico," *New York Times*, 18 April 1998, A3.

35. Jodi Bizar, "Expert Profiles Juárez Killers: Ex-FBI Man Thinks One Lives in El Paso," *San Antonio Express-News*, 6 July 1998, 1A.

36. Julia Estela Monárrez Fragoso, "La cultura del feminicidio en Ciudad Juárez," *Frontera Norte* 12, no. 23 (2000): 88–117.

37. The *El Paso Times* series, "Death Stalks the Border," puts the number of male homicides in Ciudad Juárez at 1,600 for the same period.

38. What I do not intend by setting these murders in the framework of Devil stories is the trivialization of these events. The Devil here should not be confused with devilishness, or the picaresque, a theme of the next chapter. The association with Devil stories is mine alone, and I have made this association in order to discuss broader transformations (economic, social, political, and cultural) of which the murders are indissolubly a part, not to make light of them or

dismiss their seriousness. Since I wrote the first draft of this chapter, the U.S. media has picked up on the case with a vengeance, and the U.S. public has become far more aware of the murders, unfortunately in often highly sensationalized ways. Fortunately, some journalists and academics who have written about the murders have discussed the contexual background of the case (rising violence, rapid urbanization, the shifting nature of employment, and profound changes in gender roles) and highlighted the dissimilarities as well as the similarities among the murders. See note 33, above, for sources.

39. Megan K. Stack, "Till Death Came to Her Door," *Los Angeles Times*, 11 September 2001, A1, A10. This journalistic source may provide numbers that are too high and too convenient; indeed, given the level of informality involved in Mexican urbanization, I would view any firm numbers with some suspicion.

40. Alejandro Gutiérrez, "Una ausencia: Historias de horror y muerte," *El Diario* (Ciudad Juárez, Mexico) 30 November 1999, 9A.

41. Quoted in Nancy San Martin, "To Catch a Killer: FBI to Aid Mexican Police in Series of Unsolved Homicides," *Dallas Morning News*, 5 February 1999, 37A.

42. Stack, "Till Death Came to Her Door," A10.

6. Everyday Border Heroes

1. Luis A. Urrea, *Across the Wire: Life and Hard Times on the Mexican Border* (New York: Anchor/Doubleday, 1993), 20.

2. Faith and faith-based practice surrounding Jesús Malverde and Juan Soldado are routinized in a recognizably religious framework in Northern Mexico and parts of the Southwestern United States. For example, both have chapels or shrines, protective amulets with their image are produced and sold, and there are formal prayers said to them. In the case of Elián González, there does not exist the same sort of formalization of his image within a religious framework. Importantly, too, Elián is still very much alive in Cuba. Yet I argue that his image does function within a quasi-religious framework. For example, his former Little Havana house has become a museum (an equivalent to a shrine), his name and image appear still—in early 2003—posted on bumper stickers and windows, and he is ritually invoked in local political discussions.

3. Ana López, "The 'Other' Island: Exiled Cuban Cinema," *JumpCut* 38 (1993): 7–15.

4. Kuehls, *Beyond Sovereign Territory*, 49. For another discussion of transverse space, see Francois Debrix, "Deterritorialised Territories, Borderless Borders: The New Geography of International Medical Assistance," *Third World Quarterly* 19, no. 5 (1998): 827–46.

5. For a discussion of rabbit trickster figures, including Bugs Bunny, see Margaret P. Baker, "The Rabbit as Trickster," *Journal of Popular Culture* 28, no. 2 (1994): 149–52.

6. Lewis Hyde, *Trickster Makes This World: Mischief, Myth, and Art* (New York: Farrar, Straus, and Giroux, 1998), 7.

7. Ibid., 12.

8. This story is a composite one, based on several versions of "Eye-Juggler" that I have read and heard told aloud. I don't pretend to present an authentic version of "Eye-Juggler," nor is this story, as it is recounted here, intended for any ritual purposes. By retelling it here, I intend only to illustrate. Lewis Hyde includes a version of "Eye-Juggler" in *Trickster Makes This World*, 3–4.

9. Rebert, *La Gran Línea*, 192.

10. Hyde, *Trickster Makes This World*, 13.

11. This is my translation of the standard prayer, found in leaflets distributed in the main chapel to Jesús Malverde in Culiacán, Sinaloa, Mexico.

12. Sinaloa is probably most recognizable to those unfamiliar with Mexico's geography as the state where the Pacific coast resort town of Mazatlán is located.

13. Additionally, there are rumors of shrines as far south as Guatemala and Colombia. Sergio López Sánchez, "Malverde: Un bandido generoso," *Fronteras* 1, no. 2 (1996): 32–40, and personal interview, Juan (taxi driver in Culiacán), July 2001.

14. The most detailed account of the several versions of Malverde's story is López Sánchez's "Malverde," published in Spanish. Also in Spanish, Luis A. Astorga's important *Mitología del "narcotraficante" en México* (Mexico City: Plaza y Valdés, 1995) sets the legend of Malverde and other narcoheroes into a wider cultural, political, and musical context. James Griffith has written of Malverde in English, though the text is brief and largely descriptive; see "El Tiradito and Juan Soldado: Two Victim Intercessors of the Western Borderlands," in *A Shared Space: Folklife in the Arizona-Sonora Borderlands* (Logan, Utah: Utah State University Press, 1995), 67–86. A journalistic account of Malverde is provided by Sam Quiñones in *True Tales from Another Mexico: The Lynch Mob, the Popsicle Kings, Chalino, and the Bronx* (Albuquerque: University of New Mexico

Press, 2001), esp. 225–32. Finally, Elijah Wald provides a portrait of Malverde in connection with *narcocorridos*, or ballads connected to drug trafficking, in *Narcocorrido: A Journey into the Music of Drugs, Guns, and Guerrillas* (New York: HarperCollins, 2001), esp. 47–68.

15. Personal interview, July 2001. Eligio González, the shrine's builder and primary caretaker, was hospitalized with complications from diabetes during my visit.

16. Sinaloa is a major producer of winter vegetables for the export market to the United States, and shrimp fishing is another seasonal source of livelihood in this coastal state.

17. Claim reiterated in Wald, *Narcocorrido*, 63.

18. In another version, Malverde covered himself with green banana leaves as a camouflage, while in yet another version, he wore a green military uniform.

19. López-Sánchez, "Malverde," 34.

20. José Manuel Valenzuela Arce, "Por los milagros recibidos: Religiosidad popular a través del culto a Juan Soldado," in José Manuel Valenzuela Arce, ed., *Entre la magia y la historia: Tradiciones, mitos y leyendas de la frontera* (Tijuana, Mexico: Programa Cultural de las Fronteras, El Colegio de la Frontera Norte, 1992), 76–87.

21. Olga Vicenta Díaz Castro ("Sor Abeja"), *Narraciones y leyendas de Tijuana* (Tijuana, Mexico: Vocal del Seminario de Cultural Mexicana, 1981), 44. Additionally, this piece illustrates the general disbelief and frustration of the formal Catholic Church regarding local lay saints like Juan Soldado and Jesús Malverde.

22. Valenzuela Arce, "Por los milagros recibidos," 78.

23. Ralph Rugoff, *Circus Americanus* (London: Verso, 1995), 71. Another brief descriptive account of Juan Soldado in English can be found in Griffith, *A Shared Space*, 67–86.

24. Recounted by José Manuel Valenzuela Arce, personal interview, July 2001.

25. Although Griffith remarks that he has seen shrines to Juan Soldado in the Mexican border state of Sonora, to the east of Tijuana, he makes no mention of Juan Soldado's perceived powers of intercession on the behalf of border crossers. See Griffith, *A Shared Space*, 67–86.

26. Though as urban border crossing areas became more heavily fortified throughout the 1990s, broader rural areas, such those bordering Eastern California, desert areas of Arizona, New Mexico, and Texas, and the Southern Texas scrublands, have become preferred crossing zones north from Mexico.

27. Rugoff, *Circus Americanus*, 73.

28. The ranks of Caribbean island desperados have been joined by economic refugees from across Latin America's faltering economic landscape in the late 1990s and up to the present day. While Asian and African immigrants have yet to make much of an impact on South Florida's demographic landscape, rising numbers of Russian expatriates, spanning the economic scale, have come to the region lately as well.

29. Donna Haraway, "The Promises of Monsters: A Regenerative Politics for Inappropriate/d Others," in Lawrence Grossberg, Cary Nelson, and Paula Treichler, eds., *Cultural Studies* (New York: Routledge, 1992), 295–337.

30. Ibid., 295.

7. Hatred and Beautiful Things

1. Georges Benko, "Introduction: Modernity, Postmodernity, and the Social Sciences," in Georges Benko and Ulf Strohmayer, eds., *Space and Social Theory: Interpreting Modernity and Postmodernity* (Oxford: Blackwell, 1997), 25.

2. Saldívar, *Border Matters*, 158.

3. Klein, *Frontiers of Historical Imagination*, 2–3.

4. Crispin Sartwell, "Satanic Beauty," *Harper's Magazine* 299, no. 1795 (1999): 21–26.

Index

Patricia L. Price is associate professor of geography in the Department of International Relations and Geography at Florida International University in Miami.